On Life

L. N. Tolstoy at Yasnaya Polyana with his family and guests, 1887.
Russian State Archive for Literature and the Arts (RGALI 508-8-1-6).
Seated from left to right: Lev Tolstoy, Mikhail Stakhovich, Tatiana
(Tanya) Tolstaya, Maria Kuzminsky (Tolstoy's niece), Maria (Masha)
Tolstaya, Sergey (Seriozha) Tolstoy, Sophia (Andreevna) Tolstaya.
Seated on the screen partition: Misha and Andriusha Tolstoy.
Courtesy of RGALI.

On Life

A CRITICAL EDITION

Leo Tolstoy

EDITED BY INESSA MEDZHIBOVSKAYA

TRANSLATED FROM THE RUSSIAN
BY MICHAEL DENNER AND
INESSA MEDZHIBOVSKAYA

 Northwestern University Press • Evanston, Illinois

Northwestern University Press
www.nupress.northwestern.edu

On Life, originally completed in Russian under the title *O zhizni* in 1887, was banned
the following year. The first accurate Russian version was published in 1911.

Printed in the United States of America

10 9 8 7 6 5 4 3 2 1

Library of Congress Cataloging-in-Publication Data

Names: Tolstoy, Leo, graf, 1828–1910, author. | Medzhibovskaya, Inessa, 1964–
    editor, translator. | Denner, Michael A., translator.
Title: On life : a critical edition / Leo Tolstoy ; edited by Inessa Medzhibovskaya ;
    translated from the Russian by Michael Denner and Inessa Medzhibovskaya.
Other titles: O zhizni. English
Description: Evanston, Illinois : Northwestern University Press, 2019. | "On Life
    originally completed in Russian under the title O zhizni (1886–87)." | Includes
    bibliographical references.
Identifiers: LCCN 2018025731| ISBN 9780810138032 (alk. paper) | ISBN
    9780810138049 (alk. paper) | ISBN 9780810138056
Subjects: LCSH: Life.
Classification: LCC BD431 .T5613 2019 | DDC 128–dc23
LC record available at https://lccn.loc.gov/2018025731

In loving memory of Zoya Medzhibovskaya,
Emmanuel (Monia) Goldshteyn, Iosif Medzhibovsky,
Khona Medzhibovsky (Udler), Shlomo Muchnik,
and Melvin Denner
Because there is no death

CONTENTS

ACKNOWLEDGMENTS

I would like to extend my deepest thanks to the following institutions for granting me access to manuscripts and archival materials: the Leo Tolstoy State Museum in Moscow (GMT) and its Manuscript Division, which contains the fullest depository of Tolstoy manuscripts and personal papers ("The Steel Room"); the Tolstoy Museum Estate at Yasnaya Polyana; the Russian State Archive of Literature and the Arts (RGALI); the Russian State Public Library and Manuscript Section (Pashkov Dom); the Moscow University Philosophy Department Archive; the Historical Archive of the Russian Federation; the Harvard University Archives; the Columbia University Archives; the Columbia University Bakhmeteff Collection; the New York Public Library Manuscript Division; and the Interlibrary Loan Division of New York University.

My deepest thanks are also due to the American Philosophical Society for underwriting the early stages of the research and work with manuscripts and archives in Russia; to Eugene Lang College of Liberal Arts of The New School for granting me a semester of paid leave in 2010 and in 2017 that enabled me to advance and then complete this volume; and to "Leo Tolstoy and His English Translations," a symposium at Columbia University in 2010, for inviting me to present parts of this project in the making and for the encouraging and rich feedback I received from symposium participants.

For their help, assistance, and collaboration at various stages of work, special thanks to Galina Alekseeva, Scott Barker, Valentina Bastrykina, Michael Denner, Michael Gordin, Dominika and Tom Juraszek, Natalia Kalinina, Olga Knizhnik, Joel de Lara, Joseph Lemelin, Jeff Love, Dmitry Neustroev, Tatiana Nikiforova, Dmitri Nikulin, Svetlana Novikova, Randall Poole, Vitaly Remizov, the late James Scanlan, Lubov Shevtsova, Emily Sogn, Matthew Strother, Eugene Thacker, Vladimir Tolstoy, Yuliya

Yadovker, Galina Zlobina. And to Yuriy Medzhibovskiy, Mania Gold-shteyn, Zoya Kopetman, Ruzhena Kolten, and Marina Sverdlov.

And last, my thanks to Northwestern University Press editors for their enthusiasm for *On Life*. I thank Mike Levine, who first invited this project; Trevor Perri, who approved it and signed it up for completion, and for his wise stewardship throughout; and Anne Gendler and Maggie Grossman for their kind responses to all inquiries. With her characteristic kindness and patience, Anne Gendler steered the book throughout the production process. Mike Ashby's queries and his attention to style have been incredible. Marianne Jankowski designed a cover showing an almost eighty-year-old Tolstoy whose sly smile tells us that he is sure that the approaching death cannot lay claims on what we know about life. Caryl Emerson and Victor Brombert wrote beautiful endorsements. JD Wilson did everything to launch Tolstoy's *On Life* into its published afterlife.

—INESSA MEDZHIBOVSKAYA

ABBREVIATIONS

AT GMT   The archival collection of Tolstoy's personal documents, manuscripts, and letters addressed to him held at the Tolstoy Collection of the Manuscript Division/Tolstovskoe Sobranie Otdela Rukopisei of the Leo Tolstoy State Museum [Gosudarstvennyi Muzei Tolstogo] in Moscow.

CG   *A Critical Guide to Tolstoy's "On Life" with Interpretive Essays and Historical Sources*, ed. Inessa Medzhibovskaya, a publication of the *Tolstoy Studies Journal* (special imprint), general editor, Michael A. Denner (DeLand, Fla. and Toronto: North American Tolstoy Society, 2018). A companion volume to the present edition, *A Critical Guide* provides more specialized readings of *On Life* by leading scholars. The essays in that volume complement the historical and biographical essays of this edition.

DSAT   S. A. Tolstaya, *Dnevniki* [Diaries], 2 vols., ed. S. A. Rozanova (Moscow: Khudozhestvennaia Literatura, 1978).

DTLST   T. L. Sukhotina-Tolstaya, *Dnevnik* [Diary], ed. T. N. Volkova (Moscow: Sovremennik, 1984).

GMT   The Leo Tolstoy State Museum in Moscow.

The Jubilee   L. N. Tolstoy, *Polnoe sobranie sochinenii v 90 tomakh, Akademicheskoe Iubileinoe Izdanie* [Complete Collected Works in 90 volumes, Academic Jubilee Publication], ed. V. G. Chertkov et al. (Moscow: Khudozhestvennaia Literatura, 1928–58). Unless otherwise noted, all references in the present volume to Tolstoy's texts in Russian are to *The Jubilee* and cite the respective volume and page numbers, separated by a colon.

MPS   The Moscow Psychological Society (occasionally referred to as the "Society," in appropriate contexts).

PMPS   Protocols of the sessions of the Moscow Psychological
Society.

PTAAT   *Tolstovskii Muzei, Tom 1: Perepiska L. N. Tolstogo s gr. A. A.
Tolstoi, 1857–1903* [Tolstoy Museum, Volume 1: The Correspondence of
L. N. Tolstoy and Countess A. A. Tolstaya, 1857–1903] (St. Petersburg:
Izdanie Tolstovskogo Muzeia, 1911).

PTS   *L. N. Tolstoi i N. N. Strakhov. Polnoe sobranie perepiski* [*Leo Tolstoy
and Nikolaj Strakhov: Complete Correspondence*], 2 vols., ed. A. A. Donskov,
L. D. Gromova, and T. G. Nikiforova (Ottawa: Slavic Research Group;
Moscow: State L. N. Tolstoy Museum, 2003).

VFP   *Voprosy Filosofii i Psikhologii* (journal).

Introduction

TOLSTOY'S *ON LIFE* AND ITS TIMES

Inessa Medzhibovskaya

Pro captu lectoris habent sua fata libelli
[Books have their destiny depending on a reader's reception]

—TERENTIANUS MAURUS

Tolstoy's *On Life* (*O zhizni*, 1886–87) is a philosophical reflection on life and death, reason and the choices of thought, love and the overcoming of pessimism that was begun during a period of convalescence from a life-threatening injury only a few months after the publication of *The Death of Ivan Ilyich* (1886). The present volume is the first annotated edition of *On Life* based on a study of Tolstoy's manuscripts, redactorial scholarship, and extensive archival research, and it is the first annotated translation of this work into English.[1]

The destiny of *On Life* is complex. With its freethinking treatment of the problem of personal salvation, from the earliest drafts the work contravened the chief dogmas of Russian Orthodoxy, which caused it to be censored in autocratic Russia, where it would remain banned until the revolution of 1917. Only the more innocent-looking fragments on love, the fear of death, and bodily suffering would appear in Russian legal periodicals and in later prerevolutionary editions of Tolstoy's *Collected Works*.[2]

The Soviet destiny of *On Life* was no less complicated: Tolstoy's prescriptions for a happy life did not fit the program of the builders of communism. Given its deeply subversive character, *On Life* was very rarely printed after the Bolshevik Revolution, though it appeared in volume 26 of *The Jubilee* edition of Tolstoy's *Complete Collected Works* (1928–58). That volume had the misfortune of being edited and printed in 1936 at the height of Stalin's purges and was accompanied by textual commentary unreflective of its philosophical meaning. Volume 26 of *The Jubilee* edition, itself a solemn historical testament to ruthless expurgation, a product of fear, and a monumental victim of Stalinist terror, continues to be regarded as the standard version of the work in Russian. A. I. Nikiforov, the editor of *On Life* for *The Jubilee*, perished in the purges. Tolstoy's last secretary, Valentin Bulgakov (born in 1886, the year *On Life* was begun), had to perjure himself in exchange for permission to return to the Soviet Union from emigration after World War II by claiming that *On Life* was one example of Tolstoy's abstract spiritualism. *On Life* was republished in the Soviet Union as an addendum to Tolstoy's diaries and correspondence in his *Collected Works* in the 1960s and 1980s. These editions likewise lacked adequate commentary. The situation has remained unchanged after the collapse of communism—the work is no longer suppressed, but it lingers in obscurity and has been reprinted only very occasionally. A semiclandestine unannotated version prepared before 1917 by one of Tolstoy's followers was reprinted in 2012.[3]

There have been four previous translations of *On Life* into English, the most recent of which was published in the 1930s. First, an "authorized" translation by Isabel F. Hapgood, which Tolstoy never checked, was published in 1888.[4] Second, a much poorer English translation by Mabel and Agnes Cook was published in 1902, which was based on the French translation completed in 1888 by Sophia Andreevna (Tolstoy's wife).[5] Third, Leo Wiener's translation, which was included in volume 16 of his edition of the *Complete Works of Count Tolstoy*, was published in 1904.[6] Wiener was the first American Slavist, but he was not a native English speaker, which made him a constant target of ridicule by the text's fourth (and most recent) translator, Aylmer Maude, whose translation of *On Life* was published by him with a number of Tolstoy's essays on religion in 1934. Maude first met Tolstoy in 1888, by which time *On Life* had already been banned. Maude's translation of *On Life* was not among the other Tolstoy–Maude collaborations published during Tolstoy's lifetime, in which the writer was directly involved, providing feedback and commenting on Maude's versions.[7] Maude's translation of *On Life* is not among his best; it is inconsistent and uninformed when it comes to rendering Tolstoy's terminology: his awkward Victorianisms, such as "the cleavage of consciousness" and "intellectual intercourse," are unacceptable forms of usage today.[8]

This new translation attempts to restore the original text's vibrant, melodic, meditative, and yet polemical feel. *On Life* is neither an abstract nor a technical philosophical treatise. It is a piece of literary nonfiction with many perplexing word choices, persistent and intended repetitions, and constant deployments of certain terms in expected and unexpected contexts.

The introductory comments that follow, together with detailed annotations to the text of *On Life* and historical materials included in the present edition, seek to situate the work in the larger context of Tolstoy's philosophical life project, the intellectual life of Russia and of his age. This edition contains a historical supplement that includes nine selections, arranged chronologically, offering readers a more direct immersion in the intellectual environment of Tolstoy's Russia. The historical supplement presents Tolstoy's early drafts and responses either to these drafts or to published fragments of *On Life*.

Tolstoy began *On Life* as a collection of thoughts on dying and immortality shortly before his fifty-eighth birthday, after a serious bodily injury in the summer of 1886, and he completed the work toward the end of the following year. The year 1886 began under the pall of death. The Tolstoys lost their four-and-a-half-year-old son, Alyosha, to angina pectoris on January 18, 1886. Leaving Moscow earlier than normal that season in April, accompanied by two young friends, Tolstoy walked for three days to his beloved estate, Yasnaya Polyana. *The Death of Ivan Ilyich* was selling fast in volume 12 of his *Collected Works*, which he gifted to his wife, Countess Sophia Andreevna, the managing publisher of his estate from 1885 and copyright holder for all his works written before 1880. (Aside from this gift in thanks for her effort, Tolstoy did not charge any money for anything he wrote after 1880). At Yasnaya Polyana, he threw himself with abandon into work on the estate's fields. One day, during these agricultural exertions, he was taking hay to a peasant widow, Anisya Kopylova, when he gravely injured his leg and subsequently neglected the wound. Pulling the scab prematurely, he contracted an infection. One more day and he might have developed a fatal form of septicemia, but luckily a doctor was brought in from Moscow just in time to prevent this.

Tolstoy had a difficult convalescence: he remained bedridden for almost three full months, until mid-November 1886. During these months, he could write but little. Everyone in the family knew that what Tolstoy was composing while in bed were scenes from a new play about peasant life, *The Power of Darkness*, a shocking drama in which unrelenting beastly turpitude prevails until almost the very end.[9] Madame Seuron, the French governess of Tolstoy's daughters and younger sons, watched in horror as the lord of the estate lay with drainage tubes sticking out of his suspended leg, looking both terrifying and ridiculous, as he talked to himself in the obscene peasant jargon in which the play was being written.[10] The domestics showed no signs of knowing that Tolstoy was writing a new work on life and death. Throughout 1886, Sophia Andreevna and Tolstoy's eldest daughter, Tanya, aged twenty-two—the only other diary keepers in the family besides Tolstoy at that time—mention Tolstoy's disease but do not say anything concerning *On Life*. How and why did Tolstoy manage to keep such a momentous project sub rosa? Perhaps he did so because he had become tired of his family making fun of his *Weltbesserungswahn* (mania for improving the world)—a condition they attributed to him, imitating the then-fashionable lingo of psychology, the new queen discipline in the scientific realm.[11] After the publication of *Anna Karenina* in 1878, Tolstoy told his family that he would abandon playing with the illusions of life reflected in the carefree mirror of the fine arts (an image he described in *A Confession*, begun in 1879)[12] and instead buried himself in the study of philosophy and theology. It was at that time, it seemed, that, for Tolstoy's family, "happiness faded and never revived."[13]

Tolstoy was gradually becoming a vegetarian. He was sewing shoes and experimenting with abstaining from tea, coffee, alcohol, and tobacco. The injury itself was the result of mowing hazards he himself had created on the estate.[14] Tolstoy's diary entries for 1886 and 1887 inform us best about his improved state of mind before the injury and provide early indications of the psychological turn that led Tolstoy to writing *On Life* in the genre in which it was begun. These entries are especially precious because Tolstoy's diary, in other years documented in detail day by day, is uncharacteristically thin for 1886 and 1887 (see pages 215–20 in the historical supplement).

We can observe in the diary entries completed in the spring and summer of 1886 and before the injury that Tolstoy was continuing with his exploration of Ivan Ilyich's discovery that death no longer existed. The entries in May explore the transient connections in humans between sleep, wakefulness, living, and dying. Life is a river pouring over everything; the human is also a creature from eternity, a fluid being coming out of All and going back into All constantly, not just at birth and death. In June, a month before the injury, Tolstoy introduces a new theme concerning a contradiction he saw in life between a person's discrete existence and his or her former and future belonging to All: as a discrete being, one is engaged with every breath and every step of one's finite being in a futile battle with other creatures, all of which are destined for the same prize at the end—namely, their physical annihilation and disappearance from life. The only way to avoid life's becoming a nightmare or an illusion, for Tolstoy, is if reason can justify the situation by reestablishing man's connection with that which might be invisible to the mortal eye but which is visible to the eye of the soul. Reason helps one overcome the egoistic aims of personal survival and leads toward realizing what undying happiness is.

On August 28, 1886, the day of his fifty-eighth birthday, *after* the injury and while still very ill, Tolstoy writes that the aim of life lies beyond pleasure and suffering. He sketches a graph according to which it takes passing through what looks in the drawing like the shaft of suffering to discover the meaning of living and dying (see page 218 in the historical supplement). The last entry in 1886, made on October 18, concludes the discoveries made in the diary for that year with a realization that one's expending of oneself through living is neither completed nor exhausted by "the complex activity of [one's] body."[15]

Another priceless source of information about the beginnings of *On Life* is the draft of a reflection on life and death (pages 221–23) that Tolstoy sketched *after* the injury, during the last ten days of September and the early days of October 1886, for his new young acquaintance, Anna Konstantinovna Diterikhs (1859–1927), a general's daughter, graduate of the Bestuzhev Academy for Women, and model for painter Nikolai Iaroshenko's famous canvas *A Female Student* (*Kursistka*, 1880).

The Diterikhs letter was another reason for Tolstoy's secrecy about his new work. Sophia Andreevna was dismayed by this young lady, who, in Sophia's view, was not behaving herself properly. Unmarried at twenty-seven, in late February or early March of 1886 she showed up at the Tolstoys' Moscow apartment in the company of two single men, Pavel (Posha) Biriukov[16] and Vladimir Chertkov–the first Tolstoyans to be active in the Posrednik firm, which since 1884 had been turning out cheap editions of Tolstoy's latest works by the thousands, the very works that could have been a significant source of revenue had Tolstoy not renounced copyright. During her short visit, Diterikhs made a number of rude mistakes: she did not blush or flinch when proofs of *The Death of Ivan Ilyich* were shown to her by Tolstoy with the scenes where peasant Gerasim is taking his feeble master to the commode.[17] She kept defending Tolstoy's postnovelistic worldview against the lady of the house and her uncle, Isleniev. And even though she was really fond of Posha, Sophia Andreevna was starting to detest Chertkov, who was beginning to win Diterikhs's affection.

To make things worse, two months before the injury, Diterikhs joined Tolstoy again in the slightly augmented company of young people at

Yasnaya Polyana at a time when Sophia Andreevna was not yet around for the summer. In response to her angry letters about the various visiting "demoiselles," Tolstoy agreed on May 2, 1886, that although he found them nice, they were difficult to handle and "beyond the convention" (83:566). During Dietrikhs's visit, Tolstoy and his young friends did indeed speak of very improper topics. They examined the "suicide bar" in his library, immortalized in *A Confession* (1879–82), a symbol of a nihilistic bravery that rejected other approaches to life such as happy ignorance, deliberate Epicureanism, and withdrawal into passivity. The only other option remaining was that of an active battle for the life-affirming view that confronts head-on the conclusions of Buddha and Schopenhauer: that life in this world is nothing but senseless evil. *A Confession* persists in its rebellion against pessimism from beginning to end, always upending the gloomy logic of pessimism with provocative questions, such as, "How could reason deny life when it itself is the creator of life? . . . if there were no life, my reason would not be there either" (23:29). As we have seen, this fight acquires more lyrical and mystical overtones in the pages of Tolstoy's diary in the summer of 1886.

The spectral and mystical elements of Tolstoy's art were noticed in the very same year by the French critic and diplomat Vicomte de Vogüé, who made the now-famous claim that Tolstoy had "the spirit of an English scientist" combined with the "soul of a Buddhist."[18] Note the contradiction, which would become one of the key themes of what Tolstoy would call "a split of consciousness," in *On Life*. Like a star English chemist at the forefront of science, writes de Vogüé, Tolstoy could dissolve the hardest and most impenetrable masses of matter into the minuscule elements of analysis. This is the power of his pragmatic nihilism. Only one step short of discovering the secret of the last speck of creation, Tolstoy gives up abruptly: he falls down on his knees and yields to a trance of inactivity similar to the mystical abandon of the world of a "Hindu Buddhist."[19]

Taking his cue from the concluding chapters of *A Confession*, Tolstoy and his visiting company went on talking about how through selfless living one could overcome the despair propagated by the philosophies of Schopenhauer and Hartmann.[20] Soon after the visit, and at the time when Tolstoy was writing Diterikhs a letter, she became Chertkov's fiancée.[21]

Tolstoy's letter to her develops vital existential and ontological themes of his earlier postconversion texts, including *A Confession*, Tolstoy's harmonization and translation of the Gospels (1880–81); *A Critique of Dogmatic Theology* (1879–84); *What I Believe?* (or, *My Religion*) (1882–84); and *What, Then, Should We Do?* (1882–86). The letter contains multiple frantic repetitions of "I." This "I" is literary-autobiographical: *A Confession* contains a most memorable, somewhat pathetic portrayal of it. The "I" in *A Confession* behaves like a wounded beast thrashing around in the mortal cage in which it is chained, obsessed with hearing back from God, begging to be provided with a sign promising hope that salvation is possible. The "I" of *A Confession* would be remembered for insisting on being given more encouraging advice than could be found in Kant's rationalistic ethical agnosticism, with its lack of a positive proof for God and salvation, and for something more reassuring than that provided by Kant's sinister partner, Schopenhauer, who counseled a complete renunciation of the will to live. The letter to Diterikhs makes fun of this "I" that wishes to know nothing of life in this world and of the life of other creatures outside its own struggles. Struggles for a faith that could save just you are still selfish ones.

The two drafts of the letter to Diterikhs, one of which Tolstoy sends her through Chertkov, bring together images of a *reasonable life* that unifies an individual self with the rest of creation. Tolstoy begins with examples of unconscious or semiconscious forms of a reasonable life, such as a germinating sprout. Another vivid image of a developing awareness he gives is of a horse walking in a circle and activating the grinding wheel of a mill. Conscious efforts to lead a reasonable life end with the attainment of "reasonable consciousness" (*razumnoe soznanie*), which becomes the watchful guide of one's physical existence. The Diterikhs drafts present Christ's awareness of life (*razumenie zhizni*) as the highest form of self-sacrificial understanding that overcomes self-pity, stands by the Lord's Logos, and replaces it in the world with the best and happiest acts of man.[22] And although Tolstoy rejects the idea of the resurrection of the body and the transfiguration of the bodily into the heavenly, he believes in the life that is exemplified in Christ's sacrificial love and selfless service to life—a life that resolves the aimless struggles of self-conscious life, which lacks certitude.

The "English scientist" in Tolstoy gets down to the essential elements of his being and the being of every creature. This route brings him face-to-face with the question of the soul, the nature of which is no longer confined by Church doctrine, at least not for Tolstoy, and which has become, through the development of psychology, an object of external observation. Tolstoy here recalls his earlier conversations on the topic in his *Critique of Dogmatic Theology*: "And I inevitably come to God: Nails are not I; hands are not I; head is not I; feelings are not I; even thoughts are not I. Then what is I? My soul is I."[23] He repeats these phrases in the letter to Diterikhs and in other drafts of the new work. This kind of certitude is not the knowledge of the doctrine of faith of the Pharisees or the scientific knowledge of the

Scribes.[24] This is *my* unique knowledge, says Tolstoy, about *my* relationship with life fulfilled by ends that are not narrowly material or egoistic.

Tolstoy continues to refine several ideas from the Diterikhs drafts—in particular, that "the little cells are not I," that the promise of "I cry here and rejoice there" is not for him, and that one's primary duties to life may contradict the pressures of family, society, nation, and culture, thereby creating a productive if painful split within the self. Tolstoy saves for refinement his other best-loved ideas from *My Religion* and *What, Then, Should We Do?* concerning the five truest conditions of human happiness, which, for Tolstoy, differ from the options of organized religion, liberal and scientific utilitarianism, social Darwinism, and Marxism, selections of which had been published and discussed in Russian and foreign presses. These conditions are (1) man's loving, grateful, attentive communication and cooperation with nature (the sky, the sun, the seasons, plants, animals)—a relationship that was all but lost or nearly lost in the quickly modernizing world; (2) free, uncoerced, and meaningful labor (physical, intellectual, spiritual); (3) family happiness in which children are not raised to become "coddled" and "preserved" selfish beings but ethical and spiritual members of human brotherhood; (4) free and loving communion with people and the broadest possible circle of brotherly communication in the temple of life; and (5) healthy and painless death. Known to his contemporaries as his thoughts about what constitutes happiness, the majority of which are selections from chapter 10 of *My Religion*, these ideas appeared in the first issue of the liberal journal *Russian Reliquary* in 1886, which was edited by Leonid Obolensky.[25] Obolensky had been corresponding with Tolstoy on spiritual matters for some time, and their connection was solidified by Obolensky's loss of his six-year-old daughter a few months after the death of Tolstoy's Alyosha. The letters exchanged between them in 1886 touch upon the big questions about the meaning of it all.

Also in 1886, Obolensky published in *Russian Reliquary* several articles on Tolstoy's philosophical and moral worldview—articles that, overall, supported Tolstoy's version of happiness based on the understanding of social well-being (*blago*) as an individual's service to life, as opposed to the reigning ideas of happiness as the scientifically and politically mentored participation of an individual in the work of progress.[26] Tolstoy had begun his investigations into a theory of *blago* within a sociological project, conducting a test of sociology as a potential science of happiness after a meeting in 1885 and subsequent correspondence with an American of Russian origin who was a devout follower of the Comtean religion of happiness, William Frey. In Obolensky's treatment, Tolstoy offered a more wide-ranging spiritual reform for achieving happiness through personal altruism and charity (*blagotvoritel'nost'*) than the rational-utilitarian theories of Comte, Mill, Spencer, Lewes, and Huxley. The technocrats and engineers of happiness were seeking to curtail diseases and physical degeneration, poverty, the deprivation of rights or opportunities, without regard for concerns that, according to Tolstoy, are more vital to man. For Tolstoy, these concerns are revealed in the following questions: Why am I alive? What should I do with the life given to me? How can I live a good life in which the good I do is not for me alone?

Obolensky noted that Tolstoy had deconstructed the notion of charity (*blagotvoritel'nost'*) into its constituent parts: *blago* (good, happiness, bliss) and *tvorit'* (to create). To be charitable and happy and make others happy is to create and spread what is good. Obolensky wanted to know how Tolstoy's hopeful idealism could be implemented more practically, especially in view of the visible transformation he had observed in Tolstoy's outlook. Tolstoy's youthful intoxication with earthly happiness had been overtaken by slightly more mature dreams of building a material paradise on earth—dreams that blossomed, in turn, in the discussions of the historical *blago* and the system of civil *bien publique* in *War and Peace*. These dreams would crumble in *Anna Karenina*, where hope is left alive not so much in all the metaphysical teachings that explain life nonmaterialistically but in the prompts from the peasants not to live for one's belly. These explorations culminate in recalcitrant tracts and popular parables of the early to mid-1880s that aim at shaking the established order in the minds and souls of men. Obolensky knew that Tolstoy's mind never lost its connection with reality. The excerpts from *What, Then, Should We Do?* that Obolensky's journal had published and that discuss a universal program of economic and social improvement of life had garnered praise from the noted economists and Moscow University professors Ivan Ianzhul and Alexander Chuprov.

In October 1886 or earlier, while convalescing, Tolstoy read Obolensky's studies along with attacks by democratic and conservative critics alike on Obolensky on account of his objective evaluation of Tolstoy.[27] Despite Tolstoy's relative secrecy about his new work, rumors about it had already spread. We can see this from Obolensky's request to Tolstoy on November 6, 1886, to publish the Diterikhs fragments in *Russian Reliquary*. But having decided, on November 14, 1886, to start a much longer and original work, Tolstoy refused Obolensky's offer, saying that he was still in the thick of thinking on the matter of death and life (63:409).[28] This decision was the first turning point in the development of what would become *On Life*.

It is true that Tolstoy does not at this stage use—at least not in the same way as he would in the finished work, in his diary, or in his letter to Diterikhs—one of the main concepts of *On Life*: reasonable consciousness. A rudimentary version of this concept can be found in the Diterikhs fragments. This term was properly born in the philosophical sense on the same day that Tolstoy refused Obolensky's request—November 14, 1886—by which time, incidentally, Tolstoy was back on his feet and moving around cautiously. On November 4, 1884, Tolstoy had realized suddenly, when approached for a comparison between the soul and *razumenie*, that the two are not interchangeable terms. He objected to the substitution of the word *razumenie* with the word "soul" (63:405). The "soul" means something else in the Gospels, he decided. During the decades when everyone who was not a diehard materialist or an "English scientist" was liable to being called a mystic or a spiritualist, Tolstoy rejected the majority of spiritualist concepts related to the existence of psychic substance and immortality and psychic communication and transmigration. In 1886, Tolstoy's close intellectual friend Nikolai Strakhov published an analysis of the motor function and other functions of the soul—albeit a very dull analysis, written with the pretense of clinical precision.[29] In this work, Strakhov wrote that the "I" of empirical psychology is what is revealed by the examination of the life of the spiritual monad in its interaction with reality. On November 14, 1886, Tolstoy for the first time uses the term "reasonable consciousness" in a polite objection to Strakhov's view that monads possess the real and full life of the soul. Consciousness, which is of such great interest to psychology, is a force, Tolstoy says. Material forces (physical and chemical) are inert and passive, but spiritual consciousness is *reasonable consciousness*, which is alert and active: "If it is reasonable consciousness," it is "therefore good and active."[30] Reason and consciousness, Tolstoy added, apologizing for the metaphysical flourish, are the foundational forces of the world "and the highest ones."[31] In a special hierarchy that became the signature feature of *On Life*, Tolstoy claims in this letter that the laws of reasonable consciousness subordinate and coordinate the lower laws that govern organic and inorganic life. Out of this conclusion would arise one of Tolstoy's most important decisions: that human knowledge of the self and the hierarchy of one's relationship with life is tripartite, because the human being is simultaneously a reasonable being, an animal and plant, and an assemblage of inorganic matter (*nezhivoe veshchestvo*) (see chapters 13 and 32 in *On Life*).

Here, Tolstoy might for the first time be referring to Pascal's idea of man's dignity as a "thinking reed."[32] Tolstoy did not elaborate further, but he did select as the first of the three epigraphs to *On Life* Pascal's thought about man as a thinking reed—a being that is frail but has the advantage over nature and the universe in the knowledge of its finitude. This letter to Strakhov, from a barely healed thinking reed, is written too casually and is disorganized in comparison with previous conversations between the two men that had begun in November 1870 and centered on what makes a philosophical or scientific evaluation of life true. Despite the multifaceted and complex nature of this correspondence, it owed its longevity, which was interrupted only by Strakhov's death in 1896, to the interlocutors' shared confidence that philosophy, science, and art should all give the possibility of hope to a thinking human being, a direction about how to act, and a clear explanation of what his or her meaning in the world is. What drove Strakhov, a biologist by training and a Hegelian literary critic by conviction, to start writing to Tolstoy in the first place was one of the first encapsulations of the idea in the character of Platon Karataev in *War and Peace*, whose life, as he regarded it, possessed no meaning taken by itself but only as part of the whole of life. Karataev was always *conscious* of this meaning but felt no need to explain or express it. This character, who was overwhelmingly taken by Russian readers for a model of a Slavophile-tempered, antirational monadist, was a very popular reference point for interpreting the meaning of life. The allegory of God as a perfect clockmaker, in the words of the historical-philosophical narrator of *War and Peace*, suggests that God is the creator of the best of all possible worlds, despite the cataclysms that the narrator describes. The allegory of the clockmaker appears only briefly in the earliest drafts of *On Life* and is then replaced first by the image of the rounds made by a horse turning a millstone and second by the image of a horse led out of a stable to do its work and, finally and separately, in the introduction to the work, by the image of a man running a mill at a river.

In accordance with the Leibnizian clockmaker scheme of *War and Peace*, and around 1870, Tolstoy still believed that man's freedom was more voluntaristic than real: man was little more than a force, an atom in the universe, positing and intending himself outside himself, often brusquely and aggressively, against the overwhelming powers outside him. On this point, Tolstoy was compared with Fichte, whose *Wissenschaftslehre* aimed to construct a bridge between Kant's transcendental critical method and the unknowable external world through the effort of this aggressive "I," whose life vocation is self-expansion and refinement. There is little of the tender but dignified frailty of a thinking reed in this "I." Strakhov kept reminding Tolstoy of the likeness with Fichte, but Tolstoy felt more drawn to Schelling's universalizing subjectivity—and, as such, was very optimistic about the triumph of the ideal over the prosaic real in the realization of the highest historically developing potencies of nature and man.

In 1872, Strakhov had published the first edition of his major work, a volume of his letters on nature, titled *The World as a Whole*, which developed Wilhelm Wundt's behavioristic distinction between the soul of man and the soul of animal in his renowned lectures on the topic, which were themselves a development of Herbert Spencer's theory of man's psyche as tiered.[33] Wundt had always interested Tolstoy, who couldn't have failed to see Strakhov's explicit support of this connection through a distinction between man and animal in his book, which begins with the statement that man is an animal but that man's psychic power is in his "higher animality" (*vysshaia zhivotnost*).[34] But during his work on *Anna Karenina*, and after spending about two days as a materialist, as he once joked to Strakhov, Tolstoy began to share with him the ideas of idealistic liberation, which he developed in numerous philosophical fragments that all focused on the possibility of a future life outside time and space and on the life of the soul outside the life known or visible to us.[35] Tolstoy was no longer mesmerized by the magnetism of the idea of an organic integrity to life in which spiritualists might talk amicably with materialists. Most important in this regard to Tolstoy were Kant's three questions in *The Critique of Pure Reason* (A805–6/B833–34): "What can I know? What must I do? What should I hope for?"[36] Tolstoy never claimed that we can know all about the world or ourselves; for Tolstoy, we can find ourselves in determining what to do as conscience commands.[37] This knowledge is directed, for Tolstoy, by an active religious attitude—our unique stance toward and relatedness with the world that he now defined on November 14, 1886, as reasonable consciousness.

What should we make of Tolstoy's Kantian leanings and his advocating for active conscientious reasoning guided by conscience and responsibility? Kant called lazy any reasoning that appealed to the material to define the soul. And the soul was the same as the "I" in Tolstoy's equations, as we have seen; there was nothing material about it. To explain the return to Kant here, we need to look elsewhere. Kant's three questions in the first *Critique* (1781) precede the development of an altogether new theme in his work, that of *happiness as the highest good* (A811/B839). This sense of happiness is not defined by what is material or temporal but demonstrates the goodwill of a salient mind that becomes *worthy* of being happy. Kant develops the idea further in *Groundwork for the Metaphysics of Morals* (1785) and *The Critique of Practical Reason* (1788). We cannot neglect the switch, especially because Tolstoy would select the second epigraph to *On Life* from the latter text, with its emphasis on the coupling (*Verknüpfung*) of reason and consciousness with the awareness of the moral law within. And although Tolstoy's interest in *blago* as a spiritual value and a form of spiritual experience is quite in keeping with the convictions of several factions of European neo-Kantianism that were slowly beginning to spread in Russia,[38] what was still missing in Tolstoy's new project was the idea of love.

Back in Moscow in early December 1886 and fully healed, Tolstoy went immediately to the Rumiantsev Museum to seek the opinion of Nikolai Fedorov, a librarian there. A saintly man around Tolstoy's own age, Fedorov was famous for his belief that God made an error in creating human life as horizontal and ending in death. Fedorov saw the common task of humanity as the repositioning of itself away from a horizontal plane and onto a vertical plane. Placed onto a vertical plane, humanity engages in resurrecting the lives of the perished, including ancestors. Despite their unending disputes (for Tolstoy could never believe in bodily resurrection), both men cared about conceptualizing the state of immortality, and Fedorov eagerly anticipated the completion of Tolstoy's new thoughts on life and death. While at the Rumiantsev Museum, Tolstoy ran into his younger acquaintance, Nikolai Grot, a philosopher at Moscow University. Tolstoy was elected a member of the Moscow Psychological Society (MPS) in its fifth session and had been active in the society—albeit in absentia until then.[39] Its initial sessions, which focused on the tasks of positivist science and on experimental studies of the soul, were temporarily suspended, but Tolstoy attended several soirées at Grot's place, where Grot spoke about free will—the topic of his formal talks on February 25 and March 5, 1887, at MPS, which Tolstoy also attended. According to the transcription of the society's session of the latter date, Tolstoy volunteered at this meeting to give a talk at an upcoming gathering.[40] Tolstoy indeed presented his new concept of life at MPS on March 14, 1887.[41]

Grot had just left his position at Novorossiysk University in Odessa to take a philosophy chair at Moscow University. In his two farewell lectures at the former, he all but deserts positivism. Positivism was, at the time, a dominant philosophical school in Russia: the chief procurator of the Holy Synod, Konstantin Pobedonostsev, the minister-policeman overseeing the spiritual health of the nation—who happened to be Tolstoy's long-term enemy—was an admirer of the English model of Herbert Spencer. Pobedonostsev esteemed Spencer's work in psychology, which was based on his theory of rational egoism and happiness—a theory that respected power, standardized morals informed with the aid of science, and vouchsafed public peace. Alongside positivism, which was well established in Russia, variants of monadology and other eclectic nineteenth-century spiritualist and vitalist developments of Leibniz's thought were gaining traction—especially the variegated presentations of *Lebensphilosophie* and *la philosophie de la vie* by thinkers such as Gustav Theodor Fechner, Victor Cousin, Paul Janet, Hermann Lotze, Eugen Dühring, and Gustav Teichmüller, to name a few. Most Russian monadologists were strong personalists. At least two of them—A. A. Kozlov of Kiev University, who held a master's in theology but no doctorate, and Petr Astafiev, a lecturer in the history of philosophy who was interested in the psychology of feeling and was a lawyer by training—were opposed to Tolstoy's thought. With its postulate of predestined harmony, Leibniz's monadology was a picture of the world that was not in direct conflict with Russian Orthodoxy. Lotze's celebrated teaching about the microcosm of life and Teichmüller's of the immortality of the soul were widely used in the otherwise closely monitored curricula in Russian universities and theological academies.

Grot had spoken in Odessa of the soul as an active force independent of physical forces. This force, in its flight of free will, he pressed, deserved a new field of philosophical study that would not relapse into the abstractions of German idealism and yet would also not condemn the soul to the verdicts of materialistic teachings, spiritualist and theosophical fashions, and indifferent clinical experiments. There was no question of returning the soul to the Church. But Grot was approached and congratulated by Archbishop Nikanor of Kherson and Odessa simply for bringing up the question of the soul in a university auditorium. Nikanor's approval became known, and Grot's lectures, which he had sent to Tolstoy before moving to Moscow, were published. Tolstoy finished the story of Ivan Ilyich with Grot's brochure in hand.

Tolstoy liked Grot very much as a person but did not consider him a deep thinker or a really original philosopher. In his view, repeated in the various private papers of Tolstoy's family, Grot was a typical "scribe" (*knizhnik*), although not a malevolent one. His proposal to return to Kant was not readily welcomed at that time. Following the draconian university regulations of 1884 and the reactionary restrictions on modern humanities curricula that had been ongoing since the 1870s, professors were required to have their lecture notes approved before they could be delivered to students and circulated among them in written form. These lecture notes were frequently uncritical compilations of ancient philosophy and standard surveys of the modern period.

On October 23, 1886, Nikanor wrote to Grot about Kant: "His *Critique of Practical Reason* is a joke written for the enjoyment of a God-fearing valet."[42] Grot was one of the first recipients in Russia of a doctoral degree conferred by a Russian philosophy department. In his doctoral dissertation on the reform of logic (1882), he had suggested conducting a "psychic turn" away from the slavery of formalism and positivism, guiding the course of Russian thought in the spirit of Kantian critical philosophy. Grot needed the help of Kant and Tolstoy's concept of reasonable consciousness to loosen the straitjacket that was constraining this young and still dependent discipline.[43]

The delivery and discussion of Tolstoy's talk at MPS took place behind closed doors and lasted from 8:00 P.M. until 12:30 A.M. Examination of the drafts of this talk, of which Sophia Andreevna had prepared a good copy, shows that by March 1887, *On Life* had outgrown its original intention (which was a treatise on death written on the writer's deathbed with all the plaintive and sentimental accoutrements of a threnody). Tolstoy's talk is no longer the story of how one man encounters and embraces and laments his personal death, journeys up and down his memory of life, and then makes death his own.[44] The mental exclusion of death is apparent in the work's title, and death and life become members of "the concept of life," as the title of the talk states. The meaning of our life cannot be exhausted by its physical conclusion, and what we call life is not restricted to the course and outcome of our individual life-and-death story. In personal terms, it is the supersensible and supersensory memory of our common origin and the anticipation of meaning that we should strive toward attaining during the experience of the pleasures and pains of our physical existence.

This meaning necessarily continues, according to Tolstoy. The firmer our faith is supported by reason in the meaning that will be disclosed as a reward for our active and engaged anticipation, the happier we live and die. Reason and consciousness are what we all share in our humanity. Both reason and consciousness help us in the process of developing the capacity for viewing our personal life from a greater distance and altitude and viewing the needs and aspirations of the rest of life—the life that is not our own in a narrow and selfish sense—as the sphere of our proximate responsibility.

The talk engages in dialogue with the magnificent literary-philosophical tradition of deathbed meditation or meditation in seclusion, a genre Tolstoy explored for forty years of his creative life, but it is focused less and less on its author and his reflections alone.[45] In the tone that Tolstoy had found for the talk, his concept of life develops into a series of conversations of the individual named Tolstoy (or Lev Nikolaevich, as he refers to himself in the finished text of *On Life*) with other species in the creaturely realm and its extended habitats: human beings, cells, embryos, plants, animals, saints, the starry skies, the Milky Way.

The text of Tolstoy's talk begins exactly as would the text of Tolstoy's introduction to *On Life*. The talk also foreshadows discussions that would become part of future chapters of the finished work. For example, chapter 6 describes the struggles of a lonely "I"; chapter 18 illustrates how reasonable consciousness teaches us that life cannot be death. Chapter 22 polemically sharpens Jesus's question to the Pharisees: "And who is the neighbor?" The talk used roguish turns of phrase, such as "a fish tries not to stay out of water; man tries to stay out of troubled waters," and it covered international politics, touching upon the confrontation of patriotic militarisms, Bismarck's Germany, and Russia, in particular. All political references, except for a brief mention of terrorist bombs that might be thrown at the reader (chapter 34, on suffering), would be excluded from the final version. Instead, Tolstoy would include in *On Life* a few historical and literary predecessors by name—Jesus, Buddha, Pascal, Chénier, Gogol, Lermontov, Pellico.[46]

The conservative periodical *Novoe Vremia*, edited by Tolstoy's acquaintance Alexey Suvorin, and the liberal organ *Russkii Vestnik* both published transcripts of Tolstoy's talk.[47] It was not easy for the reading public to acquiesce immediately to what Tolstoy was proposing in these transcripts, and some understood his postulates to mean that he was working out a theory of a disintegration of personality. Nothing could be further from the truth, but there was demand even for such garbled presentations of immortality, as long as they were secular and optimistic. Volume 13 of Tolstoy's *Collected Works*—which was announced in advance as containing the forthcoming essay on the concept of life—was oversubscribed. Grot effusively endorsed the work in thanking Tolstoy on March 30, 1887, on behalf of Russian philosophy and society: "You are the only solid fulcrum point in the cause of our searching for the ideals and our leader on the road to Truth."[48]

Tolstoy did not linger in the capital and left for Yasnaya Polyana as soon as he could for the summer. On April 2, 1887, he wrote to Chertkov: "A month and a half or so I have been thinking about nothing else day and night" (86:42). He did little other than write and rewrite *On Life* the entire happy summer, after having identified by mid-May 1887 what the core of the work would be. He was surrounded by family, his children, and the young children of his sister-in-law, Tanya Kuzminsky. There was a lot of singing, merrymaking, and performing. Suvorin arrived in June to seek spiritual advice after the suicide of his son in May and to speak about the translation of Wundt into Russian. Strakhov visited twice in July and then again in August to speak about a possible connection between Tolstoy's vision of life and his own recent work, *On Eternal Truths: My Argument on Spiritualism*,[49] in which he argues in favor of dialectical psychology as opposed to Darwinism, combining ideas from Plato's *Phaedo* with scientific methods of testing. Strakhov's battle on these points with Moscow University professor and botanist Kliment Timiriazev, a steadfast Darwinian, did not interest Tolstoy. Sophia Andreevna was again pregnant, at forty-three, with the couple's last son, Vanechka, who would be born March 31, 1888.

Tolstoy's presentation at MPS in March was the second turning point in his work. The vigorous response to the developing drafts of *On Life* from professional philosophers, scientists, writers, doctors, churchmen, and his own domestics and friends that he received in the spring and summer of 1887 reinvigorated the polemical tone of Tolstoy's text. An introduction, thirty-five chapters, a conclusion, and three appendixes, of which the final version of Tolstoy's text is composed, provide a detailed, high-spirited account of how we can be happy while remaining mortal, in tones now mellow, now rambunctious, always lively, never dull. Tolstoy filled the work with unforgettable imagery: anecdotes describing man as a line and as a glass; the metaphoric dispute between a Jew and a Christian; the likening of incorrect definitions of life to a pharmacy that sells vials labeled for the pharmacist's own convenience, instead of according to their true contents; adages about a minnow and a perch, a spider and a fly; numerous short and extended analogies, of the existential horse learning how to abide by the law, of the youthful reasonable consciousness as a blushing maiden, of life as a river with a mill and then as a conic structure, of a crowd thronging at the doors of life, in the Kafkaesque fashion, and forgetting to enter through them. *On Life* was also replete with all those unforgettable paeans about loving it all—the young grass and the blue sky, the dog, the horse, the cat, and a little spider in a prisoner's cell. And, of course, the text included Tolstoy's cavalier jokes about our irreducibility to an ensemble and chorus of "little cells."

Before sending *On Life* off to print, Tolstoy invited Grot to Yasnaya Polyana for an informal rehearsal. The timing was perfect, because the Kuzminskys (his in-laws) were still staying there. His second aunt, Alexandrine, a lady-in-waiting at the court, one of his keenest critics and his closest spiritual friend, a devout Russian Orthodox believer, also arrived.[50] Whereas a year before brigades of family and guests mowed the fields at Yasnaya Polyana, in the summer of 1887 a copying bureau for the drafts of *On Life* was formed and set up in several rooms of the house. Sophia Andreevna and Alexandrine took turns with Alexander (Sasha) Kuzminsky copying and taking dictation from Tolstoy of the finished drafts of *On Life*.

Since becoming acquainted with the drafts firsthand, Sophia Andreevna had fallen in love with the quality of the prose, but its central idea that one should resign one's personal life in the name of love of the whole world distressed her. To her, as she was keen on noting in her diary a few times, the *blago* and happiness of her family, her husband and children, came first.[51] In their customary teasing exchanges, Alexandrine warned Tolstoy that tidbits of his wisdom always piqued her interest, but that his philosophical compositions were as alien to her as Sanskrit. She did not hesitate to point out instances of his cryptographic grammar, yet she agreed to judge the work in its final reading at home, which lasted two hours.

Tolstoy joked that in his handpicked triumvirate of jurors, Grot represented philosophy, Alexandrine was a "representative of religion," and Sasha Kuzminsky, a lawyer, represented the legal profession.[52] Grot and Alexandrine tried to object to some points in the text, but the audience at the reading would not allow it. The resignation of the animal and the bodily was a popular theme at home. Anticipating Ilya's marriage to Sophia Filosofova, Tolstoy's family members became immersed in discussions of the nature of love and what becomes of love after marriage. Echoes of Tolstoy's mentorship of his older sons, Sergey and Ilya, about love, eternal life, and the role of marriage in governing animal instincts and sexual behavior can be heard in the final chapters of *On Life*.[53]

Biriukov took *On Life* to the printers August 3 1887, with the word "death" removed from the title page. But even that version was not yet final. Endless galley corrections would begin, resulting in the next, and final, seventh round of redactions. From the safety of distance and upon arrival at her residence at the palace, Alexandrine wrote back to Tolstoy with protests against the glorification of the primacy of reason over traditional faith.[54] Painter Ilya Repin arrived on the estate on August 9 to commence his work on what would become the now iconic image of

Tolstoy in the fields. In October, occupying pride of place in shop windows, small lithographs of the image could be purchased at major bookstores. The idea was to sell lithographs around the time volume 13 of the *Collected Works* containing *On Life* would appear. *On Life* had garnered a great deal of public anticipation. Grot volunteered to keep the proofs, and Tolstoy authorized him to enter minor corrections.[55] In October, epigraphs quoting Pascal, Kant, and the Gospel of John were added to the text. The last, the commandment of love, fortified the theme of the loving proliferation of *blago*, which comes to the fore in the final chapters. At the last minute, Tolstoy decided not to move his introduction out of the main text and place portions of it in the appendixes. He was especially enthusiastic about adding a quote from Kant.[56] In his letters written in December, we can see that he thought that the work would come out in a matter of days.

On *Life* was scheduled to appear in 1888 as part of the fifth edition of Tolstoy's *Collected Works* in volume 13. On January 25, 1888, the Moscow Censorship Committee made the first motion to ban the work and forwarded it on April 5, 1888, to the Holy Synod for the final decision. The synodal decision decreed that all published copies of the book should be relinquished to the care of the Archive of the Censorship Committee and that all printing had to stop. Of the six hundred pilot copies published, only three are known to have survived.[57] Tolstoy would not know until the end of August 1888 whether volume 13 would see the light of day. Archbishop Nikanor was one of the chief enemies of the work.[58]

On Life had already been advertised to subscribers as forthcoming in volume 13. Many disappointed readers had to be reimbursed for the subscription. This was disappointing, but, as *On Life* puts it, "live we must." Sophia Andreevna was bitterly upset. Anticipating the ban and battling against oppressive episodes of ill health during her last pregnancy, the countess rather quickly produced in early 1888 a French translation, *De la vie*, which Tolstoy read and corrected in manuscript in February 1888. This French translation, with further stylistic and idiomatic emendations by the Tastevin brothers, who were teachers of French and booksellers, would appear in France in 1889.[59] Hapgood's translation was also finished in 1888, although Tolstoy had little interest in it.[60]

What was so criminal about *On Life* that only a foreign-language edition of it was marginally tolerable to the authorities? It makes for an absorbing read whether one agrees with its author or not. It invites and even encourages a critical response. But it did not deserve to be banned and suppressed. To explain the objections to the work in Russia, it might be easier to point out what the censors decided to cut from the selections published in *Nedelia* in 1889. Omitted were the portions in which Tolstoy remarks that Christianity has long been called a teaching of happiness and of truth, as well as those sections in which Tolstoy argues for immortality as true undying endlessness, in the sense of Kant's term *wahre Unendlichkeit*. Excluded were Tolstoy's references to what Nietzsche called *Gespenster* (specters)—most frequently understood as human kin in general who are neither physically present nor in any sense close. The remarks that portrayed Tolstoy's Nietzschean spirit of praising "distant ones"—for example, in response to the question from the Pharisaic pettifogger to Christ as to whom one should consider a neighbor—were cut. And what Tolstoy explains as the happiness of the divine part of the "I" was also cut.[61] Outlawed were the sections of chapter 34 in which Tolstoy explains the connection between an individual's errors and his suffering, where one option is neglecting the connection and living with this suffering, and another option is acknowledging the connection and overcoming the grief of senseless and meaningless suffering. And certainly, Tolstoy's very antipatriotic statements about the sin of pledging one's allegiance to one's kin, one's people, or one's fatherland, instead of to all humanity, would have been unimaginable to the censors and were hence excised. The three appendixes especially invited scrutiny, with their emphasis on the importance of active capacities of cognition and decision making that are based on the skills of critical seeing, observation, and understanding.

Digital analysis of the work reveals unprecedented consistency in Tolstoy's verbal and syntactic selections. The words that Tolstoy uses most frequently (and the number of their occurrences) in *On Life* are the following: *zhizn'* (life), 1,078; *blago* (happiness, good), 409; *razum* (reason), 393; *lichnost'* and *lichnyi* (individuality, individual; person, personal), 363; *soznanie* (consciousness), 334; *liubov'* (love), 309; *stradanie* (suffering), 204; *zakon* (law, Logos), 193; *znanie* (knowledge), 171; *razumnoe soznanie* (reasonable consciousness), 164; *smert'* (death), 156; *predstavlenie* (perception, imagination, view, appearance, idea), 129; *otnoshenie* (relationship), 99; *ponimat'* and *ponimanie* (comprehend), 92; *poznat'*, *uznat'*, and *poznanie* ("know" in the imperative sense—as in "Know thyself!"—learn, comprehend, recognize, come to know, get to know, find out, attain knowledge, penetrate, knowing, cognition), 73; *poniatie* (concept), 49; *zabluzhdenie* (error), 39; *dusha* (soul), 27; *umirat'* (to die), 12; *telesnoe* (the bodily), 5; *zagadka* (riddle), 5; and *dukhovnoe* (spiritual), 3.[62] These are the key terms of Tolstoy's linguistic theology and existential ontology, but they are hardly part and parcel of traditional philosophical terminology or any denominationally specific religious doctrine.

Madame Blavatsky's journal *Lucifer* would give *On Life* a glowing review, on several occasions finding similarities between theosophy and Tolstoy's nonecclesiastical comprehension of the aims of individuality.[63] A look at the occurrences of Tolstoy's terminological usage easily substantiates fears based on views more traditional than Madame Blavatsky's about the critical and polemical character of Tolstoy's text. *On Life* proved a disturbing and uncanny piece of reading for traditional Orthodox believers as well, and Alexandrine Tolstaya was one of them. In the previously discussed letter, Alexandrine spared Tolstoy some details. But in her memoir, released in 1911, only after both she and Tolstoy were dead, she recalls how during that now-distant reading in August 1887, she had experienced something of a panic attack as if locked in an anatomical laboratory, wanting to escape, running around the cerebral hallways with no light or exit.[64]

On Life was written during years of political turmoil, seething revolutionary and student movements, and heavy censorial pressure. The Russian philosophical idiom was young and insecure. Much of it was derived from Western philosophical terminology; a great deal was borrowed from theological and nationalistic-bureaucratic vocabulary.[65] Some of Tolstoy's terms, like "reasonable consciousness," were readily adopted by *VFP* and its regular contributors. One of the notable adapters of the term was Vladimir Soloviev (1853–1900), the most original Russian philosopher of the nineteenth century. Along with Grot, he advised Sophia Andreevna on the best way to render the term in French during her work on *De la vie*.[66]

Acquainted with Soloviev since 1875, Tolstoy had acknowledged the role of his critique of positivism as a starter for his "philosophical yeast."[67] Soloviev had posited the incarnation of Christ in the body to be a guarantee of the resurrected unity between divine humanity (Godmanhood) guided by *sophia*–the philosophical wisdom of the being in God–with the All. In 1892–93, Soloviev would publish *The Meaning of Love* (*Smysl liubvi*) in *VFP*, retooling reasonable consciousness into a weapon meant to defeat Tolstoy's subjugation of carnal love to the beastly tiers of being. By 1886–87, Tolstoy knew Soloviev's long-standing view that neither the law of nature (according to which man suffers and dies like an animal without need of achieving aims beyond those having been exhausted at the end of his terminal existence) nor the law of reason and conscience can on their own lead man out of his animality toward truth. Only the vision of Christ's face in the temple of the church, where one can see with one's otherwise powerless mortal eyes Christ represented alive and incarnated, can endow man with the force that can grant him a transcending guidance toward immortality.[68] Soloviev specifically disputes Tolstoy's passion- and anger-free *willing of happiness* (*blagovolenie*) toward all.[69] If Grot was to Tolstoy a nonmalevolent scribe, Soloviev was to him a "brainy deacon's son."[70]

Grot's forewords to *VFP* in its beginning stages, and many of his other works, speak in echoes of Tolstoy's voice without necessarily being aware of the tribute owed to Tolstoy for the formation of his vocabulary and his philosophy.[71] Grot, whose letter of introduction to Tolstoy in 1885 spoke of the tasks of philosophy in unleashing the "subjective creativity" (*sub'ek-tivnoe tvorchestvo*) of an individual,[72] was also one of the first, from around 1893, to start comparing Tolstoy with Nietzsche and characterizing them as the two most essential and least traditional thinkers of modernity. The comparison was prompted in great measure by Tolstoy's own disparaging remarks, in works like *Religion and Morality* (*Religiia i nravstvennost'*, 1893), about Nietzsche's disordered paeans to overmen—*Uebermensch'ev, sverkh-chelovekov*, as Tolstoy writes (39:8–10, 20). Just as he could not accept Schopenhauer's dictum that to rid himself of suffering man should extinguish his will to live along with the autonomy of his freedom, Tolstoy could not accept the absolute voluntarism of Zarathustra's dictum that man is something that should be overcome.[73] Unlike Kant in the famous phrase, Tolstoy believed in man's capacity to straighten out the crooked timber of earthly humanity.

Is *On Life* compatible with Nietzsche's ideas? Philosophical ideas were as important for Tolstoy as the style in which they were expressed. Nietzsche's style was too footloose for Tolstoy's taste, even though the professional philosopher's shoe was too narrow. By contrast, representatives of the young philosophical tradition in Russia held on tight to their professional language, feeling something close to a possibility of gaining prideful accreditation in their self-definition as philosophers—by training and vocation. They loved using their specialist terms; they loved to designate one another as belonging to a particular philosophical faction or school or movement. From the point of view of the lack of many or all these component parts in *On Life*, they criticized Tolstoy.

After delivering his talk on the concept of life at MPS and in the first weeks of his escape to Yasnaya Polyana to write, Tolstoy shared with Sophia Andreevna, on April 7, 1887, the following opinion about the importance of lucid style in philosophical writing that best captures his antiscribe mind-set: "From the communication with professors come wordiness, difficult wordings, and lack of clarity; from the communication with the peasants come brevity, the beauty of language, and clarity" (84:22). During the first years after the completion of *On Life* and after its ban, and because of the lack of extra copies of the destroyed print run of the work, Tolstoy found it most rewarding to hold forth on the topics of *On Life* eye to eye and head-to-head through personal conversations or letter exchanges. Many of these interlocutors would never get to read *On Life*, or would read it only years later, but they would carry memories of its messages with them through their lives. *On Life* should be remembered for its Socratic approach.

Published philosophy was less exciting for Tolstoy. He disliked the first issue of *VFP* when it was released in November 1889 for its jargon, arcane disconnections, and the arguments from the point of view of "the Mother of God of Iversk," in an article on the nature of human consciousness by Prince Sergey Trubetskoy.[74] He nonetheless continued to selectively attend the sessions of MPS into the early 1900s. Tolstoy supported Grot in every sense until Grot's untimely death in 1899 at forty-seven, and he defended the activity of MPS and the autonomy of Moscow University against the authorities. At Grot's special request, Tolstoy would publish *What Is Art?* in the last issue of *VFP* of 1897 and the first issue of 1898. Several reviews of *On Life* and commentaries on them also appeared in *VFP*.[75]

The reviews and responses to *On Life* selected for the present volume give a hint as to the intense interest in and the lively spirit of responses to Tolstoy's thinking about the best solutions for mortal lives. The historical supplement contains five examples of published responses to *On Life*. Two are from ordinary readers–Tolstoy's favorite part of the audience–who were both taken with *On Life*. In the first example, somebody signing his defense of Tolstoy as "Petersburg Burgher" rises up against the reactionary writings and the rudeness and shallowness of the conservative critic Protopopov's "Lev Tolstoy, His 'Art' and 'Philosophy.'" The Burgher's aim is to disprove Protopopov's far-fetched allegations leveled at Tolstoy– namely, that he wishes happiness (*blago*) only to unkempt and bearded peasants (*volosatym i borodatym*), and that his speeches and philosophy are immoral, a criticism that Protopopov makes while reminding Tolstoy that a human being is no planet, mineral, or plant, but a man.[76]

P. K. Novitskaya, a very young woman from Bessarabia writing to *VFP* in 1895, is astonished with the journal's decision to give so much space in four issues to philosopher Kozlov's evaluation of *On Life*.[77] Novitskaya in fact questions the ability of this dry, conservative academic with a history of an ill-disposed attitude toward Tolstoy to appreciate the writer's work. A staunch supporter of philosophical personalism, Kozlov had always had a Comtean annoyance with any sort of *l'anarchie intellectuelle*. But in the middle sections of his fifteen letters on Tolstoy's *On Life*–which are rather long and dull denunciations of Tolstoy, unenlivened by the genre in which they're written with an implied epistolary partner–Kozlov confesses that what drew him to reading *On Life* was not its theory of happiness, which he found to be pieced together from eclectic bits of various systems dominated by rationalist-Epicurean impulses, but the work's stylistic brilliance.[78] As we can see, Novitskaya calls into question Kozlov's chief complaint, which was grounded in his personalist convictions against Tolstoy–namely, that "life beyond time and space is the life of lifeless spirits, which has nothing to do with us, sinners."[79]

The historical supplement contains two other responses that both belong to professionally trained philosophers–Soloviev and Grot. These two responses show how differently each of these close friends was affili-ated with the arguments in *On Life*–Soloviev from the point of belief in the doctrine of resurrection, and Grot from the point of view of radical ethics, which leads him to a comparison between Tolstoy and Nietzsche.

I place the beginning of Soloviev's letter drafts around 1889 or 1890, possibly 1891, because it is then that Soloviev sought to involve Tolstoy in the construction of a theocratic kingdom built from historical dialectics. Tolstoy's "reasonable consciousness" seemed the right- and Hegelian-sounding term to Soloviev to go with, fusing into a dialectical competition, as it does, the objectivity of observant reason with the subjectivity of the self.[80] In March 1889, Soloviev went often to speak with Tolstoy, though the conversations, according to Tolstoy's diary, did not always go smoothly. Rather than a theocratic kingdom at the center and as an end goal of historical life, Tolstoy's fulfillment of the meaning of life is in "the carrying out of the will of the Father, participating in His cause and the life of His, in availing Him of living through me" (*v predostavlenii Emu zhit' cherez menia*) (March 19, 1889; 50:54).

Tolstoy's diary explanation is thus very different from Soloviev's interpretation of reasonable consciousness. The former emphasizes the anthropocentric, horizontal plane of life, which needs to *know* the mean-ing of its existence in order to implement it by *allowing* God to use its temporal life-space. The subordination of the bodily and the material to the reasonable and the spiritual is needed (Tolstoy calls this a process of self-elevation, see chapters 14 and 31 of *On Life*) for the sake of attaining a higher level of understanding that allows for the successful carrying out of our life's business. Elsewhere, Tolstoy quotes Seneca: "Where are the dead? In the same place where the non-born are" (42:21). In effect, Tolstoy's solution to the question of immortality is best summarized in his horizontal river-plane parable in the introduction to *On Life*. The river brings man water from the past and carries the sum of man's contributions into the future, overflowing the limits of his material finality. But he alone is responsible for the maintenance of the mill entrusted to him while alive.

The vertical solution through the resurrection of mortal life to life eternal was in vogue with a large wing of Russian philosophy represented not only by the aforementioned Fedorov and Soloviev but also by many other Russian thinkers. Soloviev was the leader of the trend in the circles closest to MPS. The solutions representing this group were summed up in 1912 after Tolstoy's death by Vasily Zenkovsky's verdict on Tolstoy's denial of personality, this necessary material for resurrection, substituted by Tolstoy with the tedious repetitions of his *reasonable I*. Zenkovsky's essay is typically regarded as the final word on the problem of Tolstoy and immortality, and it states that even the naive teachings about the transmigration of souls are preferable to Tolstoy's "ethical-reasonable" agnosticism. Zenkovsky advises that anyone needing true revelation "would need to go to Church."[81]

These secular voices in Russian religious philosophy that rejected Tolstoy's philosophy should not be confused with the voice of the Church hierarchy per se. Church theology in the present work is represented by Archbishop Nikanor of Kherson and Odessa, who attempted to initiate the excommunication of both Tolstoy and Soloviev. Nikanor is chosen over other Church enemies of Tolstoy and *On Life*, such as John of Kronstadt, Archmandrite Antony (Khrapovitsky), and Theophanous the Recluse, because his involvement with Grot was more personal. In his letter to Grot, which is included here, Nikanor speaks his mind not as an official would but as a human being.[82] Readers should be the judge of the quality of the mind of this "cleric-celebrant," as he was nicknamed by Grot, Soloviev, and the Trubetskoy brothers. Nikanor may belong to a category of his own. He did cause Tolstoy to roar with laughter a few times.

W hile Zenkovsky attributed the popularity of Tolstoy's teaching on life among the general public to the collapse of religious self-consciousness,[83] Alexandrine Tolstaya thought that the sounds of her "roaring Lion's" (*rykaiushchii Lev*) laughter had won over Russia and Europe and conquered hearts as far away as America, thanks as much to his charismatic daring as to the complete incapacity of his Russian critics to offer a sophisticated analysis of his views, especially the clerical and religious intellectuals and theologians. They could not rise to Tolstoy's level of intelligence or brilliance so as to halt the advance of his captivating perversions against the divine truths ordained by the Church. According to Alexandrine, America could not really understand the essence of Tolstoy's view either.[84]

Tolstoy would again disagree. The closest American links concerning *On Life* that Tolstoy had a chance to enjoy in his lifetime occurred as a result of the energies of his two popularizers, both former lawyers, talented preachers, followers of Henry George, and activists for nonviolent social reform: Ernest Crosby (1859–1907) and Bolton Hall (1854–1938). Crosby wrote in 1904 that in embracing an active love for mankind instead of a withdrawal into self, Tolstoy had corrected the mistakes of "the Christian ascetics, of the Persian Sufis, of the Hindoo Buddhists, and of the Theosophists of today."[85] Crosby was, in addition, the one who introduced Hall to Tolstoy's texts in English. Using a rather direct application of Tolstoy's concepts of reasonable consciousness and *blago* to American democratic values and their translation into the principles of the pursuit of happiness and *e pluribus unum*, both to be found on earth, Crosby and Hall proved that *On Life* contained elements that rendered it adaptable to foreign historical and personal contexts.[86]

Tolstoy's reappraisals of *On Life* were many. In the years immediately after its ban, he felt jealous and slightly defensively critical toward it. "Yes, and I have been reading *De la vie* in French," he wrote in his diary on March 20, 1889. "It seemed very bad to me, artificial, although not false" (50:55). And then, in the last days of May of the same year, he wrote, "Aimless and obscure *blago*. [. . .] *On Life*: weak, unclear" (50:205). A year later Tolstoy felt dissatisfied with how he had explained individual immortality in *On Life*: in 1890, he replaces references to reasonable consciousness with God's consciousness as the highest form of individual consciousness. Two of his famous works—*The Kreutzer Sonata* and *Resurrection*, commenced in 1887 and 1889, respectively—hinge upon the stark juxtaposition and coexistence in every person of two elements and two choices of being: the animal and the spiritual self. Tolstoy's new approach to the question of resurrection was related to the outcome of this choice. One resurrects oneself (or rises from one's spiritual death) through consciousness, but in 1890 Tolstoy leaned toward believing that character only—not consciousness—could be revived in the flesh in future generations.[87] However, until 1892 at least, whenever the Church establishment attempted to deal blows to his theory of "inquisitive reason"—the name given by detractors to reasonable consciousness—by claiming that it was a positivist protest against the Russian Orthodox understanding of life that was destructive to the faithful and the hesitant, Tolstoy rose up vigorously in its defense (66:280).

After Soloviev adopted "reasonable consciousness" as his own term and used it more systematically in his published work in 1892 and 1893, Tolstoy retired the term, either resorting to an upgraded form of *razumenie*, a concept now endowed with a capacity for infection, or using the term in his future aesthetic theory in a basic sense, explaining that *razumenie*, when clear, helps to transmit to other people the content of one's own inner experience (50:125).[88] Some fanatical Tolstoyans also contributed to the author's cooling toward this term and its evaluation as a misstep. One witness recalls that once when a group of Tolstoyans was engaged in deciding on a fateful question—whether it is permissible, from the point of view of reasonable consciousness, to drink tea given its excitement-inducing qualities—Lev Nikolaevich turned away and asked for a cigar, but not without guilt and an excuse that he could sometimes not overcome the urge.[89]

In 1895 and 1896, Tolstoy began using another term, "freedom consciousness" or "freedom of consciousness," by which he meant the capacity of perceiving life clearly, untouched by obfuscating influences of mass hysteria and hypnosis, the vision freed from illusion. When Vanechka died at age seven in 1895, Tolstoy did not theorize this death through the schemes and graphs of reasonable consciousness, as he had done in the summer of 1886 in his diary while contemplating the pros and cons of his own potential death or in the aftermath of Alyosha's death. This time he thought that his grief was a "terrible, nay, a great spiritual event," in which nature takes back the best, seeing the world as yet unprepared for them (February 26 and March 12, 1895; 53:10). On March 31, 1895, he wrote to Alexandrine that Vanechka was sent into this life to infect everyone he touched with love and to unify the people he had touched with it (68:70–71).[90]

Unlike the retirement of "reasonable consciousness," Tolstoy maintained that *blago* in Russian remained the best option for expressing the concept of happiness for all. The following comment by him from his diary entry of February 27, 1896, is helpful for understanding how indispensable the word felt for him, especially because he writes the last six words, "what is good for every body [*sic*]," in his characteristic English: "What is *blago*? I know of only the Russian word that can express this concept. *Blago* is the true good [*istinnoe dobro*], the good for everyone [*dobro dlia vsekh*], *le bien veritable, le bien de tous*, what is good for every body" (53:82).

In 1903, Tolstoy briefly entertained the idea of radically rewriting *On Life* and creating a virtually new philosophical composition on its base. Several short drafts and plans later, he resolved that minus the awkward phrases, like "reasonable consciousness," he was satisfied with the ideas and style of the work and changed his mind, resuming a very active recommending of *On Life* without hesitation to anyone who asked for a resume of his ideas on the meaning of life. In 1889, Tolstoy stated his belief that *On Life* and *My Religion* were the two works most deserving of being translated into Esperanto;[91] by 1909, he came to think *On Life* to be most deserving of being recorded onto gramophone records. On October 17, 1909, representatives of Obshchestvo Deiatelei Periodicheskoi Pechati i Literatury [the Society of Workers of Periodic Press and Literature] and gramophone enthusiasts arrived at Yasnaya Polyana. The following day, Tolstoy's voice was recorded on five plastic records: two in Russian, the remainder in English, German, and French. Tolstoy wrote in his diary two days later, "I have reread my writings on the occasion of the phonograph: 'On the Meaning of Life,'[92] *On Life*, and so on, and it is so clear that I should not ruin what has been already done" (57:154).

On his deathbed at Astapovo, on October 31, 1910, he asked Alexandra Lvovna, his then youngest living child, to record for him his final thoughts on the human role in life in his diary. On this occasion, his diary records that man is God's "manifestation in matter, space, and time. The more of God manifested in man (life) becomes unified with the manifestations (lives) of other creatures, the more he exists. The unification within this life of one's own with the lives of other creatures is carried out through love. God is not love, but the more there is love the more (of) God man manifests, and the more he truly exists" (58:143). On November 1, 1910, he wrote to his elder children, Tatyana and Sergey, encouraging them to live by the guidance of their independently won reasonable relationship with life: "The views you have acquired about Darwinism, evolution, and the struggle for existence won't explain to you the meaning of your life and won't give you guidance in your actions, and a life without an explanation of its meaning and importance, and without the unfailing guidance that stems from it is a pitiful existence. Think about it—I say it, probably, on the eve of my death, because I love you" (82:223). In these last testaments, Tolstoy speaks in the voice of John the Theologian described by him so unforgettably in chapter 30 of *On Life*.

The most penetrating and philosophically sophisticated of the foreign responses to *On Life* came from Germany, after the appearance in 1902 of a fine translation, *Das Leben*, in volume 5 of Tolstoy's *Collected Works*, overseen from 1901 by Raphael Löwenfeld.[93] This edition was available to those older thinkers still alive at the beginning of the twentieth-century with whom *On Life* was in direct conversation originally: Eduard von Hartmann, Ernst Haeckel, and Wilhelm Wundt.[94] But it was in the works of the younger generations of German thinkers, represented by Max Weber, Georg Simmel, Max Scheler, Martin Heidegger, Ludwig Wittgenstein, and Thomas Mann, that Tolstoy's philosophy of life would strike the strongest chords. This, however, is a topic for an extended conversation elsewhere.[95]

Tolstoy duly notes in *On Life* that we live in an age of scientific and medical advancement, of faster and more comfortable means of transportation and improved means of communication, of ever proliferating networks of institutions offering pleasures, catering to all tastes and levels of income. Yet the growing volume of our obligations toward the self, family, and society are disorienting and all-consuming. The pressures of competition in modern life focus mainly on achieving prosperity and success, which are mistaken for inalienable happiness and which keep the secrets of living disconnected from the tasks of personal responsibility and discovery. Tolstoy did not write for postindustrial society, but *On Life* speaks to our postmodern age and to those who search for a happy universal individuality and who celebrate diversity but who have seen life fundamentally altered, have lost connection to their common source, and are suffering.[96] For Tolstoy, there is neither shelter nor consolation in the solipsistic security and intellectual superiority of the Cartesian cogito. And salvation is not to be found in Haeckel's recapitulation theory either, which "saves" by suggesting that in our individual ontogeny we recapitulate the evolutionary development of common phylogeny. *On Life* asks someone torn between necessity and freedom and in a state of what Tolstoy calls split consciousness, who yet hopes to become integral and whole, to pay attention to *how* one thinks and *what* one should think about his or her role in the world first, next, and last. It reminds us powerfully that we are human-animals, but that there is more to this double existence than bodily experiences and survival. We cannot deny or expel our animal nature, bodily sufferers that we all are, because that nature depends on our power of reasoning for support. We can reinforce it with our compassionate reasoning and live in the right collaborative partnership with it—and also with minerals, crystals, embryos, the young grass, horses in the shed, rivers with the mill, the starry skies, and with the singular I's of others.

The pattern of survival that *On Life* proposes and the stories that it tells share little with ancient teachings of eudaemonism,[97] little with Stoicism, which hinges on the idea of the superiority of virtue, little with Renaissance humanism and its utopias of earthly felicity, and even less with eighteenth- and nineteenth-century utilitarianism and positivism and their slogan of the greatest quantity of happiness for the greatest number. It likewise shares little with the aspirations of the New Age, the life of cyborgs, zombies, or clones and the exultations to parody dehumanized creation; it shares little with the celebrations of philosophical simulacra that claim that life is not real (not lovable or not livable). It can be said—more safely—that *On Life* is closer, in the range of problems that it raises, to existentialism and existential ontology. We can notice a resemblance between *On Life* and Kierkegaard's discussion of the modes of an individual's *unique relationship* to truth.[98] The resemblance is also clear between *On Life* and some of Sartre's ideas about the transcendence of the ego and the erasure of the phenomenology of the personal for the sake of achieving the state of a *singular universal* committed to freedom.[99] We can notice a resemblance as well with Simone Weil's celebration of the selfless impersonal,[100] and, closer to our day, with Alain Badiou's insistence on *choosing* our ontology.[101] Yet *On Life* cannot, because of its emphasis on the freedom of consciousness and on the undying uniqueness of our relation to the world, be conflated with Heidegger's *Dasein*, which depends on its progress toward death, on the certitude of its finality, and on the ejection of the language of personal consciousness.

Tolstoy thought much about the fate of books and teachings. Some arise and stay in fashion only because they speak in convenient verbiage that does not stretch the limits of the accepted worldview. But he also thought that the fates of books depend on the state of mind of their readers.[102] *On Life* is one of those books that stretch and discomfit accepted views, daring its readers toward new horizons of awareness. We hope that the present volume brings to our despairing world an important, inspirational, and properly controversial text concerning the meaning of life, one that echoes the best texts in this philosophical tradition. It belongs on the same shelf with Vauvenargues, Pascal, Montaigne, Schopenhauer, Kierkegaard, Nietzsche, Schweitzer, Weil, Frankl, and our recently lost contemporaries such as Christopher Hitchens and Oliver Sacks. We hope that *On Life*, this unsung classic of Russian thought, this passionate cry against the one-dimensionality of life and the obligations of thought in the age of the crisis of consciousness, returns at last to the transnational philosophical circle out of which it originated and where it rightfully belongs.

Notes

1. The translation of the text of Tolstoy's *On Life* in this volume was a collaboration between Michael Denner and Inessa Medzhibovskaya. Inessa Medzhibovskaya is also the author of all endnotes and annotations to the translated text, as well as the translator of Tolstoy's epigraphs and footnotes and the compiler, translator, and commentator of the entries in the historical supplement.

2. The liberal Saint Petersburg weekly periodical *Nedelia* published such excerpts from the final chapters of *On Life* in issues 1, 2, 3, 4, and 6 of 1889, bereft, of course, of the work's political and religious argument. The first Russian edition of *On Life* not to pass through the hands of the religious censors appeared in Geneva through the effort of the émigré publisher Mikhail Elpidine in 1891. Elpidine published Russian editions of many of Tolstoy's forbidden works, but he rarely edited them accurately. The first full edition of *On Life* printed in Russian appeared after Tolstoy's death, in volume 13 of his *Collected Works*, edited and released in Berlin by his biographer, Pavel Biriukov, in 1911. There were some shorter adaptations of *On Life* that Tolstoy put together in simplified formats or asked his associates to do so on his behalf—for example, Tolstoy's thoughts on life edited by Vladimir Chertkov, published in short and full versions by Chertkov through Free Age Press in England and its affiliates in New York.

3. L. N. Tolstoy, *O zhizni: Aforizmy i izbrannye mysli L. N. Tolstogo, sobrannye L. P. Nikiforovym* (Moscow: Astrel, 2012), 197–300.

4. Count Lyof N. Tolstoi, *Life*, trans. Isabel F. Hapgood (New York: Crowell, 1888).

5. Leo Tolstoy, *On Life*, trans. Agnes and Mable Cook (Hants, Eng.: Free Age Press, 1902). Tolstoy personally corrected the French translation, but he never looked at any of the English translations, except an adaptation of his thoughts by Bolton Hall in 1907.

6. Count Lev N. Tolstoy, *My Religion, On Life, Thoughts on God, On the Meaning of Life*, trans. and ed. Leo Wiener (Boston: Estes, 1904).

7. Most notable of these is L. N. Tolstoy, *What Is Art?*, trans. Aylmer Maude (London: Scott, 1898). It earned rave reviews in 1898 from G. B. Shaw, a critic who was hard to please (see G. B. Shaw, "Tolstoy on Art," *Daily Chronicle*, September 10, 1898).

8. Maude's translation of *On Life* was reprinted by Oxford University Press, unchanged, in 1950 and 1959.

9. This is Tolstoy's difficult masterpiece written that same year, the comedic-didactic drama in five acts, *The Power of Darkness, or "When the Claw Is Caught, the Whole Bird Is Lost"* (1886; 26:123–244).

10. Anna Seuron, *Graf Leo Tolstoi: Intimes aus seinem Leben* [Count Leo Tolstoy: Intimate Details from His Life], ed. Eugen Zabel (Berlin: Cronbach, 1895), 88–93.

11. As recalled by Tolstoy's elder son, Sergey, in his later memoir; see S. L. Tolstoy, *Ocherki bylogo* [Sketches from the Past], 2nd exp. ed., ed. K. Malysheva (Moscow: Gosudartsvennoe Izdatel'stvo Khudozhestvennoi Literatury, 1956), 154.

12. Tolstoy writes, "It was merry for me to look at life through this little mirror of art" (chapter 4; 23:14–15).

13. As recalled by Tolstoy's second son, Ilya; see Ilya Tolstoy, *Tolstoy, My Father: Reminiscences*, trans. Ann Dunnigan (Chicago: Cowles, 1971), 169.

14. The phrase belongs to Sophia Andreevna. For her description of the mowing hazards, see S. A. Tolstaya, *Moia zhizn'*, ed. V. B. Remizov and L. V. Gladkova (Moscow: Kuchkovo Pole / Gosudartsvennyi Muzei Tolstogo, 2011), 1:522–23, 530–33. The translation of the phrase is my own. Tolstaya's memoir is available in English: Sofia Andreevna Tolstaya, *My Life*, ed. Andrew Donskov, trans. John Woodsworth and Arkadi Klioutchanski (Ottawa: University of Ottawa Press, 2010). The events concerning 1886 that led up to the injury are described in Tolstaya, *My Life*, 459–83.

15. See the graph in Tolstoy's diary in the entry for August 28, 1886 (page 218).

16. "Posha" (a term of endearment), rather than the more customary "Pasha" (a diminutive form of the name "Pavel"), was Biriukov's nickname in Tolstoy's home.

17. A. K. Chertkova [Diterikhs], "Moi pervye vospominaniia o L. N. Tolstom" [My First Recollections about L. N. Tolstoy], in *Lev Nikolaevich Tolstoy: Iubileinyi sbornik*, ed. N. N. Gusev (Moscow: Gosudarstvennoe izdatel'stvo, 1928), 145–51, 159.

18. The phrase itself had been known since 1886, when the French edition of de Vogüé's book first appeared (see Vicomte E. M. de Vogüé, *Le roman russe* [Paris: Plon, 1886]). The actual phrase in French is "l'esprit d'un chimiste anglais dans l'âme d'un bouddhiste hindou" (the spirit of an English chemist with the soul of a Hindu Buddhist) (282).

19. De Vogüé, *Le roman russe*, 282.

20. Chertkova, "Moi pervye vospominaniia o L. N. Tolstom," 160–79.

21. Tatiana Lvovna notes, on October 12, 1886, that Chertkov is already a groom. See T. L. Sukhotina-Tolstaya, *Dnevnik* [*Diary*], ed. T. N. Volkova (Moscow: Sovremennik, 1984), 128.

22. The identification of Jesus's awareness of life with divine Logos, and of his life and death with the idea of incarnation of the life of Logos in the world,

for which Tolstoy uses the same word, *razumenie*, occurs in many fragments written by Tolstoy from 1879 and is most clearly expressed in his harmonization and translation of the four Gospels: "The awareness of life is God" (24:26). On this, see chapters 8, 9, and 10 in Inessa Medzhibovskaya, *Tolstoy and the Religious Culture of His Time: A Biography of a Long Conversion, 1845–1887* (Lanham, Md.: Lexington Books, 2008), 199–294.

23. L. N. Tolstoy, *Issledovanie dogmaticheskogo bogosloviia* (1879–84), 23:132.

24. The terms "Pharisees" and "Scribes" designate the two antihero groups of false teachers of life in *On Life*.

25. L. N. Tolstoy, "V chem schast'e?" [In What Does Happiness Consist?], *Russkoe Bogatstvo* 7, no. 1 (1886): 133–49.

26. Obolensky published these articles in a brochure format in 1886 and in a slightly expanded form a year later: L. E. Obolensky, *L. N. Tolstoy: Ego filosofskie i nravstvennye idei* [L. N. Tolstoy: His Philosophical and Moral Ideas], 2nd exp. ed. (St. Petersburg: Tsinzerling, 1887).

27. Tolstoy confirmed his knowledge of Obolensky's articles in early October 1886 (63:394).

28. This was an eventful time in the life of the family, which included the death of Sophia Andreevna's mother, just two years Tolstoy's senior, in the Crimea in mid-November.

29. N. N. Strakhov, *Ob osnovnykh poniatiiakh psikhologii i fiziologii* [On Major Concepts of Psychology and Physiology] (St. Petersburg: Zhurnal ministerstva narodnogo prosveshcheniia, 1886).

30. 63:408; *PTS*, 2:721.

31. 63:409; *PTS*, 2:722.

32. See fragment 200/347 in Blaise Pascal, *Oeuvres complètes*, ed. Louis Lafuma (Paris: L'Integrale / Seuil, 1963), 528.

33. Wilhelm Wundt, *Vorlesungen über die Menschen- und Tierseele* [Lectures on the Human and Animal Soul] (Leipzig: Boss, 1863–64).

34. See Strakhov's introductory comments in N. Strakhov, *Mir kak tseloe: Cherty iz nauki o prirode* [The World as a Whole: Outlines from the Science of Nature] (St. Petersburg: Tipografiia Zamyslovskogo, 1872), 1–34.

35. I cover these conversations in detail in Medzhibovskaya, *Tolstoy and the Religious Culture of His Time*, 131–98.

36. On Tolstoy's reading and interpretation of Kant's three questions around "the idea of the highest good," see Medzhibovskaya, *Tolstoy and the Religious Culture of His Time*, 36–37, 51–52, 161–62, 340, 355. Kant writes, "All interest of my reason (the speculative as well as the practical) is united in the following three questions: 1. What can I know? 2. What should I do? 3. What may I hope?" (Immanuel Kant, *Critique of Pure Reason*, trans. and ed.

Paul Guyer and Allen W. Wood [Cambridge: Cambridge University Press, 1998], 677–78).

37. On Tolstoy's indebtedness to Kant's second critique, see the notes to the epigraphs, note 5 to chapter 21, and note 1 to chapter 22.

38. It is worth noting that foundational texts of the German *Neokantianismus* dealing with spiritual values and spiritual experience, such as Wilhelm Dilthey's *Einleitung in die Geisteswissenschaften* [Introduction to the Human Sciences of the Spirit] (1883) and Johannes Volkelt's *Erfahrung und Denken* [Experience and Thought] (1886), had appeared shortly before Tolstoy started writing *On Life*.

39. The Moscow Psychological Society was founded in 1885 by a positivist, Matvei Troitsky, its first chairman.

40. Tolstoy is recorded present on both dates (*PMPS* February 25 and March 5, 1887). Minutes of the March 5 meeting have it thus: "Count L. N. Tolstoy proposed delivering his paper, 'On the Concept of Life,' at the nearest upcoming session."

41. See pages 224–27 in the historical supplement.

42. *Nikolai Iakovlevich Grot v ocherkakh, vospominaniiakh i pis'makh tovarishchei i uchenikov, druzei i pochitatelei.* [Nikolai Iakovlevich Grot in Essays, Reminiscences, and Letters by His Comrades, Students, Friends, and Admirers] (St. Petersburg: Tipografiia Ministerstva Putei Soobshcheniia / Tovarishchestvo I. N. Kushnerev, 1911), 324.

43. For a classic and succinct discussion of the role of Kantian philosophy for Grot and his circle, see Randall Poole, "The Neo-Idealist Reception of Kant in the Moscow Psychological Society," *Journal of the History of Ideas* 60, no. 2 (April 1999): 319–43.

44. An informative reading of *On Life* as a work of self-narration that unites states of consciousness can be found in Irina Paperno, *"Who, What Am I?" Tolstoy Struggles to Narrate the Self* (Ithaca, N.Y.: Cornell University Press, 2014), 131–34.

45. An invaluable paragon of the threnody genre was an unfinished memoir by the great surgeon and educator Nikolai Pirogov (1810–81). Titled *Voprosy zhizni: Dnevnik starogo vracha* (published in English as *Questions of Life: The Diary of an Old Doctor*, trans. and ed. Galina V. Zarechnak [Canton, Mass.: Science History Publications, U.S.A., 1991]), the memoir covered Pirogov's thoughts and reminiscences and became known in intellectual circles.

46. See note 3 to chapter 5, note 5 to chapter 21, and note 2 to chapter 33.

47. See pages 224–27 in the historical supplement for a selection from *Novoe Vremia*.

48. AT GMT, 91/7, 1–2 ob.

49. N. Strakhov, *O vechnykh istinakh: Moi spor o spiritizme* [On Eternal Truths: My Argument on Spiritualism] (St. Petersburg: Tipografiia brat'ev Panteleevykh, 1887).

50. Countess A. A. Tolstaia (1817–1904) was Tolstoy's second aunt and his correspondent for forty-seven years. As a member of the highest ranks of Russian aristocracy and a lady-in-waiting, she grew up and died at the court.

51. S. A. Tolstaya, *Dnevniki* [Diaries], 2 vols., ed. S. A. Rozanova (Moscow: Khudozhestvennaia Literatura, 1978), 1:120.

52. *PTAAT*, 41.

53. Ilya was preparing to marry Sophia Filosofova, about whom we might say that no name could be more fitting for Tolstoy's first daughter-in-law, especially when Tolstoy was at the final stages of *On Life*, in 1887. The final chapters of *On Life*, which speak about the purity of love in new avuncular and fatherly tones, are reflections of Tolstoy's conversations with his sons and daughters about the lofty elements of loving relationships. Three letters written by Tolstoy to Ilya in October 1887 (64:115–19) on marriage resonate with the proof corrections to the final chapters of *On Life*.

54. See pages 228–30 in the historical supplement.

55. This did not happen exactly as Tolstoy had intended. See my commentary on Tolstoy, Nikolai Grot, and MPS in *CG*.

56. See the notes to the epigraphs and notes 4 and 5 to chapter 21.

57. L. N. Tolstoy, *Sochineniia grafa L. N. Tolstogo. Chast' 13-ia. O zhizni* [Works of Count L. N. Tolstoy. Part 13. On Life] (Moscow: Mamontov, 1888), which includes 24 pages of introduction and front matter, 275 pages of text, and 12 blank pages. The editor was able to examine the two copies held at GMT.

58. See Nikanor's letter to Grot (pages 231–34).

59. L. N. Tolstoy, *Comte Léon Tolstoi: De la vie, seule traduction revue et corrigée par l'auteur* [Count Leo Tolstoy: *On Life*, sole translation reviewed and corrected by the author], trans. Sophia Andreevna Tolstaya, ed. Edmond Tastevin and Félix Tastevin (Paris: Marpon et Flammarion, 1889).

60. Tolstoy was already working full-time on *The Kreutzer Sonata*, the new play *Fruits of Enlightenment* (a comedy making fun of the excesses of spiritualism), and on drafts of new articles on art that would eventually become *What Is Art?* For a connection between *Fruits of Enlightenment* and *On Life*, see Michael Gordin, "Tolstoy Sees Foolishness, and Writes: From *On Life* to 'Fruits of Enlightenment,' and Back Again," forthcoming in *CG*. See also my editorial comments in *CG*.

61. See chapters 22, 23.

62. Inflected and derivative forms of these words were included in the counts.

63. Tolstoy was titled "a true theosophist" in the very first issue of the journal in September 1887. In the November issue of the same year, Madame Blavatsky translated—although rather freely—the *Novoe vremia* version of Tolstoy's talk at MPS in March. Further praises and evaluations of Tolstoy would follow. See A. I. R., "A True Theosophist," *Lucifer* 1, no. 1 (September 15, 1887): 55–62; H. P. B., "The Science of Life," *Lucifer* 1, no. 3 (November 15, 1887): 203–11; "Leo Tolstoi and His Unecclesiastical Christianity," *Lucifer* 3, no. 37 (September 15, 1890): 9–14. I discuss Blavatsky and Tolstoy in detail in *CG*.

64. *PTAAT*, 42.

65. A great resource on the intellectual atmosphere of the era is G. M. Hamburg and Randall A. Poole, *A History of Russian Philosophy, 1830–1930: Faith, Reason, and the Defense of Human Dignity* (Cambridge: Cambridge University Press, 2013).

66. On this, see S. A. Tolstaya, *Moia zhizn'*, 2:47, and Grot and Soloviev in the historical supplement. Before 1886–87, Soloviev had used the phrase only occasionally, in the Hegelian sense of historical self-consciousness objectified by reason.

67. See Tolstoy's letter to Strakhov, August 25, 1875 (62:196–97); *PTS*, 1:215–17.

68. These views are especially vivid in Soloviev's *Lectures on Divine Humanity* [*Chteniia o bogochelovechestve*] (1877–81) and *The Spiritual Foundations of Life* [*Dukhovnye osnovy zhizni*] (1883).

69. *Blagovolenie* is one of Tolstoy's most important terms in *On Life*.

70. Ilya Tolstoy, *Tolstoy, My Father*, 172.

71. This problem is covered comprehensibly in *CG*.

72. See the letter sent by Grot from Odessa on January 12, 1885 (AT GMT, 91/1, 5–6 ob.).

73. The famous phrase in *Also Sprach Zarathustra* has it thus: "Der Mensch ist Etwas, das überwunden werden soll" (Friedrich Nietzsche, *Also Sprach Zarathustra*, in *Kritische Gesamtausgabe* [Collected Works Critical Edition], ed. Giorgio Colli and Mazzino Montinari [Berlin: de Gruyter, 1968], 6:8).

74. An impatient comment about Grot and the founders of the journal and their ways of philosophizing is recorded in Tolstoy's diary on November 2, 1889 (50:172–73). Tolstoy had in mind the first issue of *VFP*, which published the first installment of Trubetskoy's four-part essay, Kn. S. N. Trubetskoy, "O prirode chelovecheskogo soznaniia" [On the Nature of Human Consciousness], *VFP* 1, no. 1 (1889): 83–126.

75. For a summary of some of these reviews (by Kozlov, Astafiev, Prince Dmitry Tsertelev, and Akim Volynsky), see James P. Scanlan, "Tolstoy among

the Philosophers: His Book *On Life* and Its Critical Reception," *Tolstoy Studies Journal*, 18 (2006): 52–69. See also James P. Scanlan, "Tolstoy's Implausible Theodicy: The Justification of Suffering in *On Life*," forthcoming in *CG*, which focuses criticism on the problem of theodicy specifically. See also Poole and Medzhibovskaya in *CG* that discuss Tolstoy's shorter publications in *VFP*.

76. For the refutation of Protopopov by the "Petersburg Burgher," see pages 235–37 in the historical supplement. The great number of quotation marks around the words "art" and "philosophy" are Protopopov's and designate both as false idols (see M. A. Protopopov, "Lev Tolstoy, ego 'iskusstvo' i 'filosofiia,' " [Lev Tolstoy, His 'Art' and 'Philosophy' "], *Severnyi Vestnik*, nos. 10 and 11 [1888], nos. 10 and 12 [1889]). I am quoting from a brochure edition of these articles assembled by the author in M. A. Protopopov, *Literaturno-kriticheskie kharakteristiki* [Literary-Critical Characteristics] (St. Petersburg: Vol'f, 1888), 154, 178.

77. See pages 244–46 in the historical supplement.

78. A. A. Kozlov, "Pis'ma o knige gr. L. N. Tolstogo 'O zhizni,' " [Letters on Count L. N. Tolstoy's Book *On Life*], *VFP* 5, no. 1 (1891): 1–33; 6, no. 2 (1891): 68–96; 7, no. 3 (1891): 69–102; 8, no. 4 (1891): 77–109. Kozlov's letters represent the monadologist, Leibnizian point of view of Russian philosophy. Other monadologists to have critiqued *On Life* include Petr Astafiev and mathematician Nikolai Bugaev. The assessment of *De la vie* by a French exponent of monadology, who was also a neo-Kantian, Charles Renouvier, was also negative.

79. A. A. Kozlov, "Pis'ma o knige" [Letter 12], *VFP* 7, no. 3 (1891): 87.

80. See pages 238–40 in the historical supplement. The controversies of Soloviev's letter to Tolstoy are discussed by me more fully in *CG*.

81. V. V. Zenskovsky, "Problema bessmertiia u L. N. Tolstogo" [The Problem of Immortality in L. N. Tolstoy], in *O religii L'va Tolstogo: Sbornik statei* [On the Religion of Lev Tolstoy; A Collection of Essays] (Moscow: Put', 1012), 44, 52, 58. An excellent introduction to major Russian theories and projects about immortality is Irene Masing-Delic, *Abolishing Death: A Salvation Myth of Russian Twentieth-Century Literature* (Stanford, Calif.: Stanford University Press, 1992). The book covers the period from the turn of the twentieth century to the early 1930s and includes a discussion of Nikolai Fedorov and Vladimir Soloviev (see 26–122).

82. See page 238 in the historical supplement.

83. Zenkovsky, "Problema bessmertiia u L. N. Tolstogo," 58. A survey of idealist readings of Tolstoy's philosophy can be found in Randall A. Poole, "Tolstoy and Russian Idealism," forthcoming in *CG*.

84. *PTAAT*, 43–45.

85. Ernest Howard Crosby, *Tolstoy and His Message* (London: Fifield, 1904), 43.

86. Bolton Hall, *Even as You and I* (London: Tennyson Neely, 1897). After Crosby's death, Hall included his friend's unpublished summary of *On Life* in Bolton Hall, *Life, and Love, and Peace* (New York: Arcadia Press, 1909), 196–204. Tolstoy endorsed Hall's paraphrase, and Hall printed the expansion of *Even as You and I*, with Tolstoy's letter of approval on the frontispiece, as Bolton Hall, *What Tolstoy Taught* (New York: Huebsch, 1911).

87. See Tolstoy's diary entry for July 25, 1890; 51:66–67. He writes, "But my consciousness is God–and not to have character" (51–66).

88. See note 3 to chapter 25.

89. N. Timkovsky, "Moe lichnoe znakomstvo s L. N. Tolstym" [My Personal Acquaintance with L. N. Tolstoy], in *L. N. Tolstoy v vospominaniiakh sovremennikov* [L. N. Tolstoy in the Reminiscences of His Contemporaries], 2 vols., ed. G. V. Krasnova (Moscow: Khudozhestvennaia Literatura, 1978), 1:437.

90. For comparison, see the descriptions of the death of his brother, Nikolenka, in chapter 31, where he writes as if nothing terrible had happened.

91. See note 13 to Tolstoy's introductory chapter of *On Life*.

92. "The Meaning of Life" (O smysle zhizni) is not a separate book or a specific edition of Tolstoy's, but a collection of his thoughts expressed in his diaries, personal correspondence, and in tidbits of his conversations that Chertkov published in a number of versions, undated and without reference. Tolstoy neither expressly objected to such publications nor felt like authorizing them.

93. Graf Leo N. Tolstoj, *Sämtliche Werke*, ed. Raphael Löwenfeld, trans. Carl Ritter (Leipzig: Diederichs, 1901–11).

94. Tolstoy's repetition of the word "riddle" in several chapters of *On Life* anticipates Haeckel's *Die Welträtsel* (1895–99). The work is known in English by its translated title: Ernst Haeckel, *The Riddle of the Universe*, trans. Joseph McCabe (London: Harper, 1900).

95. A summary of these conversations can be found in Inessa Medzhibovskaya, "Tolstoy and Heidegger on the Ways of Being," in *Heidegger in Russia and Eastern Europe*, ed. Jeff Love (London: Rowman and Littlefield, 2017), 55–94.

96. I have paraphrased here "universal singularity," a term used by Slavoj Žižek in his reworking of the Romantic notion of "singular universal." See Slavoj Žižek, *Indivisible Remainder: An Essay on Schelling and Related Matters* (London: Verso, 1996), 64. By mentioning "people and reasons," I am involving in the conversation the late Derek Parfit, *Reasons and Persons* (Oxford: Oxford University Press, 1984). Aside from these resonances, a sustained critique of

Tolstoy's rationality can be found in Jeff Love, "The End of *On Life*: Kant with Tolstoy," forthcoming in *CG*.

97. Tolstoy thoroughly revises the famous definition of eudaemonia in *The Nicomachean Ethics* that "the good is happiness" (*NE* 1094a–1099a). On the pros and cons of Tolstoy's version of impersonal life, see Eugene Thacker, "Notes on an Impersonal Life," forthcoming in *CG*.

98. See Søren Kierkegaard, *Concluding Unscientific Postscript to "Philosophical Fragments,"* 2 vols., ed. and trans. Howard V. Hong and Edna H. Hong (Princeton, N.J.: Princeton University Press, 1992), 2:48–51.

99. See especially Sartre's discussion of Kierkegaard's "singular universal" in the act of choosing freedom and sacrificing "me" in *We Have Only This Life to Live: The Selected Essays of Jean-Paul Sartre, 1939–1975*, ed. Ronald Aronson and Adrian van den Hoven (New York: New York Review of Books, 2013), 403–32.

100. See Weil's essay "Human Personality" in *An Anthology*, ed. Siân Miles (New York: Grove Press, 1986), 49–78.

101. Alain Badiou, *Being and Event*, trans. Oliver Feltham (London: Bloomsbury, 2013).

102. Tolstoy expresses these ideas most eloquently, and—from the perspective of received orthodoxy—most controversially, in his essay "On Shakespeare and On Drama" [O Shekspire i o drame, 1903–4]. It is there that he uses the phrase from Terentianus placed in the epigraph to this introduction (see especially 35:262).

A NOTE ON THE TEXT

All dates for events, publications, letters, personal and official correspondence within and from Russia before 1918, unless otherwise noted, refer to the Julian calendar then in effect in the territory of the Russian Empire. All dates in the same period covering the writings, publications, and letters of Tolstoy's correspondents, critics, and translators in the West adhere to the Gregorian calendar.

All italics in the text of *On Life* are Tolstoy's. Tolstoy's footnotes in the text of *On Life* are placed at the bottom of the page where they occur. Editor's notes and commentary appear in the endnote section after the text of *On Life*, where Aylmer Maude's explanations to Tolstoy's text in 1934 are also cited. An ellipsis without brackets indicates an omission or gap in the original. An ellipsis in square brackets indicates the editor's choice of a section of a quote or partial citation. We have stayed close to the modified Library of Congress Romanization system. For cases in which proper names and toponymics have a stable tradition of English usage and spelling (e.g., Ivan Ilyich, Yasnaya Polyana, Gogol), they are so spelled. We used "Sophia" and "Soloviev" rather than "Sofia" and "Solovyov." For "Kuzminsky" and for most names longer than one syllable, we do not use soft signs. We have translated this text using the terminology of Tolstoy's time, and for this reason "man" as it was used then is masculine gendered and stands for *chelovek*.

On Life

Survey of the Contents of
On Life by Chapters

L'homme n'est qu'un roseau, le plus faible de la nature, mais c'est un roseau pensant. Il ne faut pas que l'univers entier s'arme pour l'écraser. Une vapeur, une goutte d'eau suffit pour le tuer. Mais quand l'univers l'écraserait, l'homme serait encore plus noble que ce qui le tue, puisqu'il sait qu'il meurt et l'avantage que l'univers a sur lui, l'univers n'en sait rien. Ansi, toute notre dignité consiste donc en la pensée. C'est de là qu'il faut nous relever, non de l'espace et de la durée. Travaillons donc à bien penser voilà le principe de la morale.

—PASCAL

Zwei Dinge erfüllen das Gemüt mit immer neuer und zunehmender Bewunderung und Ehrfurcht, je öfter und anhaltender sich das Nachdenken damit beschäftigt: Der bestirnte Himmel über mir, und das moralische Gesetz in mir . . . Das erste fängt von dem Platze an, den ich in der äußern Sinnenwelt einnehme, und erweitert die Verknüpfung, darin ich stehe, ins unabsehlich-Große mit Welten über Welten und Systemen von Systemen, überdem noch in grenzenlose Zeiten ihrer periodischen Bewegung, deren Anfang und Fortdauer. Das zweite fängt von meinem unsichtbaren Selbst, meiner Persönlichkeit, an, und stellt mich in einer Welt dar, die wahre Unendlichkeit hat, aber nur dem Verstande spürbar ist, und mit welcher (dadurch aber auch zugleich mit allen jenen sichtbaren Welten) ich mich nicht, wie dort, in bloß zufälliger, sondern allgemeiner und notwendiger Verknüpfung erkenne.

—KANT, [*KRIT. DER PRAKT. VERN. BESCHLUSS*]

A new commandment I give unto you, That you love one another . . .

—JOHN 13:34

Introduction

Let us imagine a man whose only way of making a living is a grain mill. This man is the son and grandson of millers, so he knows how to tend every part of the mill so it grinds properly. Though he does not know mechanics, this man, as best as he has been able, has tuned all the parts of the mill so it grinds quickly and properly. And so the man has lived and earned his living.

But then, having heard some vague talk about mechanics, it occurs to this man to start thinking about the inner workings of the mill. He starts to observe how one part makes another spin.

From the rynd to the millstone, from the millstone to the shaft, from the shaft to the wheel, from the wheel to the water box, to the weir, and then to the water. He becomes convinced that the weir and the water are the only things that matter. The man is so delighted at the discovery that, instead of doing as he had done before—testing the grind of the flour, raising and lowering the millstones, knocking them tight, stretching and relaxing the belt—he begins studying the river. And the mill goes out of alignment. People start telling the miller that things are amiss. He argues with them, and then goes back to theorizing about the river. Having worked so long and so hard on this, and argued so hotly and so often with those who have tried to demonstrate to him that he has been thinking wrongly, in the end he becomes convinced that the river is the mill itself.

The miller responds to all proof of the wrongness of his theories by pointing out that no mill grinds without water. Consequently, to know the mill one must know how to channel water, one must know the force of its movement, and where it comes from. Therefore, to know the mill one must get to know the river.

Logically speaking, the miller's theory is irrefutable. The only way to talk him out of his error is by demonstrating to him that, in every act of theorizing, the theory itself is less important than the rank in order that the theory occupies: to think fruitfully, in other words, one ought to know what to think about first, and what next. One would need to demonstrate

51

to him that a reasonable endeavor differs from an insane one only inasmuch as a reasonable one distinguishes its theories according to their relative importance—what theory should come first, second, third, tenth, and so on. An insane endeavor neglects this order. One would also need to point out to him that the determination of this order is not arbitrary but instead depends on the aim of the theorizing.

What qualifies all acts of theorizing as reasonable is that the aim of the theorizing imposes an order in which each separate theory is ranked.

And a theory disconnected from the general aim of the theorizing is insane, no matter how logical it might be.

The miller's aim is to grind grain properly, and this very aim—if he keeps it in focus—will determine for him the indubitable order and sequence of his theorizing about millstones, the wheel, the dam, and the river.

Without this relationship toward their ultimate aim, no matter how beautiful and logical, the miller's theories will be incorrect and, more important, they will be frivolous. They will turn out like Kifa Mokievich's theorizing about how thick the shell of an elephant's egg would have to be if elephants hatched like birds.[1] In my view, the theories of contemporary science about life are precisely like Kifa Mokievich's.

Life is the mill that man wishes to study. A mill is necessary to the extent that it does a good job grinding; life is necessary only inasmuch as it is good. And one cannot forget this aim of study, not for a single moment, without being punished. If he forgets it, his theories will fall out of their proper sequence and they will become like the frivolous theories of Kifa Mokievich about what sort of gunpowder you would need to break through the shell of an elephant egg.[2]

One studies life only to make it better, just as people who have advanced humanity along the path of knowledge have investigated life. But together with these genuine teachers and benefactors of humanity there are, and always have been, theorizers who have abandoned the aim of theorizing and instead deliberate about how life originates, and what makes the mill spin around.[3] Some say it's because of the water, while others say it has to do with the way the mill is designed. A debate flares up, and the subject of the theory fades further and further away and is completely eclipsed by irrelevant topics.

There is an ancient joke: A Yid and a Christian are arguing. The Christian, responding to the convoluted subtleties of the Yid, slaps the Yid's bald spot, making a smacking sound. The Christian asks, "What made the sound, my hand or your bald head?" Their debate on faith was thus replaced by a new insoluble question.[4]

Something similar to this joke has, since antiquity, taken place along-side the search for authentic human knowledge.

We have long theorized about how life originated: Did it arise from immaterial origins? Or from various combinations of matter? And these theories continue to this day, and there seems to be no end to them—precisely because the aim of this theorizing has been abandoned, and all the theories go on independent of life's aim. When they say "life" they do not mean life, but what causes life, or what accompanies it.

When talking about life nowadays, not just in scientific books but also in regular conversations, they do not talk about the life as we know it—I mean the life of which I am conscious because of the suffering that I fear and hate and the pleasures and joys that I desire. Instead they speak about something that appeared out of randomness, in accord with the laws of physics, or perhaps something that arose from a miraculous cause.

They now ascribe the word "life" to something problematic, something that does not contain the hallmarks of life like consciousness of suffering and pleasures and the pursuit of happiness.

"La vie est l'ensemble des fonctions, qui résistent à la mort. La vie est l'ensemble des phénomènes, qui se succèdent pendant un temps limité dans un être organisé."[5] "Life is a twofold process of decomposition and composition, common to all, and at the same time uninterruptible. Life is a certain combination of heterogeneous changes that occur in sequence. Life is an organism in action. Life is a special activity of organic matter. Life is adaptation of inner relations to external ones."[6]

Let us leave aside the imprecision and tautologies that pervade these definitions. They are essentially the same: they do not define what everyone undoubtedly understands by the word "life" but instead define some processes and other phenomena that accompany life.

The majority of these definitions apply equally to the formation of crystals; some of them are applicable to fermentation and rotting. Moreover, all the definitions are valid for every separate cell within my body, for which nothing exists—neither good nor bad. Processes occurring in crystals, in protoplasm or the nucleus of protoplasm, and in the cells of my body and in those of others—these things they call by the very same name as that thing which, for me, is inseparably bound with the consciousness of pursuing my own happiness.[7]

Theorizing about certain conditions of life as if they were really life is no different from theorizing about the river as if it were a mill. These theories may be very useful for something, but they do not touch upon the very subject they would like to discuss. Therefore, all conclusions about life deduced from such theories cannot help being false.[8]

The word "life" is very short and very clear and everyone understands *what* it means.[9] And precisely because everyone understands *what* it means, we must always use it in that universally clear meaning. This word is clear to everyone not because it has been defined very precisely by other words and concepts but, on the contrary, because this word signifies the main concept from which many if not all concepts derive. Therefore, to make conclusions based on this concept, we are obliged foremost to accept this concept in its central, indisputable meaning. And this very thing, it seems to me, has been left out of debates about life. The basic concept of life, because it was initially not used in its general sense, has during all the debates lost its basic meaning and has acquired another, incongruous meaning. It is as though the center that was first used to inscribe the geometric shape has been abandoned and shifted to another point.

They debate whether there is life in a cell or in a protoplasm or somewhere even more primitive like in inorganic matter. But before arguing we should ask ourselves, do we have the right to ascribe the concept of life to a cell?

We say, for instance, that there is life in a cell and that a cell is a living thing. However, the fundamental concept of human life and the concept of life in that cell are completely different and moreover incompatible. One concept excludes the other. I am told that my whole body, without exception, consists of cells, and that these cells possess the same quality of life as do I; they are living creatures like myself. However, I consider myself alive only because I am conscious of myself—and of all these cells of which I am composed—as a single, indivisible living creature. And yet I am being told that, without exception, I am made up of living cells. To what, then, am I to attribute the quality of life—to the cells or myself? If I admit that the cells have life, then I ought to exclude from the concept of life the main sign of my own life—my consciousness of myself as an integral living creature. If I admit, though, that I have life as a distinct creature, then it is obvious that I cannot attribute the same quality to the cells that make up my body, cells whose consciousness I know nothing about.[10]

Either I am alive and there are nonliving elements within me called cells, or there is a host of small living cells and my consciousness of life is not life but only an illusion.

After all, we do not say that cells "jive" but that they are "alive."[11] We say the cell is alive not to imply some unknown quantity but to imply a definite quantity that we all know equally, that we know solely from within ourselves, as our consciousness of ourselves with our integral body that is something indivisibly whole. This concept is therefore inapplicable to the cells that make up our body.

No matter what investigations and observations a person undertakes, to express the results of his observations he must use the commonsensical meanings of words, the ones that others indisputably have in mind, and not just choose some convenient concept that fails to align with the main and universal concept. If one could use the word "life" so that it made no difference whether it indicates equally the quality of the whole object and the quite different qualities of all its constituent parts—which is what is being done with regard to a cell and the animal composed of cells—then one could use other words similarly. One could then say, for example, that since all thoughts are composed of words and words of letters and letters of little scribbles, making scribbles is the same as thinking and little lines are the same thing as thoughts.

It is a commonplace in the world of science, for example, to hear and read theories about life originating out of the play of physical and mechanical forces.

It might well be that the majority of men of science embrace this . . . how shall I put it? . . . this opinion or paradox or, speaking plainly, this joke or riddle.

They assert that life originates from a play of physical and mechanical forces—calling these forces of physical nature physical and mechanical just to juxtapose them to the concept life.

Obviously, as it has been incorrectly applied to concepts that are alien to it, the word "life" has shifted further and further from its principal meaning. It is now at such a distance from its center point that it is now assumed to be located somewhere that life cannot possibly be, according to our concept of it.[12] It is as though someone were proposing a circle or sphere the center point of which lies outside its periphery.

And indeed life, which I cannot imagine otherwise than as a striving away from evil toward happiness, takes place somewhere where I can see neither happiness nor evil. Clearly, the concept of life has had its center point completely shifted. What is worse, when I look into these studies of this thing called life, I see that they do not even touch upon concepts that are familiar to me.

Everyone [in the scientific community] understands the concept of life differently from the way that I understand it, and the concepts that have been deduced from it furthermore do not correspond to customary concepts; instead, these new conditional concepts have received suitably artificial names.

Human language is increasingly rare in scientific investigations. Instead of using words as a means for expressing existing objects and concepts, a scientific jargon or Volapük reigns. It differs from the real Volapük in that the real Volapük assigns names to real objects and concepts using common words, while scientific Volapük assigns names to nonexistent concepts using nonexistent words.[13]

Words are the only means of intellectual communication among people, and to make this communication possible, one has to use words so that every word universally evokes corresponding and exact concepts. If one were free to use words as one pleases and imply anything at will, then it would be better not to speak at all but to refer to everything using signs.

I will agree that defining the world's laws based solely on reasonable deductions, with no recourse to experience and observation, is a path both false and unscientific. But is it not worse to study the phenomenal world by means of experience and observation while at the same time, rather than being guided by fundamental and commonplace concepts, instead being guided by conditional concepts and describing the results of your experiments with imprecise words? The best pharmacy would inflict great injury if the vials were labeled according to what the pharmacist found convenient instead of according to their contents.

They will tell me: science does not, as it were, assign itself the task of studying the sum total of life, which would include the will, the desire for happiness, and the spiritual world; it abstracts from the concept of life only those phenomena that are subject to its experimental investigations.

This would all be fine and legitimate. We know, though, that scientists of our time see it otherwise. Were the concept of life accepted in its central, universally understood meaning, and then were it made clear that science, having put aside all aspects of the concept save the one that is subject to external observation, would examine the phenomena from this one aspect, for which it has its own method of inquiry . . . well, that would be just fine and another matter altogether. The place that science would then occupy, and the results at which we would arrive based on science, would be quite different. One should talk straight, instead of hiding what we all know. Do we not know that the majority of those who investigate life by means of scientific experiments are quite certain that they study not just one side of life but the whole of life?

Astronomy, mechanics, physics, chemistry, and all the other sciences, taken together and each on its own, elaborate a particular and appropriate aspect of life, and they make no conclusions about life in general. Only when they have gone wild—that is, during times of imprecision and indefiniteness—did some of these sciences try to embrace, from their point of view, all the phenomena of life; and they got confused and invented new concepts and words. Such was the case with astronomy when it was formerly known as astrology; the same could be said of chemistry when it was known as alchemy. The same thing is happening nowadays with experimental evolutionary science, which, by investigating one or several sides of life, claims to study the whole of life.

People with an erroneous view of their science will not admit that only certain aspects of life are subject to their investigation. They insist that they will investigate the totality of life, with all its phenomena, using external experimentation. "If," they say, "the human psyche"—they love this indefinite, Volapük word—"is at present unknown to us, it will be known someday." By investigating one or several sides of life's phenomena, we will get to know it from all sides; thus, in other words, by gazing at an object long and hard from one side, we shall eventually see the object from all sides, and even from within.

No matter how astonishing it might be, this strange doctrine exists; it can be explained only as a fanatical superstition. Like all wild, fanatical doctrines, it produces its murderous influence by channeling human thinking along a false and frivolous path. Wasted are the lives of conscientious laborers who dedicate their lives to the study of something nearly useless; wasted are the material forces of people, which are directed where there is no need; and wasted are the young generations, directed as they are toward the idlest activity of the Kifa Mokieviches, an activity that has been placed on a pedestal as the highest service to humanity.

It is commonly said that science studies life from every side. But, really, every object has as many sides as there are radii in a circle—that is, innumerable. Since one cannot study something from every side, one needs to know which side is more important and more necessary, and which side is less important and less necessary. Just as you cannot approach an object from all sides at once, you cannot study the phenomena of life from all sides. One way or another, things fall into an order, and this order is the heart of the matter. This order is provided only by an awareness of life.

Generally speaking, as well as for every particular science, only the correct understanding of life provides the necessary meaning and direction to science. It arranges this meaning and direction according to their relative importance for life. If our awareness of life is not the same as the one that has been instilled in all of us, then the science itself will be likewise false.

What we call science does not define life; rather, our concept of life determines *what* should be regarded as science. For science to become science, we need to resolve the question of *what is* and *what is not* science, and to do so, the concept of life must be clarified.

Let me tell you frankly my thought on the matter: we all know the basic dogma of faith for this false experimental science.

Matter and its energy exist. Energy begets movement; this mechanical movement is transformed into molecular movement; and the molecular movement manifests itself as heat, electricity, and activity of the nervous system and brain. And, without exception, all phenomena of life are explicable by reference to energy. All this is so lovely, simple, clear, and—most important—convenient. And so, if what we so desire, if what simplifies our life, does not exist at all, then we must simply make it up one way or another.

And here is the whole daring thought of mine: most of the energy and the passionate activity of experimental science derive from its desire to invent whatever is needed to confirm this convenient perception.

In all the activity of science, you see not so much a desire to study the phenomena of life as you see a single and omnipresent anxiety to prove the justice of its basic dogma. How much effort has been wasted on attempts to prove the origin of the organic from the inorganic and of psychic activity from the processes of an organism? So the organic does not transition into the inorganic. In which case, let us search the sea bottom and we shall find this whatsit that we will call a nucleus or a monera.[14]

So it is not there, either; let's assume we'll find it, especially since we have the infinitude of the ages where we can stick everything that ought to exist, according to our faith, but that, at present, does not.

The same thing happens with the transition of organic activity into psychic activity. Still do not have it? But we believe that we will find it, and we will martial all our mental efforts to prove at least its possibility.

These arguments about things irrelevant to life, particularly debates about why life occurs—be it animism, vitalism, or some concept of some other special force—have concealed from people the main question of life, the question without which the concept of life loses its meaning. These debates have brought men of science, the very people who must lead others, to the state of someone headed somewhere who hurries but who has forgotten where he is headed.[15]

Perhaps, though, I am deliberately trying to ignore the impressive results that science has yielded in its current direction? But, really, no results can possibly correct a false direction. Let us entertain the impossible: All that the science of today wishes to learn about life, all that it asserts that it will discover (without really believing it), let us imagine that it has all been discovered and is all clear as day. It is clear how something organic is brought into existence, through adaptation, from inorganic matter; it is clear how physical energies are transformed into feelings, will, and thought. Let us imagine that all this is clear not only to high school students but also to peasant lads from the village school.

I know that these particular thoughts and emotions originate from these particular movements. Well, so what? Can I, or can I not, control these movements in such a way as to stir these or other thoughts in myself? The question of what thoughts and feelings I need to stir in myself and in others remains not only unresolved but also in fact not even touched upon.

I know that men of science do not trouble themselves to answer this question. The answer to this question seems very simple to them, just as the answer to a difficult question always seems simple to someone who does not understand it. Answering the question of how to arrange life, when it is within our power to do so, seems very simple to men of science. They say it should be arranged in such a way that people can satisfy their needs. Science first works out the means to measure out correctly the satisfaction of needs. Then it figures out how to produce these means in such quantity and with such ease so as to render all needs easily satisfied. And everyone will be carefree.[16]

But if you ask them what is meant by "need" and what are the limits of these "needs," they merely respond, That is just what science does. It assigns categories to needs—physical, mental, aesthetic, and even ethical ones. It further clearly defines which needs are legitimate and which are illegitimate, and to what degree.

Given time, science will determine this. If you ask what will determine whether needs are legitimate or illegitimate, then they will answer you boldly: The study of needs. But the word "need" has only two meanings: either it is a condition for existence—and there are countless conditions and therefore all the conditions cannot be thoroughly studied—or it is what a living creature needs for its happiness, something that can be known and defined only through consciousness and therefore something that can hardly be studied thoroughly by experimental science.

There is an institution, a corporation, a convocation, if you will, of people or minds that is beyond reproach. It is called science. In time, it will define everything.

Is it not obvious that the answer to the question is nothing less than a paraphrased Kingdom of the Messiah, wherein science plays the role of the Messiah? For this explanation to explain anything, one must believe in the dogmas of science as vehemently as Jews believe in the Messiah, which is precisely what orthodox sciences always do, with one difference: The Orthodox Jew imagines in the Messiah a messenger from God who will, through his authority, arrange everything excellently. The orthodox scientist, on the other hand, cannot believe that by means of external study one can solve the one and only question about life.

CHAPTER 1

The Main Contradiction
of Human Life

Every person lives only to feel good, for his own happiness. Were a person not to wish for his own happiness, he would not feel alive. Man cannot imagine life without wishing happiness for himself. Being alive for every person is precisely the same thing as wanting to acquire this happiness; wishing for and acquiring this happiness is the same thing as being alive.

A person senses life only in himself, in his own individuality. A person, therefore, initially imagines that this happiness that he desires is only individual happiness. Initially, it seems to him that he, alone, truly lives. The life of other creatures seems to him not at all like his own—it seems to him to be a mere semblance of life; he only observes the life of other creatures and only from these observations does he learn that they live. A person knows about the life of others when he wants to think about them; but about himself he knows that he is alive and cannot stop knowing this even for a second. He therefore perceives his own life alone to be authentic. The life of other creatures around him appears to be merely one of the conditions of his own existence. The only reason he does not wish evil on others is that the sight of their suffering disturbs his happiness. When he wishes others well, he does so for reasons entirely different from the reasons that he wishes it for himself—not because he wants those that he wishes well to feel good but only so that the happiness of other creatures increases his own happiness. The only happiness that is important and necessary to a person is the one he feels as his own—that is, his own happiness.

And so, as he pursues the attainment of this happiness of his, he notices that this happiness depends on other creatures. By observing and watching these other creatures, a person sees that they—people and even animals—have the same view of life as he does. Each of these creatures senses—just as he does—only its own life and happiness, considers only its own life to be important and authentic. It views the life of all other creatures merely as a means for achieving its own happiness. A person sees that, just like him, every living creature should, for the sake of its own small happiness, be ready to deprive all other creatures of a greater happiness, even to deprive them of their life—including even the life of the person who is contemplating the matter. And having understood this, the person involuntarily reflects that if this is so—and he knows that this is so—then not just one creature, nor a dozen creatures, but all the innumerable creatures of the world, each seeking to achieve their own aim, are ready to destroy him, that one person for whom life exists. Having realized this, a person sees that his individual happiness, which is the only way that he understands life, not only cannot be easily obtained by him but also likely will be taken away from him.

The longer a person lives, the more this theorizing gets substantiated by experience. Man sees that the life of the world in which he participates—a life composed of interconnected individuals who are ready to destroy and eat one another—not only cannot offer him happiness but also will surely be a great evil.

What is worse, even when a person finds himself in a situation so advantageous that he can successfully fight against others without fearing for himself, very soon his reason and experience demonstrate that these mere semblances of happiness that he snatches away from life in the form of individual pleasures are not happiness. They are somehow merely patterns of happiness, given to him only so that he feels evermore acutely the sufferings that always accompany pleasures. The longer a person lives, the more distinctly he sees that the pleasures are fewer and fewer, while boredom, satiety, toil, and suffering are greater and greater. What is even worse, when he begins to experience illnesses and the atrophying of his strength, and looks at the illnesses, senility, and deaths of others, he also notices that his own existence, in which alone he senses authentic and full life, with every hour and with every move, gets closer to atrophy, senility, and death. He sees that his life is subject to thousands of chances of destruction by those other creatures that are fighting against him and that it is subject to ever-increasing suffering; and he sees that his life, in essence, is only an incessant approach to death, an approach to that state in which not only is his individual life destroyed but also the very possibility of happiness is in all likelihood destroyed. Man sees that he, his individuality—that thing where alone he senses life—does nothing save struggle against what it is impossible to struggle against, the whole world. He sees that he seeks pleasures that yield the mere semblance of happiness and always end in suffering. And he sees that he wishes to hold fast to something beyond his reach: life. Man sees that he himself, his very own individuality—the thing for which alone he wishes happiness and life—can possess neither happiness nor life. What he wishes to possess—happiness and life—are possessed only by those creatures that are alien to him, those creatures that he does not and cannot sense, cannot and does not want to know.

His individuality—that which for him is the most important thing, that which alone is necessary, that which alone seems to truly live—that thing will first die, then there will be bones and worms. It is not he, not what is necessary, not what is important, not what he senses is alive, but rather this whole world of the struggling creatures, one replacing the next—it is this thing that is the real life, the thing that will last and will live eternally. Thus the only life that man senses, the one he directs all activities toward, turns out to be something deceptive and impossible, while the life outside him—the life that is unloved, that he does not feel, that is unknown to him—is the only true life.

The thing that he does not sense—that alone possesses the qualities that he wishes to possess. This perception is not one that occurs only in black moments of bleak moods, nor a perception that can be avoided; it is instead such an obvious and indubitable truth that if it ever occurs to a person, or if others ever explain it to him, he will never be rid of it. Nothing burns this truth out of his consciousness.

Humanity Has Been Aware of the Contradiction of Life since the Remotest Antiquity. Enlighteners of Humanity Have Revealed the Definitions of Life to People. These Definitions Have Solved This Inner Contradiction, but the Pharisees and Scribes Have Kept Them Concealed from People

The only aim for life that initially occurs to someone is his individual happiness, but there is no such thing as individual happiness; were there something in life like happiness, then life, in which alone happiness is possible—individual life, that is—with its every movement, every breath, is drawn inexorably toward suffering, evil, death, and destruction.

This is so obvious and so clear that every thinking person—young and old, educated and uneducated, everyone—sees it. This theorizing is so simple and natural that it appears to every reasonable person and has been known to humanity from remotest antiquity.

"The life of a person, as an individual merely pursuing his own happiness among an innumerable multitude of other such individuals, each destroying the other and destroying itself, is evil and nonsense. True life cannot be thus." Man has said this to himself since remotest antiquity. This inner contradiction of human life has been expressed with unusual force and clarity by Hindu, Chinese, Egyptian, Greek, and Hebrew sages. Human reason has been directed, since remotest antiquity, at comprehending a human happiness that cannot be destroyed by strife among creatures, by suffering or by death. Ever since we have been aware of life, all forward movement of humanity has consisted of an ever-greater illumination of this happiness, free from doubt and impervious to strife, suffering, and death.

Since remotest antiquity, and in the most diverse of nations, the teachers of humanity have revealed to people ever-clearer definitions of life that try to resolve life's inner contradiction. They have directed people toward the true happiness and true life that are natural for people. The human condition in the world is everywhere the same, and therefore the contradiction of a man's pursuit of individual happiness, and the realization of its impossibility, is also the same for everyone. All definitions of true happiness—and therefore all definitions of true life—that have been revealed to people by the greatest minds of humanity are thus essentially the same.

"Life is the proliferation of the light that has descended from heaven for the benefit of people," said Confucius, six hundred years B.C.

"Life is the journey and perfection of souls that are achieving ever-greater happiness," said the Brahmins around the same time. "Life is self-renunciation for the sake of the blessed nirvana," said Buddha, a contemporary of Confucius's. "Life is a path of humility and humiliation for the attainment of happiness," said Laozi, also a contemporary of Confucius's. "Life is what God breathed into man's nostrils in order that man, in fulfilling His law, should receive happiness," Hebraic wisdom says.[1] "Life is submission to reason, which gives happiness to man," said the Stoics. "Life is love for God and neighbor, bringing happiness to man," Christ said, encompassing in his definition all the above.[2]

Such are the definitions of life that, thousands of years before our time, by directing people away from a false and impossible individual happiness toward a real, indestructible happiness, have resolved the contradiction of human life and imposed a reasonable meaning upon it. One can disagree with these definitions of life, one can claim that they could be expressed more precisely and clearly, but one cannot help seeing that these definitions, once accepted, will annihilate the contradiction of life. By replacing the pursuit of an unattainable individual happiness with a different kind of pursuit, one that seeks a happiness that cannot be destroyed by suffering or by death, these definitions give life a reasonable meaning. One cannot help seeing that, being theoretically correct, these definitions are confirmed by life's experience and that the millions and millions of people who have accepted and still accept these definitions have proved, and still prove, that it is possible to substitute, in place of pursuit of individual happiness, a pursuit of a happiness that is impervious to suffering and death.

But besides those people who have understood and still understand, and live by, the definitions of life revealed by its great enlighteners, there has been and still are a vast majority of people who, at a certain period of their life, and sometimes during their entire life, have lived and continue to live solely for the satisfaction of their animal life. They not only do not understand the definitions that resolve the contradictions of human life but also do not even see these contradictions. There have always been among people those who, because of their exclusive standing, consider themselves elected to lead humanity. Without understanding the meaning of human life, they have taught and still teach other people about life, a life they do not understand. They teach about a life that is nothing more than individual existence.

These false teachers have always existed, and they exist in our own age. Some of them verbally profess the teachings of the enlighteners of humanity in whose traditions these teachers were educated. However, not understanding the teachings' reasonable meaning, they turn them into supernatural revelation about people's past and future life and demand only the observation of rites. This is Pharisaic teaching in its broadest sense—that is, these are the people who teach that our life, unreasonable in itself, can be corrected by faith in another life, a life attainable through the fulfillment of external rites.

Others reject the existence of any life save the perceptible one. They deny all miracles and everything supernatural and boldly declare that a person's life is nothing but his animal existence from birth to death. This is the teaching of the Scribes, people who teach that in human life, as in animal life, there can be nothing unreasonable.

No matter that the teachings of both groups of false teachers are based on the same crude misunderstanding of the main contradiction of human life, they have always quarreled and still quarrel with one another. Both teachings hold sway over our world, and, as they quarrel with one other, they fill the world with their disputes. These disputes conceal from people the definitions of life that reveal to them the path toward their true happiness, definitions that were given to humanity thousands of years ago.

The Pharisees, misunderstanding the definition of life that was handed down to people by the very teachers in whose traditions the Pharisees were raised, replace the true definition of life with their own false interpretations of a future life. At the same time, the Pharisees try to conceal from people the definitions of life by other enlighteners of humanity, exhibiting them in most crude and cruel distortions. They hope thereby to maintain the exclusive authority of that teaching on which they base their own interpretations.*

The Scribes, not even suspecting that there might be reasonable foundations to the Pharisaic teaching, bluntly refute all teachings about future life, boldly declaring that all such teachings are baseless and merely boorish customs left over from barbarity and that the forward march of humanity depends upon not asking oneself any questions about life exceeding the bounds of animal existence.

---

* The unanimity of reasonable meaning in the various definitions of life by other enlighteners of humanity does not appear to them as the best proof of the truth of their own teaching because it undermines the faith in those unreasonable and false interpretations that they have substituted for the [true] essence of the teaching. —Tolstoy

CHAPTER 3

The Errors of the Scribes

What an amazing thing! All the teachings of the great minds of humanity have always so struck people with their greatness that coarse people have often attributed to them a supernatural character and made demigods of their founders. The very thing that has served as the chief sign of the significance of these teachings serves, for the Scribes at least, as the best proof of their falsity and backwardness. The insignificant teachings of Aristotle, Bacon, Comte, and others have always been, and still are, the legacy of a small number of their readers and admirers; these teachings, because of their wrongness, could never influence the masses and have therefore never become subjects of any superstitious distortion or accretion. The very sign of their insignificance is recognized as proof of their being genuine. The teachings of the Brahmins, Buddha, Zoroaster, Laozi, Confucius, Isaiah, and Christ, on the contrary, are considered to be prejudice and errors precisely because these teachings have upended the lives of millions.[1]

That billions of people have lived by these superstitions because, even in their distorted form, they provide people with answers about life's true happiness; that these teachings are not only widely held but also have served as the basis of thought for the best people of all ages, while the theories acknowledged by the Scribes are held true only among them, are always disputed, and at times do not even last a decade before being forgotten almost as quickly as they come into being—none of this bothers them in the least.

Nothing more clearly demonstrates the false direction of knowledge that contemporary society has taken than the place occupied in this society by the teaching of those great teachers of life who have provided and continue to provide guidance for life and education to humanity. In almanacs one can find in their statistical information sections that there are some one thousand faiths professed by the inhabitants of the globe. Among these faiths are Buddhism, Brahmanism, Confucianism, Taoism, and Christianity. So there are a thousand faiths, and people in our age quite sincerely believe this to be true. There are a thousand faiths, all of them are nonsense, so why study them? People in our age are ashamed if they do not know the latest wise utterances of Spencer, Helmholtz, and others, but of the Brahmins, Buddha, Confucius, Mencius, Laozi, Epictetus, and Isaiah? They sometimes know their names, though sometimes do not even know that much. It never crosses their mind that rather than a thousand, there are only three faiths professed in our time: the faiths of the Chinese, the Hindus, and the Judeo-Christians (with the Muhammadan faith as its offshoot). It never crosses their mind that the books explaining these faiths one can buy for five rubles and read in two weeks, and that these books that have guided all humanity then and now—with the exception of those 0.07 percent we barely know about—contain the whole wisdom of humanity, all that has made humanity into what it is. It is not enough that the crowd does not know these teachings: men of science do not know them unless it is their specialty, and professional philosophers do not consider it necessary to glance into these books. Why bother studying those people who have resolved what reasonable people have acknowledged as the contradiction of life, who have defined true happiness and the life of the people? The Scribes, who have failed to understand the contradiction that constitutes the principle of reasonable life, boldly proclaim that, because they do not see it, there is no contradiction and that the life of man consists only of his animal existence.

The man with sight understands and defines what he sees before him; the blind man pokes about with his cane and claims that there is nothing there, save what the touch of his cane tells him.

The Teaching of the Scribes Substitutes the Visible Phenomena of Man's Animal Existence for the Notion of the Whole of Human Life and Thus Derives Conclusions about the Aim of His Life

"Life is what goes on in the living creature from the time of his birth until his death. A man is born—a dog, a horse; each has its own particular body, and this particular body lives and then dies; the body decomposes, enters other creatures, and that former creature will no longer exist. There used to be life, and then life ended. The heart beats, the lungs breathe, the body does not decompose—this means that a person is alive, a dog is alive, a horse is alive; the heart has stopped beating, breathing has ceased, the body has started decomposing—this means they have died, life is no more. Life is what occurs in the body of man, just as it is for an animal, in that span of life between birth and death. What could be clearer?" Thus have the crudest illiterate people, those who have barely exited their animal state, always looked and still look upon life. So in our time the teaching of the Scribes, which calls itself science, acknowledges this crudest and most primitive view of life as the only true one. Availing itself of all those tools of applied science that humanity has acquired, this false teaching shows a systematic will to lead humanity backward into the darkness of ignorance, an ignorance from which it has, for thousands of years, been straining and laboring to escape.

This teaching says we cannot define life in our consciousness. We go astray trying to examine it within ourselves. That concept of happiness, the pursuit of which constitutes life in our consciousness, is a deceptive phantom. One must not understand life in this consciousness. To understand life one ought only to follow its manifestation as a form of material movement. Only through these observations and the laws derived from them will we find the law of life itself, and the law of human life.*

Having thus substituted the visible part of life–its animal existence–for the understanding of the whole of human life–the one known to man through his consciousness–this false teaching begins to study these visible manifestations of life first in the human animal, then in animals proper, then in plants, then in matter. All the while it asserts that it is studying not just the manifestations of life but also life itself. These observations are so complex, so manifold, so convoluted, so much time and effort are expended on them, that little by little people begin to forget the original mistake of having substituted part of an object for the whole, and they finally become fully convinced that the study of the observable properties of matter, plants, and animals is the study of life itself; they forget that life can be really knowable to man only in his consciousness.

What happens is a little akin to someone who is pointing to shadows and wants to prolong the spectators' state of error.

"Do not look anywhere," says the person doing the pointing, "save in the direction where the reflections appear. Most important, do not look at the object itself; there is no object, there is only its reflection."[1]

This is the very thing that the false science of the Scribes does when it caters to the crude crowd, looking at life without considering its main definition–that is, the pursuit of happiness, which is available only within human consciousness.† Beginning directly from definitions of life independent of the pursuit of happiness, false science makes observations about the aims of living creatures and, finding in these aims things that are foreign to man, imposes them on him.

---

* Physical science speaks about the laws and relationships of forces, never asking what force is and never trying to explain the essence of force. Chemical science speaks about interrelationships of matter, never asking what matter is and never trying to define the essence of matter. Biological science speaks about the forms of life, never asking what life is and never trying to define its essence. Force, matter, and life have been accepted by genuine sciences not as subjects of scrutiny but as axiomatic supports, taken from other spheres of knowledge; these have become the pillars upon which the edifice of each science, taken separately, is being built. This is the view of life of genuine science, a science that cannot have a pernicious influence on the crowd, one that returns them to ignorance. But the false clericalism of science does not look at its subject in this way. "We study matter, and force, and life; and because we study them, we can cognize them," they claim, never imagining that they do not really study force, matter, or life but only their interrelationships and forms. –Tolstoy

† See appendix 1, about a false definition of life. –Tolstoy

It seems to external observation that the aim of living creatures is the preservation of one's individuality, preservation of one's species, reproduction of your ilk, and the struggle for existence, and this farcical aim of life is imposed on man.

Beginning from this backwards perception of life—one that obscures the main contradiction of human life, its main feature—false science in its most recent conclusions comes to what the crude majority of humankind demands, the recognition that the happiness of one's individual life is possible, and the recognition of the animal existence as the only human happiness.

False science goes even further than the demands of the crude crowd, for which it wants to furnish an explanation: it arrives at an assertion that is rejected by any reasonable consciousness at the idea's first glimmer—that human life, just like the life of any animal, consists of the struggle for individual existence, the genus, and the species.*

* See appendix 2. —Tolstoy

CHAPTER 5

The False Teaching of the Pharisees and the Scribes Offers Neither an Explanation of the Meaning of True Life nor Guidance for Life; the Inertia of Life Is the Only Guidance for a Life without Reasonable Explanation

"Do not bother defining life. Everyone knows what it is . . . Enough! Let us live." So say people who, deluded, get their bearings from false teachings. Not knowing what life is, nor what constitutes its happiness, they think they live, just as it may seem to someone carried away by the waves that he is really swimming where he needs to and where he wants to.

A child, born in either poverty or wealth, gets an education from the Pharisees or the Scribes. For a child or a youth, the contradiction of life and its question do not yet exist, and therefore neither the explanations of the Pharisees nor those of the Scribes are of use to him, nor can they guide his life. He learns solely from the example of the people around him, and the examples set by the Pharisees and the Scribes are the same: both groups live only for the happiness of their individual life, and they teach him to do the same.

If his parents live in poverty, the child learns from them that the aim of life is acquiring more bread and money with as little work as possible, so that things are as good as possible for his animal individuality. If he is born into luxury, he learns that the aim of life is wealth and esteem so that he might spend his time as pleasurably and enjoyably as possible.

All the knowledge that a poor man gets is required only inasmuch as it improves his individual welfare. The knowledge of the sciences and the arts that the rich man gets—whatever the eloquent words about the significance of science and the arts—is required only inasmuch as it battles boredom and makes time pass pleasantly. The longer either of them lives, the more thoroughly they absorb this reigning view of worldly people. They enter into marriage, start a family, and the selfish drive to obtain the happiness of animal life increases, now reinforced by familial justifications: the struggle with others gets fiercer and the (inertia), the habit of living only for individual happiness, becomes established.

Even if one or the other, the poor man or the rich one, has doubts about the reasonableness of such a life, even if questions occur to the one or the other about this pointless struggle for existence, a struggle that my children will continue,[1] or about this deceptive hunt for pleasures that end in suffering for me and my children—even so, there is little chance that he would discover the definitions of life, given long ago to humanity by its great teachers, who had found themselves, thousands of years before him, in the same condition. The teachings of the Pharisees and the Scribes so completely hide these definitions that one rarely manages to glimpse them. Asked, "What is the point of this miserable life?" the Pharisees answer, "Life is, has always been, and must be such; the happiness of life lies not in its present but in its past—prior to life—and in the future, after life." The Brahmin, the Buddhist, the Taoist, the Jewish, and the Christian Pharisees always say the same thing. Life in the present is evil, and the explanation of this evil is in the past, in the story of genesis and man's creation; the correction of this existing evil lies in the future—beyond the grave. All that man can do to acquire happiness—not in this life but in a future one—is to believe in this teaching that we impart to you, and to perform the rites that we prescribe.[2]

The doubter—seeing the life of people who live for individual happiness and the life of the Pharisees who live for the same thing, and the falsity of their explanation—does not delve into the meaning of their answer, outright refuses to believe them, and turns to the Scribes. "All teachings about any life other than the one we can observe in animal life is the fruit of ignorance," the Scribes say. "All your doubts about the reasonableness of your life are but idle dreams. The life of worlds, of the earth, of man, of the animal, of the plant—they have their laws, and we study those laws, we investigate the origin of worlds and of man, of animals and plants, and of all physical matter; we investigate what will happen to worlds, how the sun will grow cold, and so on, and what has been and will be with man and with every animal and plant. We can demonstrate and prove that it has been and will be as we say; moreover, our investigations also contribute to the improvement of human welfare. We can tell you nothing about your own life, nothing about your pursuit of happiness, aside from what you know without our help. You are alive, so live however best you can."

And the doubter, having received no answer to his questions from the one or the other, remains as he has been, with no guidance for life except the promptings of his individuality.

Some of the doubters, as Pascal observed, say to themselves, "What if they are true, all those things that the Pharisees frighten us with for not following their rule?" So, in their spare time, they observe all the Pharisees' rules. (There is no loss, and the gain could be significant.) Others, agreeing with the Scribes, bluntly reject all future life and all religious rites and tell themselves, "It is not just me, all live like this. That's the way it will be." Their differences offer neither group any advantage: both groups remain without any explanation of the meaning of their real life.[3]

But live we must.

Human life is a series of acts from the time we rise until bedtime. Man needs every day to choose, without hesitation, what acts he will commit from among the hundreds of possible acts. Neither the teaching of the Pharisees, which explains mysteries of heavenly life, nor the teaching of the Scribes, which explores the origin of worlds and of man and makes predictions about their future fate—neither group provides the required guide for actions. Without a guide to choose his acts, man cannot live. At this point, our fellow submits willy-nilly not to theories but to that external guidance of life that has always existed and continues to exist in every human society.

This guidance has no reasonable explanation, but it directs the vast majority of all men's acts. This guidance is the habit of human social life, and it exerts control proportionate to the degree that people do not understand the meaning of their life. This guidance cannot be expressed definitively because it is composed of very diverse deeds and acts, varying according to time and place: for the Chinese, candles set on plaques for their parents; for the Muhammadan, pilgrimage to certain sites; for the Indian, a certain number of prayer words; it is loyalty to his flag and the honor of the uniform for the military man, a duel for the worldly man, blood feuds for the Caucasian mountaineer; certain foods for certain days, a certain upbringing for their children; it is paying visits, a certain interior decoration, a certain observance of funeral rites, births, and weddings. It is an endless number of deeds and acts that fill up our life. It is called propriety, custom, habit, and most often it is called duty—even sacred duty.[4]

It is precisely to this guidance that most people submit—besides the explanations of life of the Pharisees and the Scribes. Beginning in childhood, a person sees how people perform these deeds with complete certainty and outward solemnity. Lacking a reasonable explanation of his life, a person not only starts performing similar deeds but also tries to attribute reasonable meaning to these deeds. He would like to believe that people who perform these deeds possess an explanation for why they do whatever they are doing. He begins to persuade himself that these deeds have a reasonable meaning, and if he lacks complete knowledge of their meaning, then it must be known to others. Most other people likewise lack a reasonable explanation of life and find themselves in a situation quite like his. They perform these deeds, however, only because it seems to them that others, who have an explanation for these deeds, demand these deeds from them. Thus unwittingly deceiving one another, people get all the more used to performing deeds that lack a reasonable explanation, and they get used to ascribing to these deeds some miraculous, incomprehensible meaning. And the less they comprehend the meaning of the deeds they perform and the more questionable these deeds are to them, the more importance they ascribe to them. They perform these deeds with greater pomp. The rich and the poor man alike behave like those around them, and they call these deeds their duty, their sacred duty, and they console themselves that this has long been done by so many, and is so highly valued by them, that it must be their life's purpose. People live to a ripe old age, to their dying day, trying to persuade themselves that if they themselves do not know why they live, then other people know—those very people who know just as little about why they live as those who look to them.

New people are conceived, born, and grow up, and as they gaze into this crush of existence called life—in which old, dignified people, upon whom respect is lavished, also take part—and become convinced that this insane ruckus is life itself, and that there is no other, and then they retreat after clamoring a bit at its doors. Thus a man who has never before been to an assembly, upon seeing a pushy, loud, and animated crowd at the entrance, decides that this must be the assembly itself, and having tussled a bit at the door, returns home with bruised ribs, fully convinced that he has been to the assembly.

We cut roads through the mountains, we fly all around the globe; we have electricity, microscopes, telephones, wars, parliament, philanthropy, party politics, universities, learned societies, museums . . . All this is not life?

All this complex, seething activity of people with their trade, wars, road networks, science, their arts—all this is, for the most part, just the stampede of the raving crowd at the doors of life.[5]

CHAPTER 6

Split Consciousness in
People of Our World

"Verily, verily, I tell you, the hour is coming, and is now here, when the dead will hear the voice of the Son of God, and those who hear will live."[1] And this time is coming. No matter how much one may try to persuade oneself, or others may try to persuade one, that life can be happy and reasonable only beyond the grave, or, conversely, that only individual life can be happy and reasonable—man cannot believe in this. In the depths of his soul, man has an indelible need for his life to be happy and to have a reasonable meaning; a life with no other aim before it other than life beyond the grave, or an unattainable individual happiness, is evil and nonsense.

You ask whether you are to live for a future life. But if that life, that sole sample of life that I know—my life as it is now—must be meaningless, then this not only fails to convince me that another, reasonable life is possible but also persuades me, on the contrary, that life is essentially meaningless, and that there can be no other life but a meaningless one.

Am I to live for myself? But my individual life is evil and nonsense. Am I to live for my family? For my community? For the fatherland? Perhaps, even for humanity? But if my individual life is disastrous and senseless, then the life of every other human individual is equally meaningless, and an infinite number of meaningless and unreasonable individuals, put together, fails to add up to a single blessed and reasonable life. Shall I live, without knowing what for? Shall I do what others are doing? Yet I know that these other people, just like me, do not know why they are doing what they are doing.

The time is nigh when reasonable consciousness surpasses false teachings, and man stops in the thick of life and demands an explanation.[2]

Only the rare person who lacks interaction with people from other spheres of life, or someone who is constantly locked in an intense struggle with nature to sustain his existence in the flesh, could believe that the performance of these senseless acts, what he calls his duty, could be the real and natural duty of his life.*

The time is coming, and has now come, when these shams that deny this life supposedly to prepare us for the future life, that claim that one's animal existence alone constitutes life itself, and that tell us so-called duty is actually life's task—these shams become clear to most people. And only those hardened by need or made stupid by their depraved life can still exist without sensing the meaninglessness and disastrousness of their existence.

More and more often, people are roused to reasonable consciousness, come to life in their graves—and become aware of the main contradiction of human life despite all the efforts by people to conceal it from themselves. It is becoming clear with terrible force to the majority of people.[3]

"My whole life has been a desire for my own happiness," says a man upon awakening. "While my reason tells me that there can be no happiness of this sort for me, whatever I have done, whatever I have achieved—all this will end the same: suffering and death, and destruction.[4] I want happiness, I want life, I want some reasonable meaning, but within me, and in all that surrounds me, there is evil, death, meaninglessness. How am I to be? How am I to live? What am I to do?" And there is no answer.

Man looks around himself, seeking some answer to his question, but finds it not. What he finds are teachings that offer answers to questions he has never asked himself, but not an answer to the question he has posed. There is nothing but the vanity of people who, not knowing why, are doing the things that other people are doing, not knowing why.

Everyone lives as though they do not realize the disastrousness of their condition and the meaninglessness of their activity. "Either *they* are insane or *I am*," says the man who has been roused from sleep to himself. "But they cannot all be insane, so it must be I. But no, that reasonable *I* that tells me this, it cannot be insane. Let it stand alone athwart the whole world, I cannot help but believe it."

And man realizes that he is alone in the whole world with the terrible questions that rend his soul apart. And yet he must live.

One *I*, his individuality, commands him to live.

And the other *I*, his reason, tells him, "You cannot live."

Man feels that he is split in two. And this split torments and rends his soul.

Man sees his reason as the cause of this split and suffering.

---

* See appendix 3. —Tolstoy

Reason, man's highest capacity, which is necessary for his life, that which provides him, naked and helpless, means for both existence and pleasure in the midst of the forces of nature that would destroy him—this same capacity poisons his life.

All about us, living creatures are endowed with shared, natural abilities that are necessary for them all and that contribute to their happiness. By each obeying its own law, plants, insects, and animals live a blessed, joyous, and quiet life. And now, suddenly, this highest attribute of his nature produces such a tormenting state in a person that often—more and more often of late—he cuts the Gordian knot of his life, kills himself, just to be rid of that tormenting inner contradiction that in our time has reached the utmost degree of intensity, a contradiction produced by reasonable consciousness.

CHAPTER 7

The Split of Consciousness Takes Place Because of the Confusion between Animal and Human Life

It seems to a person that this awakened reasonable consciousness is tearing him apart and bringing his life to a halt because he perceives his life to be what it has never been, is not, and could not be.

Born and bred amid false teachings of our world that confirm his conviction that life is nothing more than his individual existence that began at birth, it seems to a person that he was living when he was a toddler, a child; then it seems to him that he was living continuously when he was a youth and a mature adult. He has been living, so it seems to him, for a very long time, living all along, when suddenly he has reached a point when it becomes indubitably clear that the way that he has been living previously is impossible, and that life has stopped and been torn apart.

The false teaching has affirmed his idea that his life is a period from birth to death, and, looking at the visible lives of animals, he has mixed up the perception of visible life and his own consciousness. He has become completely convinced that the life that is visible to him is, in fact, really his life.

With its awakening, his reasonable consciousness makes the kinds of demands that fail to satisfy his animal life, and thereby it indicates the incorrectness of his idea of life. But the ingrained false teaching does not allow him to acknowledge his mistake: he cannot give up his view of life as animal existence, and so it seems to him that his life has been brought to a halt by reasonable consciousness. But what he calls his life—the thing that seems to him to have stalled—has never existed. What he calls his life, his existence from birth, has never been his life; his perception that he has lived the whole time from birth up to this minute is the mere trickery of consciousness, which is akin to the trickery of consciousness during dreams: there have been no dreams before awakening, all these dreams

were assembled at the moment of awakening. Before the awakening of
reasonable consciousness there was no life; the idea of a past life was
assembled when reasonable consciousness awoke.

Man lived like an animal during childhood, when he knew nothing of
life. Had a man only ten months to live, he would know nothing about his
own life or any other life; were he to die in his mother's womb, he would
know just as little. Just like a baby, an unreasonable adult and a complete
idiot can know nothing about the fact that they live and that other creatures live. They therefore do not have a human life.

Human life begins only with the manifestation of reasonable
consciousness—the same consciousness that simultaneously reveals to man
his own life in the present and in the past and the life of other individuals
and everything that inevitably flows forth from the relationships of these
individuals, suffering and death. This is the very same consciousness that
produces in him a rejection of individual happiness and the contradiction,
so it seems to him, that halts his life.

Man wishes to define his life using time, the way he defines the existence that he sees around himself, and suddenly a life is born from within
him that does not coincide with the time of his birth in the flesh. He is
unwilling to believe that something could be life that you cannot define
using time. But no matter how long a person might search for a point in
time to start counting the beginning of his reasonable life, he will never
find it.*

He will never find this point, this beginning of reasonable consciousness, in his recollections. It seems that reasonable consciousness has always
been within him. If he indeed finds something akin to the beginning of
this consciousness, then he finds it not at all in his birth in the flesh but

---

* There is nothing more commonplace than to hear theorizing about the origin and
development in time of human life and life in general. It seems to people who think
this way that they are on the firmest ground of reality; yet there is nothing more fantas-
tic than thinking about the origin of life in time. These theories are like a person who,
wishing to measure a line, doesn't start to measure from the one point known to him
upon which he stands but instead picks imaginary points at various and undefined distances, and from them measures toward himself. Is not this precisely what people do
when they think about the origin and development of life within man? Indeed, where
are we to locate that arbitrary point on this infinite line from which we may begin the
illusory story of the development, starting from the past, of a person's life? Do we
begin with the birth or conception of a child, or his parents, or even further away in
the primeval animal, or in the protoplasm, or in the first bit of matter that broke off
from the sun? All these theories will remain the most arbitrary fantasies—like making
measurements without having a ruler. —Tolstoy

in a sphere that has nothing to do with birth in the flesh. He is aware of his reasonable origin in a completely different way from the way he sees his birth in the flesh. Asking himself about the origin of his reasonable consciousness, a man can never imagine that he, as a reasonable creature, was the child of his father or mother and a grandchild of his grandfathers and grandmothers, who were born in such and such a year. Rather than a son, he is aware of himself as something fused with the consciousness of reasonable creatures quite alien to him in space and time, who could well have lived thousands of years earlier, on the other side of the globe. In his reasonable consciousness, a man does not even see some sort of individual origin; he is instead aware of his extratemporal and extraspatial merging with other reasonable consciousnesses. They penetrate him and he penetrates them. This same awakened reasonable consciousness in man brings to a halt that semblance of life that deluded people consider to be life; it seems to deluded people that their life stops exactly when their life awakens.

CHAPTER 8

There Is Neither a Split nor a Contradiction; They Emerge Only If the Teaching Is False

Only the false teaching that human life is an animal existence from birth to death, the teaching by which people are raised and maintain themselves, produces the tormenting split state that people enter when they first discover their reasonable consciousness.

To a man who finds himself in this deluded state, it seems that the life within him splits in two.

A person knows that he has but one life, but he feels as though there were two. When a person rolls a ball between two fingers, he knows that there is one ball, but he feels two of them. Something similar happens to a person who has absorbed a false view about life.

Man's reason has been falsely directed. He has been taught to think of his life as his individual existence in the flesh alone, which cannot be life.

Given this false view of an imaginary life, he has taken a look at life and has seen two of them—the one that he has imagined and the one that really is.

It seems to such a person that reasonable consciousness's rejection of the happiness of individual existence, and its demand for another type of happiness, is something painful and unnatural.

But for man as a reasonable creature, rejecting the possibility of individual happiness and life is an inescapable consequence of the conditions of individual life and of the character of reasonable consciousness connected with individual life. For a reasonable creature, rejecting the happiness and life of one's individuality is just as natural as it is for a bird to fly using its wings rather than running on its legs. If a fledgling uses its legs to run, this is no proof that it is not natural for it to fly. If we see around us people whose consciousness has not awakened and who identify their life with individual happiness, this is not proof that it is uncharacteristic of man to live a reasonable life. If man's awakening to his true and natural life in our world is accompanied by these painful exertions, it is only because the false teaching of the world attempts to convince people that the phantom of life is life itself, and that the revelation of true life is really a violation of it.

What happens to people of our world who come into true life is something like what might happen to a girl who has been left ignorant of feminine nature. Having felt the first signs of sexual maturity, this girl would mistake the state that beckons her toward her married life, with the duties and joys of motherhood, for an unwell and unnatural state that would reduce her to despair.

That very same despair is experienced by the people of our world at the first signs of their awakening to true human life.

A person in whom reasonable consciousness has awakened but who nonetheless understands his life only as individual life finds himself in the same tormenting condition that an animal might find itself in when, having acknowledged the movement of matter to be its life, would not acknowledge its own [animal] law of individuality and would see its own life solely in obeying the laws of matter, laws that occur even without its efforts. This animal would feel a painful inner contradiction and split.

By submitting itself to material laws, the animal would perceive the aim of its life to be lying about and breathing, but its individuality would demand otherwise: eating, procreating—and then it would seem to the animal that it suffers a split and a contradiction. "Life," it would think, "means obeying the laws of gravity—that is to say, not moving around, lying about, giving in to chemical processes taking place within the body; and this is what I am doing, but one also needs to move, to eat, to look for a mate."

The animal would suffer and would see in this condition a tormenting contradiction and split. This is what happens to a person who has been taught to acknowledge the inferior law of his life, his animal individuality, to be the law of his life. The superior law of life, the law of reasonable consciousness, demands something else from him. Meanwhile, the environment and false teaching hold him back in deceitful consciousness; and he feels a contradiction and split.

To stop its suffering, the animal must acknowledge its individual law, and not the law of matter; fulfilling this individual law, it must make use of the law of matter to satisfy its individual law. So, too, must a man think of his life not according to the inferior individual law but according to its higher law, one available to his reasonable consciousness, a law that subsumes the individual law. The contradiction will be destroyed, and his individuality will freely submit itself to reasonable consciousness, and serve it.

CHAPTER 9

The Birth of True Life in Man

Contemplating the passing of time, observing the manifestation of life in the human creature, we notice that true life is always preserved in man as it is preserved in a seed: the time arrives, and life is revealed. The manifestation of true life occurs when the animal individuality draws man toward its own happiness while reasonable consciousness, on the other hand, demonstrates to him the impossibility of individual happiness and identifies another kind of happiness. Man stares intently at this distant happiness, but he is powerless to see it. At first he does not believe in this happiness and goes back to individual happiness. Though it identifies its own happiness very indefinitely, reasonable consciousness so undeniably and persuasively demonstrates the impossibility of individual happiness that the person once again renounces his individual happiness and again scrutinizes this new happiness that has been identified for him. Reasonable happiness may be invisible, but individual happiness is so undeniably destroyed that it is impossible to continue one's individual existence. His animal consciousness establishes a new relationship toward his reasonable consciousness. The person begins to be born into true human life.

What happens is something like what happens in the material world at every birth. A fetus is born not because it wishes to be born, not because it is better for it to be born, not because it knows that it is good to be born, but because it has ripened, and it is no longer able to maintain its former existence. It ought to give itself over to the new life not so much because the new life calls upon it but because the possibility of the former existence has been destroyed.

Reasonable consciousness, growing imperceptibly in a man's individuality, finally grows to the point when life within the bounds of individuality becomes impossible.

What happens is exactly like what happens at the birth of all things, the same destruction of the seed, of a previous form of life, and the emergence of a new sprout; the same appearance of a struggle between the previous decaying form of the seed and the growth of the sprout, and the same feeding of the sprout at the expense of the decaying seed. For us, the difference between the birth of reasonable consciousness and the visible, corporeal birth is this: while we can observe, in time and space, whence, how, when, and what gets born from the embryo, and we know that the seed is a germ, and that under certain conditions a plant will grow out of a seed, that it will bloom, and then a fruit that is the same as the one that bore the seed—in front of our very eyes the whole cycle of life takes place. We do not see the growth of reasonable consciousness in the passing of time; we do not see its cycle. We do not see the growth of reasonable consciousness and its cycle because we are the ones who are accomplishing it: our life is nothing but the birth of a creature that is invisible to us, that is being born within us, and that therefore we can never see.[1]

We cannot see the birth of this new creature, this new relationship of reasonable consciousness toward the animal one, just as the seed cannot see the growth of its stalk. When reasonable consciousness exits its latent state and reveals itself to us, it seems to us that we are experiencing a contradiction. There is no contradiction, however, just as there is none in the sprouting seed. In the sprouting seed we see only that the life that has been abiding in the hull of the seed is now in its shoot. It is precisely the same in a person upon the awakening of his reasonable consciousness: there is only the birth of a new creature, of a new relationship of reasonable consciousness toward the animal one.[2]

If a person exists without knowing that other individuals live, and without knowing that pleasures fail to satisfy him, that he will die—he does not even know that *he* lives and therefore no contradiction arises in him.

But if a person has observed that other individuals are the same as him, that sufferings threaten him, and that his existence is a slow death, and if his reasonable consciousness has started to break down the existence of his individuality, then he cannot put his life in this decomposing individuality and should unavoidably place his stake in the new life that is being revealed to him.[3] Once again there is no contradiction, as there is none in the seed when it puts forth a sprout and therefore decomposes.

CHAPTER 10

Reason Is That Law Recognized by Man according to Which His Life Should Be Fulfilled

The true life of man, revealing itself in the relationship of his reasonable consciousness toward his animal individuality, begins only with the rejection of the happiness of animal individuality. This rejection of this animal individuality begins when reasonable consciousness awakens.

But then what is reasonable consciousness? John's Gospel begins by saying that this word "Logos" (Reason, Wisdom, Word) is the beginning, and that all is contained within it and originates from it; therefore reason is what defines everything else—but cannot be defined by anything.[1]

Reason cannot be defined and we have no need to define it. Not only do we all know it but also reason is the only thing we know. When interacting with one another we rest assured—more than in anything else—in the identical necessity of this reason for us all. We are convinced that reason is the sole basis that unites all of us living creatures into one. We know reason prior to and more certainly than anything, and so all that we know in the world we know only because what we are cognizing coincides with the laws of this reason, laws that are indubitably known to us. We know reason and cannot but help knowing reason. We cannot help knowing it because reason is the law according to which reasonable creatures—people—should necessarily live. For man, reason is the law according to which his life is fulfilled; just as this law exists for an animal according to which it eats food and multiplies; just as this law exists for a plant, according to which grass and trees grow and bloom; just as this law exists for the celestial body, according to which the earth and celestial bodies move. The law we know from within as the law of our life is the very same law according to which all external phenomena in the world take place, with the difference that we know this law as something that we ourselves should perform, while in the external phenomena we know it as something taking place, without our participation, according to that law. All we can know about the world is the visible subordination to reason taking place outside of us in celestial bodies, in animals, in plants, in the whole world; in ourselves, we know this law as something that we ourselves should perform.

The usual error about life lies in this: We take our human life to be the obedience of our animal body to the law governing it, a law that we are not fulfilling but that is visible to us. This law of our animal body, though, with which our reasonable consciousness is connected, is within our animal body; it is being fulfilled as unconsciously for us as it is fulfilled in a tree, crystal, or celestial body. The law of our life, the obedience of our animal body to reason, is the law that we can nowhere see—because it has not yet been fulfilled but is being fulfilled, by us, in our life. Our life is fulfilling this law in making our animal [self] obedient to the law of reason to attain happiness. By not understanding that happiness and our life consist in making our animal individuality obey the law of reason, and by mistaking the happiness and the existence of our animal individuality for the whole of our life, and by refusing our life's intended work, we forfeit our true happiness and our true life and substitute in their stead the visible existence of our animal activity, which takes place independent of us and that therefore cannot be our life.

CHAPTER 11

The False Direction
of Knowledge

It is an old error that the law we can see being worked out in our animal individuality is the law of our life; people have always fallen into this error and continue to fall into it. This error, which conceals from people the main subject of their investigation—making their animal individuality obey reason to attain the happiness of life—puts in its stead the study of a human existence that is independent of the happiness of life.

False knowing directs its efforts toward the study of merely the happiness and living conditions of the animal individuality of a person, with no regard for the main subject of knowledge—making the animal individuality of man obey the law of reason to attain the happiness of true life. It should instead study the law that a person's animal individuality should obey to attain its happiness and, only after having fully understood this law, study on this basis the rest of worldly phenomena.

False knowledge, ignoring the main subject of knowing, directs its effort toward the study of the animal existence of people, from the past and the present, and the study of conditions of existence for man in general, as an animal. It seems to this way of knowing that from such studies one can also discover guidance for the happiness of human life.

False knowledge theorizes this way: People exist and have existed before us; let us have a look at how they have existed, what kinds of changes have taken place through time and space during their time, and where these changes are headed. We shall discover the law of their life from these historical changes in their existence.

Ignoring the main aim of all science—the study of the reasonable law that one's individuality should, for its own happiness, obey—with the aim that they have set for their study, the so-called learned men of this sort utter a verdict on themselves, rendering their study void. If indeed human existence changes only as a result of the general laws of animal existence, then the study of these very laws, to which human existence is already subject, would be quite useless and futile. Whether or not people know the law responsible for changes in their living conditions, this law fulfills itself in the same way as it is fulfilled in the life of moles and beavers—as a product of the conditions in which they find themselves. If indeed knowledge of the law of reason—that law that should govern his life—is possible, then the only place where one can attain this knowledge is wherever it is revealed to him: in his reasonable consciousness. Therefore, no matter how much one might study how people *used to exist*, as animals, one will never discover about human existence anything more than what would have happened to these people, regardless of that knowledge [of material change]. And never, no matter how much one might study the animal *existence* of man, will one discover the law that the animal existence, for its own happiness, should obey.

This is one type of the idle human theorizing about life that we call historical and political sciences.

Another kind of theorizing, particularly widespread in our time, in which the principal subject of knowledge is amiss, runs as follows: Taking man as an object of observation, we see, the scientists say, that he eats, grows, breeds, gets old, and then dies like any other animal; yet there are some phenomena, the so-called psychic ones, for instance, that stand in the way of precise observation and present too great a difficulty. Therefore, to better comprehend a human, we shall first consider his life through its more elementary manifestations, those similar to what we see in animals and plants, which are devoid of this psychic activity. To do this, we shall observe the life of animals and plants in general. On examining animals and plants, we see that there are even more elementary material laws that they all share. Since the laws of animals are simpler than the laws of human life, and the laws of plants are even simpler, and the material laws are simpler still, then our investigations should also be based upon the simplest—the material laws. We can observe that what happens in plants and animals also takes place in the same manner in man, they say, and therefore we conclude that all that happens in man is explained by what happens in the simplest thing, inanimate matter, something visible and amenable to our experiments; moreover, all particularities of human activity are always dependent upon the forces operating within matter. Each material change in a person's body alters and disturbs his entire conduct. Therefore, they conclude, material laws are the causes of human activity. They are not bothered by the idea that there might be something in a human that we find neither in animals nor in plants, nor in dead matter, and that this something is the sole object of knowing, without which everything else is futile.

It never crosses their mind that if material changes in a human's body disturb his activity, it only proves that material changes represent one of the causes that affect human activity, but by no means does it prove that material change is the cause of human activity. Similarly, the harm done when you remove the soil from the roots of a plant indicates that soil is not necessarily everywhere, and not that a plant is the product of the soil alone. So they study in man a thing that also happens in dead matter, in a plant, and in an animal, all the while assuming that the clarification of those phenomenal laws that take place alongside human life will also clarify human life itself.

To understand human life, to understand the law that a person's animal individuality should obey to attain its happiness, people examine the following: the historical existence, but not the life, of man, or the unconscious yet observable subordination to laws by animals, plants, and matter. In other words, they do what people who seek some unknown but desired destination do when they study the location of unknown objects.

It is entirely fair to say that the knowledge of the observable manifestations of human existence through history can be instructive for us; just as the study of the laws governing the animal individuality of a human being and of other animals can be instructive, as can the study of those laws to which matter itself is subject. In its ability to show him, like a reflection, what has necessarily been happening in his life, the study of all this is important. Obviously, however, knowledge of what has been happening and can be observed, no matter how complete, cannot offer the chief knowledge we need—an understanding of the law that a person's animal individuality should obey to attain its happiness. Knowing the laws that are in force is instructive, but only when we acknowledge the law of reason that our animal individuality should obey, and not when this law is completely disregarded.

No matter how well a tree might have studied—if it could study—all the chemical and physical phenomena that are taking place within it, the tree could not gather from those observations and facts that it is necessary to collect sap and distribute it in the trunk, leaf, blossom, and fruit so that these things might grow.

And, no matter how well a person might know the law that governs his animal individuality and the laws that govern matter, these laws offer him not the faintest indication of what to do with the piece of bread he holds in his hand: Should he give it to his wife, a stranger, the dog, or eat it himself? Should he guard this piece of bread, or give it to the one who asks for it? Human life, meanwhile, consists entirely of such questions.

Studying the laws that govern the existence of animals, plants, and matter is not only useful but also indeed necessary for the clarification of the law of human life, yet only when this study has as its aim the main object of human cognition: illumining the law of reason.

Presuming that the life of man is tantamount to his animal existence, and that the happiness that is indicated by reasonable consciousness is impossible, and that the law of reason is only a phantom—the study of that life is rendered not only idle but also in fact ruinous, for it blocks from man the cardinal subject of knowledge. It furthermore reinforces in him the error that through the study of an object's representation he can somehow get to know the object itself. Such study is like someone who carefully studies all the changes and motions of the shadow of a living creature, assuming that the cause of movement in a living creature lies in the changes and movements of its shadow.

The Cause of False Knowledge Is the False Perspective in Which Objects Are Represented

True knowledge, says Confucius, means knowing we know what we know, and we do not know what we do not know. False knowledge, on the other hand, means thinking that we know what we do not know, and that we do not know what we do know. It is impossible to give a more precise definition to the false way of knowing that reigns among us. It is assumed by the false knowledge of our time that we know what we cannot know, and that we cannot know the only thing that we do know. A person possessed of false knowledge imagines that he knows all that appears to him in space and time, and that he does not know that which is known to him through his reasonable consciousness.

This person imagines that happiness in general, as well as his own happiness, is the most unknowable thing to him. His reason, his reasonable consciousness, appears to him almost as unknowable; he seems more knowable to himself as an animal; animals and plants appear as even more knowable objects, and an all-pervasive inert matter appears to him as something most knowable.

Something similar happens with a person's vision. We always and unconsciously direct our vision toward objects that are most distant and that therefore seem to be the simplest in color and contour: the sky, the horizon, the distant fields, and the forests. The more distant these objects are, the more definite and simple they appear and, vice versa, the closer the object the more complex its contour and color.

If a person were incapable of ascertaining the distance of objects, if he were to view the objects not in their perspectival arrangement and instead were to consider a greater simplicity and definiteness of contour as indicating a greater degree of visibility, then the infinite sky would seem to him to be the simplest and most visible thing; then the complex lines of the horizon would seem less visible; and the even more variously colored and shaped houses and trees would seem even less visible; his own hand, moving before his eyes, still less visible; and light itself would appear the most invisible.

Is not precisely the same thing going on with a person's false cognition? What is known to him beyond a doubt—his reasonable consciousness—seems unknowable to him because it is not simple, while what is absolutely unknowable to him—infinite and eternal matter—seems to him the most knowable of things, because, owing to its distance from him, it seems simple.

But the exact opposite is true. Prior to everything, and most undoubtedly, man can know and knows that happiness that he pursues; just as undoubtedly, he knows reason, which directs him toward this happiness; then he knows his animal [self], which is subject to reason; finally he sees, but does not know, all the other phenomena that appear to him in space and time.

Only to someone with a false notion of life does it seem that he knows objects better and more precisely when they are defined by space and time; in reality, we adequately know only what is defined neither by space nor by time—happiness and the law of reason. Regarding external objects, we know less about them the less our consciousness participates in their cognition; as a consequence, an object gets defined only by its position in space and time. Therefore, the more exclusively the object is defined by space and time, the less it renders itself to human cognition (the less comprehensible it is for man).[1]

True human knowledge ends with the knowing of our individuality, our animal [self]. A person knows his own animal [self], which pursues happiness and obeys the law of reason, in a way completely different from the way he knows all things that are not his individuality. He truly knows himself in this animal, and he knows himself not because he is something bound by space and time (on the contrary, he can never know himself as a spatial and temporal manifestation) but because he is something that must, for its own happiness, obey the law of reason. He knows himself within this animal as something independent of space and time. When he asks of himself about his position in space and time, it appears first of all that he stands in the midst of time, infinite on both sides, and that he is the center of an orb whose surface is everywhere and nowhere. Man really knows this self, which exists outside time and outside space, and his real knowledge ends there, on this, his I. Everything that is located outside this individual I man does not know but can only observe and define in a conditional, external way.

By temporarily renouncing his knowledge of himself as a reasonable center that pursues happiness—that is, as an extratemporal and extraspatial creature—man can temporarily and conditionally admit that he is part of the observable world made manifest temporally and in space. By so regarding himself in space and temporally, and in his connection with other creatures, man unites his true inner knowledge of himself with an external observation of himself and gains a notion of himself as a man in general who is like all other men. Through this conditional knowledge about himself, man acquires some external notions about other people but does not know them.

The impossibility of truly knowing other people stems from the fact that we do not see these people as one person but as hundreds, thousands. We know that there are, have been, and will be people whom we have never seen and will never see.

Looking out even farther away, beyond other people, man sees animals in space and time that are different from people and from one another. These creatures would be completely incomprehensible to him had he no knowledge of man in general; but bearing this knowledge, and subtracting reasonable consciousness from the concept of man, he gains a certain notion about animals, too. This notion bears for him even less semblance to knowledge than his notion about men in general. He sees vast multitudes of various animals, and the greater their quantity, obviously, the less possible it is for him to attain knowledge of them.

Looking further out he sees plants, and the prevalence of these phenomena in the world is even greater, and with it increases the impossibility of his knowing them.

Still further out in space and time—beyond animals and plants—man sees inanimate bodies and—hardly distinguishable or completely indistinguishable at this point—various forms of matter. Matter he understands least of all. The cognition of material forms is a completely indifferent business for him: Not only does he not know these forms of matter but also he actually merely imagines a knowledge of them. Moreover, matter appears to him to be infinite in space and time.

Things Become More Knowable Not Because of Their Manifestation in Space and Time but Because of the Unity That We, and All the Things We Study, Obey

What could be more comprehensible than these words: a dog is in pain; a calf is gentle—it likes me; a bird is joyous, a horse is afraid, a kind man, a wicked animal? All these very important and clear words are not defined by space and time. On the contrary, the more a law that a phenomenon obeys is incomprehensible to us, the better this phenomenon is defined by time and space. Who can say that he understands why the law of gravity that controls the movement of the earth, the moon, and the sun occurs? The solar eclipse is most precisely defined by space and time.

We know completely only our life, our pursuit of happiness, and reason, which indicates for us this happiness. The next most reliable knowledge is knowledge of our animal individuality, which pursues happiness and obeys the law of reason. Spatial and temporal conditions already make themselves present in our knowledge of our animal individuality—visible, tangible, observable but inaccessible to our comprehension. The next most reliable knowledge is knowledge of animal individualities that are like us and in whom we recognize a common pursuit of happiness and a common reasonable consciousness. Inasmuch as the life of these individuals converges with the laws of our life—our pursuit of happiness, our obeying of the law of reason—the better we know them. Inasmuch as their lives are made manifest in spatial and temporal conditions, we do not know them. And in this way, we by and large know people. The next most reliable knowledge is our knowledge of animals. We can perceive in these animals an individuality that, just as ours does, pursues its own happiness; but we can hardly recognize anything like our reasonable consciousness, and we cannot interact with them using our reasonable consciousness. Beyond animals we see plants, in which we can recognize only with difficulty an individuality that pursues its happiness as we do. These creatures appear to us largely through temporal and spatial phenomena and are therefore even less accessible to our knowledge.

We know them only because in them we see an individuality similar to our animal individuality that pursues its happiness, just as ours does, and makes its matter obey the law of reason that is manifest in it according to the conditions of space and time.

Even less accessible to our knowledge are objects inanimate and impersonal; we find no likeness to our individuality in them and see no pursuit of happiness. We see only temporal and spatial manifestations of the laws of reason to which these things are subject.

The validity of our knowledge is independent of how well objects can be observed in space and time; on the contrary, the more observable the manifestation of an object is in space and time the less it is clear to us.

Our knowledge about the world flows from a consciousness of our pursuit of happiness and the necessity, in order to achieve this happiness, of making our animal [self] obey reason. If we know animal life, it is only because also in animals we observe a pursuit of happiness and the necessity of obeying the law of reason, which in the animal is represented by the law of its organism.[1]

If we know matter, we know it—though its happiness is incomprehensible to us—because we see in it the same phenomenon that we see in ourselves: the necessity of obeying the law of reason that governs it.

The cognition of anything at all for us depends on transferring into other objects our understanding of life as a pursuit of happiness, a happiness obtainable through obedience to the law of reason.

We cannot cognize ourselves based on the laws that govern animals; we can cognize animals only through a law that we know in ourselves. And even less can we come to know ourselves based on laws for our lives that have been applied to material phenomena.

All a person knows about the external world he knows only because he knows himself, and within himself a person finds three relations to the world: a relation of his reasonable consciousness, another relation of his animal [consciousness], and a third relation of the matter that makes up the body of his animal [self]. He knows in himself these three different relations, and therefore everything that he sees in the world arrays itself into three distinct planes: (1) reasonable creatures, (2) animals and plants, and (3) inanimate matter.

Man always sees these three categories of objects in the world because he contains within himself these three objects of cognition. He knows himself (1) as reasonable consciousness that makes the animal [self] obey it; (2) as an animal that obeys reasonable consciousness; and (3) as matter that obeys the animal [self].

It is not through a knowledge of material laws that we can come to know the laws of organisms, as is commonly believed; nor is it through a knowledge of the laws of organisms that we can know ourselves as reasonable consciousness. It is the other way around. First, we can and we must know our own selves—that is, that law of reason to which our individuality must be obedient for the sake of our happiness; only then can and must we know the law of our own animal individuality and those like it and, at a greater remove from ourselves, the laws of matter.

We need to know, and we know, only ourselves. The animal world is already a reflection of what we know from within ourselves. The world of objects is then a reflection of a reflection, as it were.

Material laws look to us especially clear because they are uniform for us; and they are uniform for us because they are especially removed from the apparent law of our life.

Likewise, the laws of organisms seem to us simpler than the law of our life because of their remoteness. But in them, too, we only observe the laws but do not know them in the way that we know the law of our reasonable consciousness that we should fulfill.

We know neither the former nor the latter existence but only see them, observe them as something external to us. We undoubtedly know the law of our reasonable consciousness, because we need it for our happiness, because we live by it; however, we do not see this consciousness, because we lack the vantage from which to observe it.

Only if there existed higher creatures who would make our reasonable consciousness obey in the way that our reasonable consciousness makes our animal individuality obey and the way that our animal individuality (our organism) makes matter obey—these higher creatures could see our reasonable life just as we see our animal existence and the existence of matter.

Human life appears to be inextricably connected with the two kinds of existence that it includes within itself: the existence of animals and plants (organisms) and the existence of matter.

A person makes his own authentic life and lives it out; but we can have no part in those two types of existence connected with his life. The body and matter, of which we consist, have their own existence.

The two types of existence appear to a person as though they had preceded him, as though they had already been lived by other lives—as though they were memories of former lives.

These two types of existence offer a person in his true life the tool and material for his work but not his work itself.

It is useful for man to study the material and tool of his work. The better he gets to know them the more he will be fit to do the work. Studying the types of existence included in his life—his animal self and the matter that makes up the animal—demonstrates to man, as if through reflection, the general law of all that exists, obedience to the law of reason; and thereby this realization of the general law affirms in man the necessity of making his animal [self] obey the law. However, man neither can nor should confuse the material and the tool of his work with the work itself.

No matter how much one has studied the life that is visible, tangible, and observable within his own life and in others' lives—a life that takes place without his effort—this life will forever remain a mystery. One will never derive from these observations an understanding of a life of which he is not himself conscious. Observations of this life, forever concealed from him in the infinity of time and space, will never shed light on his own true life, which is accessible to him in his consciousness and which consists of making his animal individuality—which is unique from all others and most familiar to him—obey the law of reason; this law is unique from other laws and most familiar to him. He does all this, moreover, to attain a happiness that is unique and most familiar to him.

CHAPTER 14

The True Life of Man Does Not Take Place in Space and Time

Man knows life from within himself as the pursuit of happiness, attainable by making his animal individuality obedient to the law of reason.

He knows no other human life and cannot know one. Man, after all, recognizes an animal as alive only when the matter that forms the animal obeys not only its own laws but also the higher law of the organism.

If in a given conglomeration of matter there is an obedience to the higher law of the organism, then we recognize life in this conglomeration of matter; if not, if this obedience has not begun or has ended and nothing sets this matter apart from all other matter in which only mechanical, chemical, and physical laws operate, then we do not recognize animal life in this matter.

Similarly, we recognize persons like us, and our own self, as living only when, in addition to obeying the law of its organism, our animal individuality also obeys the supreme law of reasonable consciousness.

Whenever this obedience of one's individuality to the law of reason is missing, whenever only the law of individuality—the law that subjugates to itself the matter that forms man—is active in man, we do not know and do not see human life in others, nor in ourselves, just as we do not see animal life in matter that obeys only its own [material] laws.

No matter how strong or quick a person's movements are in a state of delirium, or in a spell of madness or agony, or while intoxicated, or even during a spasm of passion—we do not take this human being to be alive, we do not treat this human being as a living person, and we grant only that there is the possibility of life in him. No matter how weak or motionless a person might be, as soon as we see that his animal individuality is obedient to reason, we recognize him as alive, and we treat him as such.

We cannot comprehend human life otherwise than making our animal individuality obedient to the law of reason.

This life manifests itself in space and time; it is, however, defined by neither spatial nor temporal conditions but only by the degree of animal individuality's obedience to reason. Defining life by temporal and spatial conditions is like defining the altitude of an object by its length and width.

An object that is ascending while moving along a flat plane offers an exact model of the relationship of true human life toward the life of animal individuality, or of authentic life to the temporal and spatial life. The upward movement of an object is independent of its movement along the other plane, neither increasing nor decreasing because of it. So it is with the definition of human life. True life is always made manifest through individuality, but it is independent of this or that individual existence, neither increasing nor decreasing because of it.

The temporal and spatial conditions where a person's animal individuality finds itself cannot influence true life, which consists of making the animal individuality obedient to reasonable consciousness.

Someone who wishes to live is powerless to destroy or stop the spatial or temporal movement of his existence; but his true life is the attainment of happiness by obeying reason, irrespective of these visible spatial and temporal movements. This ever-greater attainment of happiness through obedience to reason is the only thing that constitutes [true] human life. When this obedience stops increasing, human life continues along the two visible directions of space and time and is just mere existence. When there is upward movement, an increasing obedience to reason, then a relationship is set up between these two forces [of time and space] and the [upward movement], and a greater or a lesser movement takes place along the resulting force, elevating human existence into the sphere of life.

Spatial and temporal forces are forces that are defined, finite, and incompatible with an understanding of life; the force of pursuing happiness through obedience to reason is the force that elevates—the very force of life for which neither temporal nor spatial limits exist.

It appears to man that his life comes to a halt and is divided, but these halting stops and vacillations are just deceptions of consciousness (similar to the way external feelings may be deceived). There is not and cannot be halting or vacillation in true life; it only appears to us thus when we look falsely upon life.

A person begins to live a true life—that is, he rises to a certain height above animal life—and from this height he sees the illusory nature of his animal existence that inevitably ends in death; he sees that his existence on the flat plane ends on all sides with chasms. Refusing to admit that his rise to a higher level is life itself, the person is terrified by what he sees from this height. Instead of admitting that the force lifting him to this height is in fact his life and continuing in the direction that has become open to him, he becomes terrified at what has been revealed before him from above and purposely goes back down, settling somewhere as low as possible, trying not to see the chasms around him. But the force of reasonable consciousness again raises him, he sees it all again, again is terrified, and, so as not to see, he falls to earth. And this continues until he finally admits, to save himself from the terror of the ruinous life that draws him along, that he needs to understand that his movement on the flat plane—his spatial and temporal existence—is not his life, and that his life is only the upward movement, that the possibility of happiness and life abides only in the obedience of his individuality to the law of reason. He must understand that he has wings that raise him above the chasm, and were he to lack these, he would never have risen high, nor seen the chasm. He must have faith in his wings and fly wherever they take him.

The halting of true life and the splitting of consciousness—these initially strange phenomena of vacillations in one's true life—take place only because of a lack of faith.

Only a person who understands his life as limited to his animal existence, defined as it is by space and time, can believe that reasonable consciousness would at times appear in animal existence. By thus regarding these manifestations of reasonable consciousness within himself, a person might ask himself when and under what conditions his reasonable consciousness would manifest itself in him. No matter how long this person examines his past, he will never discover the moments when reasonable consciousness appeared: it always seems that either it has never been there or that it has always been there. If it seems to him that there had been periods of reasonable consciousness, it is only because he does not recognize the life of reasonable consciousness to be life as such. Understanding his life only as an animal existence, defined by spatial and temporal conditions, a person would want to use the same yardstick when measuring the awakening and the activity of his reasonable consciousness. Man asks himself, When, how long, and under what conditions did I find myself in the sphere of reasonable consciousness? But such gaps between the stirrings of reasonable life exist only for a person who understands his life as the life of animal individuality. For a person who understands his life for what it is—the activity of reasonable consciousness—there can be no such gaps.

There is a reasonable life. There is only one. Momentary gaps, be they one minute or fifty thousand years, make no difference to it because for it, time does not exist. The true life of man, the one from which he forms his notion of any other life, is his pursuit of happiness, attainable through obedience of his individuality to the law of reason. Neither reason, nor the level of obedience to it, is defined by space and time. The true life of man takes place outside space and time.[1]

CHAPTER 15

Renouncing the Happiness of the Animal Individuality Is the Law of Human Life

Life is the pursuit of happiness. The pursuit of happiness is life. All people have and will always understand life in this way. And therefore human life is the pursuit of human happiness, and the pursuit of human happiness is human life itself. The crowd, the unthinking people—they understand human happiness as something residing in the happiness of one's animal individuality.

By excluding the concept of happiness from the definition of life, false science understands life as animal existence and therefore identifies the happiness of life only with animal happiness and joins in with the error of the crowd.

In both cases, the error derives from the confusion of what science calls individuality and reasonable consciousness. Reasonable consciousness subsumes individuality. Individuality does not subsume reasonable consciousness. Individuality is both a human and an animal quality. Reasonable consciousness is a human quality alone.

An animal can live merely for the sake of its body—nothing prevents it from living thus; it takes care of its individuality and serves its kin unconsciously and does not know itself to be an individual. But a reasonable person cannot live merely for the sake of his body. He cannot live thusly because he knows himself to be an individual and therefore knows that other creatures are individuals just like him, and he knows all that must proceed from the relationships of these individuals.

Were someone to pursue only his own individual happiness, loving only himself, his individuality, he would never know that other creatures also love themselves, just as animals do not know this; but if man knows himself to be an individual who pursues the same thing that other individuals around him are pursuing, he then can no longer pursue that happiness that appears evil to his reasonable consciousness, and his life can no longer consist of pursuing his individual happiness. It only occasionally seems to someone that his pursuit of happiness has as its object the satisfaction of his animal individuality's demands. This deception results from someone's having mistaken what is going on in his animal [self] for the aim of the activity of his reasonable consciousness. What happens in this case is similar to what a person might do were he to allow his dreams to govern his wakeful hours.

When this deception is bolstered by false teachings, individuality becomes confused with reasonable consciousness.

But reasonable consciousness always reveals to a person that the satisfaction of his animal individuality's demands cannot be his happiness, and therefore neither can it be his life; and his reasonable consciousness draws him irresistibly toward that happiness, and therefore that life, that is particular to him, one that does not fit within his animal individuality.

It is usually thought and said that the renunciation of individual happiness is a heroic feat, a mark of honor for a person. Well, renunciation of individual happiness is neither an honor nor a feat but an unavoidable necessity of human life. As one becomes conscious of himself as an individual distinct from the whole world, he simultaneously comes to know other individuals as distinct from the whole world, their shared connection; he comes to know the illusory nature of his individual happiness and that the only real happiness is the one that can satisfy his reasonable consciousness.

For an animal, any activity that does not have individual happiness as its aim but instead has an aim directly in opposition to this happiness would be the negation of life. It is quite the opposite for a human. When a person directs his activity solely at the attainment of individual happiness, this is the complete negation of human life.

For an animal lacking a reasonable consciousness that could show it the misery and finality of its existence, individual happiness and the survival of its species are the highest of life's goals. For a person, his individuality is merely a stage of existence from which the true happiness of his life opens up to him, a happiness that does not coincide with his individual happiness.

For a human, this individual consciousness is not life but the boundary from which his life begins, a life that consists of a greater and greater attainment of the happiness that is particular to him, one that does not depend on the happiness of his animal individuality.

According to the pedestrian notion of life, human life is the slice of time from birth to the death of his animal [self]. This is not human life; this is only human existence as an animal individuality. Human life, on the other hand, is something made manifest in animal existence, much in the same way that organic life is something made manifest in material existence.

Initially, the goals of a person's life seem to him to be the visible goals of his individuality. These goals are visible and therefore seem clear.

The goals that his reasonable consciousness indicates, however, seem unclear because they are invisible. At first, it is frightening to reject what is visible and give oneself over to the invisible.

The animal self's demands get fulfilled automatically, and they are visible in oneself and in others, so to a person perverted by the false teachings of the world, they seem simple and clear; the new imperceptible demands of reasonable consciousness appear contradictory; they do not take place automatically but instead he himself must accomplish them, and they seem to him complex and unclear. It is frightening and horrifying to renounce the visible ideas of life and give oneself over to an imperceptible consciousness of it, just as it would be frightening and horrifying for a baby to be born if it could feel its birth—but there is no helping it when it becomes obvious that the visible idea draws one forward into death while the invisible consciousness alone grants life.

CHAPTER 16

The Animal Individuality
Is the Tool for Life

No amount of theorizing can conceal from us the obvious and indubitable truth that individual existence is something that is endlessly dying, pursuing death, and that therefore there can be no life in our animal individuality.

Man cannot help seeing that his individual existence, from birth and childhood until death, is nothing but a constant loss and diminishment of this animal individuality that ends in inevitable death; a consciousness of his individual life, which contains within it the desire for its own augmentation and indestructibility, cannot therefore help being a ceaseless contradiction and torment—it cannot help being an evil. One then sees that the sole meaning of his life is the pursuit of happiness.

Whatever a person's true happiness, his renunciation of the happiness of his animal individuality is inevitable.

Renouncing the happiness of one's animal individuality is the law of human life. If it does not take place freely, expressing itself as obedience to reasonable consciousness, then it takes place by force for each person at the moment when his animal [self] experiences death in the flesh. It happens when, because of the burden of suffering, he wishes for one thing: to get rid of the tormenting consciousness of the perishing individuality and to be transformed into another type of existence.

A person's entry into life, and human life itself, is like what happens to a horse when the owner leads it out of the stable to harness it. The horse leaves the stable and sees the light and senses freedom, and it seems that somehow life is contained in this freedom. But instead the horse is being harnessed and then geed-up. It feels the burden, and if it thinks that life consists of running around in freedom, then it starts thrashing, falls down, and sometimes kills itself. If it does not kill itself, it has only two options: either it goes forth and carries the load, learning that the load is not great, that giving a ride is no torment but joy; or it breaks free. In that case, the master breaks it on the wheel, tying it up to the wall with a lasso. As the wheel rotates under its feet, it will walk in place in the darkness. It will suffer, but its forces will not be wasted. It will do its involuntary work, and the law will be carried out. The only difference will be that the first horse will work joyfully while the second will do so unwillingly and in torment.

People who believe that their animal existence is their life will say, "But what is the use of this individuality, the happiness of which, as a human being, I should renounce so that I can receive life?"

Why then has man been given this individual consciousness that resists the manifestation of his true life? One might respond to such a question with a similar question that might be asked by an animal that pursues its goals of preserving its life and kin.

"What good," it would ask, "is this matter and its laws—mechanical, physical, chemical, and others—with which I must struggle in order to achieve my goals?" "If my calling," the animal would say, "is the realization of my animal life, what good are these obstacles that I have to overcome?"

It is clear to us that all matter and its laws against which the animal struggles and that it overcomes for the existence of its animal individuality are not in fact obstacles but instead are means for the animal to attain its goals. An animal lives only by processing matter and by means of matter's laws. The same is true of a person's life. The animal individuality in which he finds himself, and that he is called upon to make obedient to his reasonable consciousness, is not an obstacle but a means to attain the goals of his happiness: The animal individuality is the tool a person uses to work. The animal individuality is a person's spade, given to a reasonable person so that he can dig and, in digging, make it first blunt then sharpen it; use it up, rather than keep it clean and stored away. This is his talent to nurture, and not to hoard. "Those who find their life will lose it, and those who lose their life for My sake will find it."[1]

These words mean that it is impossible to save what must perish, what never stops perishing, and that only by renouncing what will perish and must perish—our animal individuality—do we receive our true life, which will not perish and cannot perish. It is said that our true life begins only when we stop thinking that life is something that it has never been and cannot be—our animal individuality. It is said that the one who spares his spade, which he possesses so that he can make the food that sustains him—that he who spares his spade will lose both food and life.

CHAPTER 17

Birth in the Spirit

"You must be born anew," said Christ.[1] No one ordered that a person be born, but a person is inevitably led to this. To have life, he ought to be born anew in this existence—through his reasonable consciousness.

Reasonable consciousness is given to man so that he can put his life into the happiness revealed to him through reasonable consciousness. Whoever puts his life into this happiness has life; whoever does not and instead puts his life into the happiness of his animal individuality deprives himself of life. In this consists the definition of life given by Christ.

When those who consider life to be the pursuit of individual happiness hear such words, they do not so much fail to acknowledge them; rather, they just do not understand them. To them it seems that these words either are meaningless or mean very little, that the person is putting on airs of a sentimental and mystical mood, as they like to call it. They cannot comprehend the meaning of these words that explain a state they cannot attain, just as a dormant, dry seed cannot understand the state of a seed that has been watered and has already sprouted. For dry seeds, the sun that illuminates them with its rays so as to bring them forth into life is nothing more than a meaningless accident—a bit more warmth and light. For the germinating seed, however, this sun is the reason for its birth into life. So it is for people who have not yet lived long enough to reach the internal contradiction between their animal individuality and reasonable consciousness, for them, the sunshine of reason is nothing but a meaningless accident, sentimental and mystical words. The sun brings to life only those in whom life has already germinated.

How it germinates, why, when, where—not only in man but also in animals and plants—nobody has ever discovered. Of life's germination in man, Christ has said that nobody knows this, and they cannot know it.

Indeed, what can man know about how life germinates in him? Life is man's light, life is life—the beginning of it all; how can man know how it germinates? Whatever germinates and dies for man is something that does not live, something that is made manifest in space and time. True life is; therefore, for man, it can neither germinate nor perish.

CHAPTER 18

What Reasonable
Consciousness Demands

Yes, reasonable consciousness tells a person certainly, irrefutably that the way he sees the world from his own individuality—for him, for that individuality, there can be no happiness. His life is a desire for happiness for himself, precisely himself, and he sees that this happiness is impossible. Strangely enough, although there can be no doubt that happiness is impossible for him, he goes on living solely for this impossible happiness—happiness only for himself.

If he does not kill himself, a person whose reasonable consciousness has awakened (only just awakened) but whose animal individuality has not yet been made obedient will still live for this impossible happiness: the person lives and acts so that he alone will have this happiness, so that all people, and even all creatures, live and act solely so that he is content, so he has enjoyment, so that there is no suffering and no death for him.

And here is the strange thing: despite his experience, despite his observations of those around him, despite reason having undeniably demonstrated to him and to every person the impossibility of forcing other living creatures to stop loving themselves and instead to love only him—despite all this, every person's life is spent forcing all creatures to love him alone and not themselves, using wealth, power, honors, glory, flattery, deception, this way or that.

People have done and are doing all they can for this goal, and yet they see that they are doing the impossible. "My life is the pursuit of happiness," someone tells himself. "Happiness is possible for me only when all other creatures love me more than themselves, and yet all other creatures love only themselves; so, all that I do to force them to love me is useless. It is useless, and yet I can do nothing else."

The ages pass. People discover the distance to celestial bodies, figure out how much these bodies weigh, find out the composition of the sun and the stars—yet how to reconcile the demands of individual happiness with the life of the world, which excludes the possibility of this happiness?

This question remains for the majority of people as unsolved as it was for people five thousand years ago.

Reasonable consciousness tells every person yes, you can have happiness, but only if everyone loves you more than they love themselves. And the same reasonable consciousness demonstrates to man that it cannot be so, because they all love only themselves. And so reasonable consciousness reveals the one happiness to man, and then conceals it again.

Ages pass and the riddle of happiness for human life remains for the majority of people the same insolvable riddle. Yet this riddle was solved long ago. And for those who figure out the riddle, it seems surprising that they had failed to solve it sooner by themselves—it seems they had known it all along and had just forgotten it. How simple and self-evident the answer is to a riddle that has seemed so difficult amid the false teachings of our world.

You want everyone to live for your sake, for everyone to love you more than themselves? There is only one way for your wish to come true: if every creature lived for the sake of others' happiness and loved others more than themselves. Only then would you and all creatures be loved by all, and you, in their midst, would receive the very happiness you are seeking. If happiness is possible for you only when all creatures love others more than they love themselves, then you, too, as a living creature, must love other creatures more than yourself.

This is the only way that happiness and human life are possible, the only way that the thing that used to poison the life of man—the struggle for existence among creatures, the agony of suffering and the fear of death—is destroyed.

After all, what made the happiness of individual existence impossible? First, the struggle with every other creature seeking individual happiness; second, the deception of pleasure that leads to a wasting of life, satiety, sufferings; and third, death. But one need only mentally admit that man can replace the pursuit of individual happiness with the pursuit of the happiness of others, and the impossibility of happiness is destroyed and happiness appears possible. Looking at the world from his notion of life as a pursuit of individual happiness, a person once saw in the world an irrational struggle of creatures bent on destroying one another. But all it takes for someone to see quite a different thing is to admit that his life is the pursuit of others' happiness: aside from accidental cases of creatures struggling with one another, one sees instead creatures constantly serving one another, something without which the existence of the world is unthinkable.

All it takes is allowing this, and the former insane activity aimed at an unobtainable individual happiness gets replaced by another sort of activity, one that corresponds to the law of the world and is aimed at achieving the utmost happiness possible for oneself and the whole world.

Another reason for the poverty of individual life and the impossibility of human happiness has been the deceptive character of enjoyment, which lays waste to life, leading, as it does, to satiety and sufferings. All it takes is recognizing that life is the pursuit of others' happiness, and the deceptive thirst for enjoyment is annihilated; the tormenting and idle activity aimed at filling the bottomless pit of individual appetite is replaced with an activity that corresponds to the laws of reason, one that consists of sustaining the life of other creatures, something necessary for one's own happiness. Thus the torment of individual suffering, something that destroys life's activity, is replaced by a feeling of compassion for others, one that causes activity that is doubtlessly fruitful and most joyous.

The third reason for the poverty of individual life was once the fear of death. It only takes man to acknowledge that he lives not for the sake of the happiness of his animal individuality but for the happiness of other creatures, and the specter of death disappears forever from his sight.

The fear of death, after all, stems merely from the fear of losing the happiness of life with its death in the flesh. If a person could put his happiness in the happiness of other creatures—that is, if he could love them more than himself—then death would no longer seem to him an end of happiness and life, as it appears to someone living only for himself. For a man who lives for others, death could never appear as a destruction of happiness and life because the happiness and life of other creatures are not destroyed when the life of that person who serves them ends; rather, they only increase and are often strengthened by the sacrifice of his life.

CHAPTER 19

Confirmation of the Demands of Reasonable Consciousness

"But this is not life," the deluded human consciousness indignantly responds. "This is a renunciation of life, suicide." "I do not know any of this," reasonable consciousness responds. "I know that such is human life, and there is no other, nor can there be. I know moreover that this life is [true] life, it is happiness—for a person and for the whole world. I know that my old view was one in which my own life, and the life of all that exists, was evil and meaninglessness, while my new view of life reveals the realization of that law of reason that is implanted in man. I know the greatest happiness of every creature, something that can be increased infinitely, can be achieved through this law of each serving all and therefore all serving each."

"While it is possible to imagine such a law, it is not the law of the real world," the deluded human consciousness indignantly responds. "Presently, others do not love me more than they love themselves, and therefore I cannot love them more than myself and for their sake deprive myself of enjoyment and submit to suffering. I want nothing to do with the law of reason. I want pleasures for myself and want to rid myself of suffering. Now there is a struggle going on among creatures, and if I alone do not do battle with them, others will trample me I do not care about the path that, at least theoretically, achieves the maximum happiness of all. What I now need is the utmost and real happiness that is my own," says false consciousness.

—"I know nothing about this," reasonable consciousness responds.

"I know only that what you call your pleasures will become your happiness only when you are not the one who takes these pleasures but when others give them to you; otherwise, your pleasures will remain an extravagance and a source of suffering, as they are now when you are grasping at them. You will rid yourself of suffering only when others rid you of it, not when you try to do so yourself—just as it is presently, when out of fear of some imagined suffering you deprive yourself of life itself.

113

"I know that individual life, a life that requires that everyone love me alone and I love only myself, a life in which I receive as much pleasure as possible and rid myself of suffering and death, is the greatest, most constant suffering. The more I love myself and struggle with others, the more they will hate me and fight me; the more I try to shield myself from suffering, the more painful it will be; the more I guard myself from death, the more terrifying it will be.

"I know that no matter what a person does, he will not receive happiness until he lives in accordance with the law of his life. And this law of his life is not the law of struggle but, on the contrary, the mutual serving of one another."[1]

"But I know life only through my individuality. It is impossible for me to stake my life in the happiness of other creatures."

—"I know nothing about this," says reasonable consciousness. "I know only that my life and the life of the world, which previously appeared to me to be wicked nonsense, now appear to be a reasonable whole, living and pursuing one and the same happiness by becoming obedient to the same law of reason that I know in myself."

"Well, that is not possible for me!" the deluded consciousness says. Meanwhile no one would refuse to do this most impossible thing, no one would refuse to stake the very best happiness of his life on this impossible thing.

"It is impossible to stake your own happiness in the happiness of other creatures." Meanwhile no one is unfamiliar with this state when what is happiness for other creatures becomes his own happiness. "It is impossible to put your own happiness in toiling and suffering for another." Yet all it takes is for someone to surrender himself to compassion, and individual pleasure stops making sense, and his force of life is transferred into toiling and suffering for the happiness of others, and toiling becomes happiness. "It is impossible to sacrifice your life for the happiness of others." Yet all it takes is for someone to recognize this feeling, and death is not only invisible and not terrifying but also appears as the highest happiness that he can achieve.

A reasonable person cannot help seeing that, when he imagines the possibility that instead of pursuing his own happiness he seek the happiness of other creatures, his life becomes reasonable and happy, instead of its former unreasonableness and misery. He cannot help seeing likewise that if he admits the same understanding of life in other people and creatures, the life of the whole world, which once appeared to be madness and cruelty, becomes the highest reasonable happiness that a man could wish for—it takes on a reasonable meaning for him instead of its former meaninglessness and aimlessness. To such a person, the goal of the life of the world appears to be the infinite enlightening and unification of the creatures of the world, which is where life is headed. As they become more and more obedient to the law of reason, all creatures will eventually understand something that, at first, only man is able to understand: that the happiness of life is not attained by each creature seeking only its own individual happiness but by each creature seeking, according to the law of reason, the happiness of all others.

But there is more. As soon as someone has admitted the possibility of pursuing the happiness of other creatures instead of pursuing his own happiness, he cannot help also seeing that this very renunciation of his individuality, gradual and ever growing as it is, and the shifting of the goal of his activity from himself to other creatures, is indeed the whole forward movement of humanity and all living creatures that are closest to man. One cannot help noticing in history that the movement of our shared life does not consist of an intensification and expansion of conflict among creatures but instead consists of its opposite, the diminution of disagreement and the weakening of struggle. One cannot help noticing that the movement of life consists of this: that the world, in its obedience to the law of reason, moves away from hostility and disagreement and toward greater and greater harmony and unity. Having admitted this, man cannot help seeing that people who once devoured one another have ceased eating one another; that those who once killed their captives and their own children have now stopped killing them; that the military that once proudly murdered has stopped taking pride in that; that those who used to condone slavery have now begun to destroy it; that those who used to kill animals have started taming them and killing them less often; that they have begun feeding on eggs and milk instead of animal flesh, and that they have begun to diminish the destruction of the plant world. One sees that the best people denounce seeking pleasure, that they call on people to exercise restraint, and the very best people, those praised by posterity, offer examples of sacrificing their existence for the happiness of others. A person sees that what he had admitted only because reason demands it in fact really takes place in the world and is confirmed by the past life of humanity.

But there is still more. Still more powerful and convincing than reason and history is something that seems to be from a completely different source, something that shows man what his heart pursues, that draws him onward, as one is drawn to some spontaneous happiness, toward the very activity that his reason has pointed out to him, something that in his heart is expressed as love.

CHAPTER 20

Individual Demands Seem Incompatible with the Demands of Reasonable Consciousness

Reason, judgment, history, and inner feeling—all these seem to convince a person of the justness of this understanding of life; but to a man raised on the teachings of this world, it still seems that the satisfaction of the demands of his reasonable consciousness and feelings cannot possibly be the law of his life.

"Not to struggle with others for my individual happiness, not to seek pleasures, not to avoid suffering, and not to fear death! This is impossible, this is a renunciation of my entire life! How is it that I renounce my individuality when I feel its demands, and when do I learn about the legitimacy of these demands on reasonable grounds?" So say the educated people of our world, full of confidence.

And here is a remarkable fact: working people, the simple ones who have practiced their intellect but little—such people almost never assert their individual demands, and they always feel internal demands that run contrary to individual ones; only among the rich, the refined, and those with a developed intellect do we find a complete negation of the demands of reasonable consciousness and, to the point, a refutation of the legitimacy of these demands and an assertion of individual rights.

A developed, refined, and idle person will always prove that an individual has inalienable rights. A starving man will not go about proving that man needs to eat; he knows this is common knowledge and that this can be neither proved nor disproved: he will just eat.

This happens because a simple person, a so-called uneducated person who has always used his body to do work, has not corrupted his reason and has retained it in its full purity and strength.

But someone who has been thinking his whole life not only about things petty and trifling but also about things quite unnatural for someone to contemplate has corrupted his reason. His reason is not free. His reason is busy with a task that is unnatural to it: contemplating his individual needs—their development, augmentation—and devising means for their satisfaction.

"But I feel the demands of my individuality; these demands are there-fore legitimate," the so-called educated people, who have been raised according to worldly teaching, will say.

And they cannot help feeling the demands of their individuality. For these people, their entire life is aimed at the ostensible increase in individ-ual happiness. And for them, individual happiness consists of satisfying needs. They call these conditions of individual existence, toward which their reason has been directed, individual needs. They are conscious of these needs—the ones at which their reason is directed—and such needs always run rampant, to infinite proportion, as a result of consciousness. And satisfying these rampant demands obstructs from their view the demands of true life.

So-called social science places at the basis of its inquiry a doctrine of human needs and overlooks a most inconvenient circumstance for this doctrine—namely, that every person has either no needs whatsoever—for example, someone who is killing himself, or someone on a hunger strike—or literally innumerable demands.

There are as many needs for the animal existence of man as there are facets of this existence, and there are as many facets as there are radii in a sphere. Demands for food, drink, breath, exercise for muscle and nerves; demands of labor, rest, pleasure, married life; demands of science, art, religion, as well as a diversity of all these needs. In all these cases, there are then the differing needs of a child, a young man, an adult man, an old man, a maiden, a woman, and an old woman; the demands of a Chi-naman, a Parisian, a Russian, a Lapp; the demands that correspond to the habits of the breed, to illnesses . . .

One can go on making this list until the end of days and still not list all the demands of someone's individual existence. All conditions of existence may count as demands, and the conditions of existence are innumerable.

What we call needs, however, are only the conscious conditions. These conscious conditions, as soon as we become conscious of them, lose their real meaning. When reason is directed at them, they acquire an exagger-ated significance, and they obstruct true life.

What we call needs—that is, the conditions of the animal existence of man—can be compared to the countless inflatable balloons that could fill a certain body. All these balloons are equal and have room until they start to inflate—just as all the demands are equal and each has room and cause us no pain so long as we are not conscious of them. But as soon as you begin to inflate a balloon, that balloon begins to take up more space than the others, and it begins to crowd against the others and is itself crowded. The same thing happens with demands: as soon as reasonable consciousness is directed at one, this conscious need occupies the whole of life and causes the whole of the human creature to suffer.

CHAPTER 21

What Is Necessary Is Not the Negation of Our Individuality but Obedience to Reasonable Consciousness

Yes, to claim that man does not feel the demands of his reasonable consciousness but only the demands of his individuality is nothing other than an acknowledgment that our animal passions, which our whole reason is directed toward intensifying, are now in control of us and have obscured our true human life. The weed of our overgrown vice has stifled the sprouts of true life.

How could it be otherwise in our world where those whom we consider teachers have directly acknowledged, and continue to acknowledge, that the highest perfection of man consists of the comprehensive development of refined individual needs, that the happiness of the masses consists of their having many demands and the ability to satisfy them, and that the happiness of people consists of their demands being satisfied.

How could people raised on this teaching fail to assert that they do not feel the demands of reasonable consciousness but only the demands of their individuality? How on earth are they to feel the demands of reason when their whole reason, without exception, has been devoted to intensifying their lustful drives? How are they to renounce their lust when it has completely swallowed their life?

These people usually say, "It is impossible to renounce one's individuality." They try purposely to tamper with the question by substituting the renunciation of individuality for its obedience to the law of reason.

"This is against nature," they say, "and therefore impossible." But nobody is talking about renouncing one's individuality. One's individuality is, for a reasonable person, the same thing as breathing and blood circulation for an animal individuality. How can an animal individuality renounce blood circulation? It is impossible to speak of this. You cannot talk to a reasonable person about renouncing his individuality.

Individuality for a reasonable person represents the same necessary condition for life as blood circulation represents for the existence of his animal individuality.

Individuality, as animal individuality, cannot and does not make any claims. These claims are made by a falsely directed reason, one that is directed not toward governing life or its illumination but toward inflating individual lust.

It is always possible to satisfy the demands of the animal individuality. A person cannot say, What am I going to eat? what am I going to wear? These needs are provided for, just as they are for a bird or a flower, so long as he lives a reasonable life. And really, what thinking person can believe that he might alleviate the misery of his existence by taking care of his individuality?

The misery of the human condition occurs not because someone is an individual but because he understands his individual life to be his life and his happiness. Only then do the contradiction, the splitting, and the suffering appear.

A person begins to suffer only when he uses the power of his reason to enhance and increase the infinitely increasing demands of his individuality in order that the demands of his reason are obscured.

It is impossible and unnecessary to reject our individuality, just as it is to reject the conditions in which a person exists, but one can and should reject the idea that these conditions are the same thing as life itself. One may and should make the best of the given conditions of life, but one must not and should not look on these conditions as if they were the goal of life. Not by renouncing individuality but by renouncing individual happiness, and by refusing to acknowledge one's individuality as the same thing as life itself—this is what a person must accomplish to return to harmony, what he must do so that the happiness that he seeks, which constitutes his life, becomes available to him.

Ever since ancient times, great teachers of humankind have preached that by acknowledging life as existing only in our individuality we destroy life, and that renouncing individual happiness is the sole path to attaining life.

"Yes, but what is this? It's nothing but Buddhism!" This is how people of our time usually respond. "This is Nirvana, it is standing on a pole!" And when they have said this, it seems to people of our time that they have successfully refuted something everyone knows very well, something that is impossible to conceal from anyone: that individual life is misery prone and that it has no meaning whatsoever.[1]

"This is Buddhism, nirvana," they say. And it seems to them that with these words they have refuted all that has been acknowledged and is acknowledged by billions of people, something that each of us knows very well in the depth of our soul, namely that a life lived in pursuit of individual aims is ruinous and meaningless and that if there is any way out of this ruinous meaninglessness, it must undoubtedly involve renouncing individual happiness.

It does not bother them that the majority of humankind has understood life and continues to understand life in such a way—that the greatest minds have understood life in such a way, and that an understanding to the contrary is quite impossible. They are certain that the questions of life, if they are not soon solved in the most satisfactory of ways, then they will be made irrelevant by telephone, silly musicals, bacteriology, electric light, roburite, and so forth.[2] So, the idea that individual happiness must be renounced seems to them only an echo of some ancient ignorance.

These unfortunates do not suspect that the crudest Indian who stands for years on one leg to show that he has renounced his individual happiness and achieved nirvana is, by any comparison, more alive than are they, the bestialized people of our contemporary European society who fly around the world by rail, who put their bovine state on exhibit under electric lights, and who use the telegraph and telephone to make known to the world their beastly state.[3] This Indian has become conscious of the contradiction between the life of his individuality and reasonable life, and he resolves that problem in his own way. People of our educated world not only have not understood this contradiction but also do not even believe in its existence. The belief that human life is not the same as the existence of one's individuality—a belief produced by the thousand-year spiritual work of humanity—has become for people (but not for animals) a truth in the moral world that is not merely as indubitable and indestructible but also in fact more indubitable and indestructible than the earth's rotation and the laws of gravity. Every thinking person—a savant, an ignoramus, an old person, a child—understands and knows it; it is concealed only from the most savage people in Africa or Australia and from well-to-do people who have gone wild in the European cities and capitals. This truth has become an achievement of all humanity, and if humanity does not go backward in its merely auxiliary knowledge of mechanics, algebra, and astronomy, then it is even less likely that it can go backward in its basic and central understanding of life. The attempt to restore the savage, antediluvian view of life as the existence of individuality, something that preoccupies the so-called science of our European world, merely demonstrates more clearly how the reasonable consciousness of humanity has grown, and how humanity has outgrown its childhood britches. Philosophical theories of self-destruction, and the fad of suicide that now spreads with terrible speed, show how it is impossible for humanity to return to the state of consciousness that it has outlived.

Humanity has outgrown life as the existence of individuality, and returning to it is impossible; it is out of the question that we will forget that the individual existence of man has no meaning. Whatever we might write or say or discover, however we may perfect our individual life—the impossibility of individual happiness remains the unshakable truth for every reasonable man of our time.

"And yet it does move."[4] Refuting the ideas of Galileo or Copernicus is not the point, nor is thinking up new Ptolemaic circles. That is impossible. The point is to go a step further and to draw new conclusions from the position into which the shared consciousness of all humanity has already entered. The same holds true regarding the belief that individual happiness is impossible, something advanced by the Brahmins, by Buddha, by Laozi, by Solomon, by the Stoics, and by all true thinkers of humanity. One should neither conceal this premise from oneself nor try to somehow avoid it, but instead one should acknowledge it courageously and openly, and then draw further conclusions from it.[5]

The Feeling of Love Is the Manifestation of Individual Activity That Has Been Subordinated to Reasonable Consciousness

It is impossible for a reasonable creature to live for individual goals. It is impossible because all roads are off-limits to it; all the aims toward which the animal individuality of man is drawn—all are obviously unattainable. Reasonable consciousness points out different goals—and these goals not only are attainable but also provide full satisfaction to the reasonable consciousness of man. Initially, however, and under the influence of the false teaching of this world, it may appear to someone that these goals are contrary to his individuality.

No matter how hard he tries to recognize himself in his reasonable I, a person who has been raised in our world—with his developed, exaggerated individual lusts—will not feel in that I the same pursuit of life that he feels in his animal individuality. It seems as though the reasonable I had contemplated life but had not itself lived, that it had no appetite for life. The reasonable I feels no appetite for life, while the animal I must suffer, and therefore one thing remains: to be rid of life.

The negative philosophers of our time (Schopenhauer, Hartmann) approach this issue dishonestly, denying life and yet remaining alive, never taking advantage of the possibility of exiting life. And so, those who commit suicide honestly resolve the question, leaving a life that, for them, represents nothing but evil.

Suicide appears to them the sole way out of the unreasonableness of human life in our time.[1]

The theorizing of pessimist philosophy, and that of most ordinary suicide, goes like this: There is an animal I, in which there is appetite for life. This I and its appetite cannot be satisfied. There is another, reasonable

I, with no appetite for life, however, that merely critically contemplates the false thrill of being alive and the passion of the animal I—and rejects it fully.

If I give myself over to the former, I see that I live insanely and come to misery and sink deeper and deeper into its sea. If I give myself over to the latter, to the reasonable I, there remains no appetite for life in me. I see that living merely for the sake of what I desire to live for, for individual happiness, is ludicrous and impossible. Where reasonable consciousness is concerned, one could live, but why bother, why have any desire for it? To serve that beginning whence I started, God. But why? Without me He'll find servants. Why bother? You can watch this game of life until it gets boring. And when you get bored you can take your leave, kill yourself. That is what I am doing.

Here is this contradictory view of life that humanity had reached prior to Solomon and Buddha, the view that the false teachers of our time wish humanity to return to.

Individual demands are driven to extremes of unreasonableness. The awakened reason denies them. But individual demands have grown to such a degree, and have so encumbered the consciousness of man, that it seems to him that reason denies all life. It seems to him that once his consciousness rejects everything that his reason denies, nothing remains. He is no longer capable of seeing what remains. The remainder, that remainder where life abides, appears to him as nothing.

But light shineth in darkness, and the darkness cannot overcome it.

The teaching of truth understands this dilemma—either insane existence or the rejection of it—and resolves it.

The teaching that has long been called a teaching of happiness, the teaching of truth, has shown people that in place of that treacherous happiness they seek for their animal individuality real happiness is inalienable and always attainable, and not sometime or somewhere but always here and now, at hand.

This happiness is not something deduced from a conclusion and not something that needs to be sought somewhere; it is not the happiness promised somewhere and at some point but that happiness already familiar to man, toward which every pure human soul is spontaneously drawn.

Everyone knows, from the earliest years of their childhood, that besides the happiness of the animal individuality there is another, better happiness of life, one that not only is independent of the gratification of animal lust but also, on the contrary, grows greater the more one rejects his animal happiness.

The feeling that resolves all contradictions of human life and that grants man the greatest happiness is known to all people. This feeling is *love*.

Life is the activity of an animal individuality, obedient to the law of reason. Reason is that law that the animal individuality of man, for its own happiness, should obey. Love is the only reasonable activity of man.

The animal individuality is drawn toward happiness; reason points out to man the treachery of individual happiness and leaves only one path open. The activity on this path is love.

The animal individuality of man demands happiness, reasonable consciousness demonstrates to man the misery of all creatures fighting among themselves and demonstrates to him that the only happiness possible for him would be one without struggle among creatures, without end, without satiety, without premonition and terror of death.

And just like a key custom-made for a lock, a person finds in his soul the feeling that gives him the same happiness that his reason indicates is the only possible one. Not only does this feeling solve the former contradiction of life but also it is as though the feeling had discovered in this contradiction the very possibility of its own manifestation.

For their own purposes, the animal individualities would like to make use of human individuality. But the feeling of love leads a person to devote his own existence for the benefit of other creatures.

The animal individuality suffers. These sufferings, together with their easing, constitute the main object of love's activity. Pursuing happiness, the animal individuality pursues with its every breath its greatest evil—death—and the premonition of death has disrupted every individual happiness. But the feeling of love not only destroys this fear but also draws one toward the final sacrifice of his existence in the flesh for the sake of others' happiness.

Manifesting the Feeling of Love Is Impossible for Those People Who Do Not Understand the Meaning of Their Life

Every person knows that there is something uncommon in the feeling of love, something special that resolves all life's contradictions and fills a person with that complete happiness, the pursuit of which amounts to life. People who do not comprehend life respond, "But this feeling visits us only occasionally; it lasts only a short while, and, worst of all, it sometimes results in even worse sufferings."

Love does not appear to these people as the sole legitimate manifestation of life, as it does to reasonable consciousness; it instead appears as merely one in a thousand sundry accidents that happen in life. Love appears to these people as one of a thousand sundry moods in which man finds himself during his existence: sometimes a man struts his stuff, then he takes up science or art, then sometimes his work at the office distracts him, or ambition, or material things, and then sometimes he loves somebody. To people who do not comprehend life, the emotion of love does not appear as the essence of human life but as a transitory mood—as independent of his will, just like all those other moods that a person is prone to. One often reads and hears the opinion that love is some false, tormenting mood, something that disrupts the correct course of life—much as sunrise must seem to an owl.

Granted, these people feel that there is something extraordinary about the state of being in love, something more important than all the other moods. But by not comprehending life, these people cannot comprehend love either, and the state of being in love appears to them as disastrous and treacherous, as all other states do.

> "To love?.. But whom, then?
> For a short time not worth it,
> And you cannot love eternally..."[1]

These words express the dim consciousness in people of the fact that there is salvation from the misery of life in love, something there that is similar to true happiness, but in these words there is also the acknowledgment that, for those who misunderstand life, love cannot be the saving anchor. There is no one to love, and every love passes. And therefore love is happiness only when there is someone to love and love eternally. Because such a thing does not exist, there is no salvation in love; love is merely the same sham and the same suffering as all the rest of life.

This and only this way is life understood by people who teach and are taught that life is nothing but animal existence.

For these people, love fails to correspond to the notion that we all involuntarily attribute to the word "love." Love is not an act of kindness that brings happiness to lovers. People who believe that their life is nothing more than their animal individuality often imagine that love is the same kind of feeling that leads a mother, in looking out for the happiness of her own child, to take from another hungry and anxious child his mother's milk; or the same feeling that compels a father, tormenting himself, to take the last piece of bread from starving people to sustain his own children; or the same feeling that causes a woman's lover to suffer because of this love and forces her to suffer by seducing her, or to destroy himself and her because of jealousy; or the same feeling that sometimes even leads a man to exercise force on a woman, [supposedly] out of love;[2] the feeling that causes one company of men to inflict harm on others to get what they want; the feeling that makes a man torment himself with his favorite pursuit and cause grief and suffering to the people around him on account of this pursuit; that feeling that keeps people from ignoring an insult to their beloved fatherland and litters the field with bodies of the killed and the wounded—their own bodies and the bodies of others.

Moreover, for people who consider their life to be nothing more than the happiness of the animal individual, loving activity presents such complications that its manifestations become not merely torment but also frequently impossible. "One should not theorize about love," say those who do not comprehend life. "Just submit to that immediate feeling of preference that you experience toward people. This is real love."

They are right that it is impossible to theorize about love, that any theorizing about love destroys love. But only those who have already put their reason to work understanding life and who have sworn off the happiness of individual life can manage not to theorize about love. Meanwhile, those who have not understood life and who exist for the happiness of their animal individuality cannot help theorizing. They need to theorize to be able to give in to that sentiment that they call love. Without a little theorizing, without trying to solve the unsolvable, any manifestation of this sentiment is impossible for them.

Indeed, people prefer their own children, their own friends, their own wives, their own fatherland to all other children, wives, friends, fatherlands; and they call this feeling love.

To love generally means to wish to do what is good. This is how we all understand love and cannot otherwise understand it. So I love my child, my wife, my fatherland—that is, I want happiness for my child, wife, and fatherland, more so than I want it for other children, wives, and fatherlands. I can never love only my child, or wife, or only my fatherland—it is never thus and never can be thus. Each person loves simultaneously his child, and wife, and children, and fatherland, and people in general. However, the conditions necessary for happiness, which he wants, out of love, for his various loved ones, are interconnected in such a way that a person's loving activity for the sake of one of his loved ones not only hinders his activity for others but also actually does them harm.

And so questions arise: In the name of what love and how should one act? In the name of what love should one sacrifice his other love? Whom shall I love more, and to whom shall I do good: my wife, or my children? My wife and my children, or my friends? How shall I serve the beloved fatherland without violating my love for wife, children, and friends? How can I sacrifice my individuality, which I need to serve others? To what extent shall I take care of myself, so that I can serve others, out of love for them? All these questions seem very simple to anyone who has not tried to account for that feeling they call love; but these questions are not only far from simple but also completely unsolvable.

It is not for nothing that the pettifogger posed this very question to Christ: who is my neighbor? Only people oblivious to the real conditions of human life find it easy to answer such questions.[3]

If only people were the gods we imagine them to be, then they would be able to love only a select few; only then would a preference for some over others be true love. But people are not gods, and they find themselves in the same conditions of existence where all living creatures find themselves when they devour one other, literally and figuratively; and a person who is a reasonable creature should know and see this. He should know that every boon of the flesh is acquired by every creature at another's expense.

No matter how much religious and scientific superstition might try to assure people of some future golden age when everyone shall have everything aplenty, a reasonable person sees and knows that the law of his temporal and spatial existence is that of struggle of all against one and one against each and against all.

In this crushing struggle of animal interests that constitutes the life of the world, it is impossible for man to love a select few the way that people who do not comprehend life imagine to be possible. Even when one might love a select few, no one can ever love just a single person. Every man loves his mother and wife and child, and friends, and fatherland, and perhaps all people. Love is not merely a word—we all agree on this—but also an activity aimed at the happiness of others. This activity does not proceed in any particular order, so that the demands of his strongest love come first, then the weaker ones, and so on. The demands of love make themselves known all at once and without cessation, without any sort of order. Now here comes a hungry old fellow whom I somewhat like, and he begs for food, which I hoard for my beloved children's supper. How shall I weigh the demands of this moment's lesser love versus the future demands of a more powerful love?

The pettifogger posed these very questions to Christ: "And who is my neighbor?" Indeed, how shall we decide whom to serve first, and to what extent? People or fatherland? Fatherland or friends? Friends or wife? Wife or father? Father or children? Children or oneself? (Certain conditions must be met to serve others when necessary.)

These are all demands of love, and all of them are intertwined such that satisfying some renders other demands impossible to satisfy. If I admit that a freezing child can be left unclothed because my children might one day need the dress that you are asking for, then I can refuse to give in to other demands of love in the name of my future children.

The same holds true for the love of my fatherland, chosen occupations, and the love for all people. If a person is capable of rejecting the demands of some insignificant love, at the present moment, in the name of a demand placed by some greater love in the future, is it not clear that this person, even if he willed it with all his might, would never be able to determine how much he might deny the demands of the present in the name of the future? Therefore, being unable to resolve this issue, he will always choose the love that brings him the most pleasure—that is, rather than acting in the name of love, he will be acting in the name of his individuality. If a person decides that it is best for him to resist the demands of the present insignificant love in the name of an expression of greater love in the future, he deceives either himself or others and loves nobody but himself.

There is no love in the future; love is something happening only in the present. Someone who does not express love in the present has no love.

The same thing happens when one imagines the life of people who do not have [true] life. If people were animals and had no reason, they would exist like animals and would not theorize about life, and their animal existence would be legitimate and happy. That is true for love, as well. If people were animals and without reason, then they would love whomever they loved—their wolf cubs, their herd—and they would be unaware that they love their own wolf cubs and their own herd, not knowing that other wolves also love their wolf cubs and other herds also love their herd mates. Their love would be that love and that life that is possible for the stage of consciousness where they find themselves.

But people are reasonable creatures. They cannot fail to see that other creatures have the same love for their own, and that therefore these feelings of love will lead to a confrontation and produce something that is unhappy and quite contrary to the concept of love.

If people use their reason to justify and reinforce this unhappy, animal feeling that they call love, assigning this feeling abnormal proportions, then this feeling not only becomes not good but also transforms man—and this is common knowledge that is long established—into the most malevolent and terrible animal. What happens is described in the Gospels: "If then the light in you is darkness, how great is this darkness!"[4] If it were not for love of himself and his children—provided there were nothing else in man—ninety-nine percent of the evil we find among people today would cease.[5] Ninety-nine percent of all evil in people occurs because of this false feeling that, when singing its praise, they call love, and that is as much like love as the life of the animal is like the life of man.

What people who do not comprehend life refer to as love is only a certain preference for certain conditions of their own individual happiness over the happiness of others. When someone who does not comprehend life says that he loves his wife or child, or a friend, he says only that the presence of his wife, his child, or his friend in his life increases the happiness of his individual life.

These preferences relate to love the same way that existence relates to life. And so in the same way that people who do not comprehend life refer to existence as life, these people refer to a preference for one set of conditions over another as love.

These feelings—a preference for certain creatures, for example our children, or even for certain vocations, for example science or the arts—we likewise refer to as love. These feelings of preference, which are infinitely variable, make up the entire complex nature of the visible, tactile animal life of men. It cannot be called love because these things lack the main feature of love—the activity that has happiness as its goal and as its consequence.

The passion that marks these preferences only demonstrates the energy of the animal individuality. The passion with which some people are preferred to others, which is incorrectly called love, is only the crabapple tree onto which true love can be grafted to yield fruit. Just as a crabapple is not quite an apple tree, since it does not bear fruit or yields only bitter fruit instead of sweet, so is preference not love. Preference does no good for people, or it creates an even greater evil. And therefore this much-vaunted love for a woman, for children, and for friends yields the greatest evil in the world, not to mention the love for science, art, the fatherland. These things are nothing but a temporary preference for certain conditions of animal life over others.

CHAPTER 24

True Love Is a Consequence of Individual Happiness Rejected

True love becomes possible only on condition that the happiness of the animal individuality is renounced.

True love becomes possible only when someone has realized there can be no happiness for his animal individuality. Only then do the juices of his life flow up into the ennobled scion of true love, which grows with all the vigor possessed in that crabapple rootstock of the animal individuality. The teaching of Christ is a grafting of this love, just as He said. He said that He, His love, is the sole vine that can yield fruit, and that every branch that fails to yield fruit should be pruned off.

Only one who has not merely understood intellectually but instead comprehended with his whole life that "whoever would save his soul will lose it; whoever loses his soul for Me will save it"; only one who has understood that whoever loves his soul will ruin it, and whoever hates his soul in this world will save it for life eternal—only he will comprehend true love.

"He who loves father or mother more than Me is not worthy of Me. And he who loves son or daughter more than Me is not worthy of Me. If you love those who love you, this is not love; but love your enemies, love those who hate you."[1]

It is commonly thought that one's individuality is renounced because of the love one feels for a father or son or wife or friends or kind and sweet people. But it is in fact a consequence of the realization that the existence of the individual is futile, a realization that its happiness is impossible. By rejecting the life of the individual, a man learns true love and can truly love father, son, wife, children, and friends.

Love is a preference for other creatures above yourself—your animal individuality.

Forgetting the immediate interests of the individual to attain remote goals for that very same individual, which is what happens with so-called love that has not grown out of self-renunciation, is only a preference for certain creatures over others to attain your individual happiness. Before becoming an effective feeling, true love must first be a genuine state. The beginning of love, its root, is not an impulsive emotional burst that clouds reason, as is usually believed. Love is a most reasonable, luminous, and therefore quiet and joyous state, which is natural for children and reasonable people.

This state is goodwill toward all, a natural state for children, but which in a grown man arises only when he rejects his individual happiness, a state that intensifies in a way that is proportionate to the degree of this renunciation. How often we hear the words, "It's all the same to me, I need nothing," only then to witness an unloving attitude toward people. But let anyone try at least once, at the moment he feels unkindly, to say to himself sincerely and from the bottom of his heart, "It's all the same to me, I need nothing"—and then, at least for a time, to will nothing for himself. Through this simple inner experience, anyone can discover that the ill will wanes immediately, and in a way that is proportionate to the degree that the renunciation is sincere. The goodwill toward all that had been locked up in his heart will flow forth.

Indeed, love is the preference for other creatures over oneself. This is how we all understand love, and it cannot be otherwise understood. The amount of love is the amount of a fraction in which the nominator, my preference, my sympathy toward others, is not in my power; the denominator, my love toward myself, can be increased or reduced by me ad infinitum, depending on the significance that I grant to my animal individuality. Calculations made by our world about love and its degrees—these are the calculations of the value of a fraction based on its nominator, disregarding the denominator.

True love always has at its basis a renunciation of individual happiness and the resulting goodwill toward all. True love toward certain people, your kin or strangers, can grow only from this goodwill toward all. And only this love provides the true happiness of life and solves the seeming contradiction of animal and reasonable consciousnesses.

Love without the renunciation of one's individuality, one that therefore lacks the goodwill toward all, is only an animal life that is subject to even greater misery and greater unreason than life without this fake love. The feeling of preference, which is called love, not only does not prevent the battle for existence, does not free a person from pursuit of pleasure, and does not save him from death—it only further dims life, makes the battle even more brutal, increases the greed for pleasure for oneself and others, and increases the terror of death for oneself and others.

Someone who stakes his life in the existence of his animal individuality cannot love because love would appear to him as an activity directly opposed to his life. The life of such a man resides in the happiness of his animal existence, while love demands above all the sacrifice of this happiness. Even if someone who does not comprehend life really and sincerely wanted to devote himself to the activity of love, he would be unable to do so until he understood life and changed his attitude toward it. Someone who stakes his life in the happiness of animal life spends his life increasing the means for his animal individuality's happiness by acquiring more wealth and preserving it and by forcing others to serve his animal happiness. He then distributes these goods among those individuals who prove most necessary for his individual happiness.[2] How is he to devote his life when he cannot support his own life and needs other people? And it is still more difficult for him to choose, from among his preferred people, to whom to give the goods he has amassed, and whom to serve.

To be able to give up his life, he should first give away the surplus that he takes away from others for his own happiness. And then he must again do something impossible: decide whom he should spend his life serving. Before he is able to love, before he is able to do good by sacrificing himself, he must stop hating—that is, stop doing evil—and he must stop preferring some people over others for his own individual happiness.

The possibility of loving activity, something that will always satisfy him and others, arises only when someone rejects the possibility of happiness in individual life and therefore does not concern himself with this false happiness and has liberated from within himself the goodwill toward all, a desire that is natural to man. The happiness of this person's life is in love, as the happiness of the plant's life is in light. A plant that is not shaded by anything cannot and does not ask what direction it should grow and whether the light is good enough, nor whether it should wait for another, better light. It rather accepts the single light that is in the world and reaches out toward it. In just such a way, a man who has renounced his individual happiness does not theorize about what he should receive from others, nor what his loved ones should receive, nor whether there might be some other, even better love than the one now making its demands. He devotes himself, his whole existence, to whatever love is available to him and stands before him. Only this love gives full satisfaction to the reasonable nature of man.

CHAPTER 25

Love Is an Integrated and Complete Activity of True Life

There is no other love than "giving one's soul for the ransom of many."[1] Love is only love when it is a sacrifice of the self. Only when man gives to another, not only his time and effort but also when he expends his own body for the sake of the object of love, gives it his life—only this do we recognize as love, and only in this love do we all find happiness, love's reward. It is only because such love exists in people that the world still stands. A mother breastfeeding a child devotes herself directly, gives her body as nourishment to children who could not otherwise live. This is love. In the same way any worker devotes himself, gives his body as nourishment for another, when he works for another's happiness, wearing out his body through work and bringing himself closer to death. Such love is possible for someone only when there is no barrier between the possibility of sacrificing himself and those creatures whom he loves. The mother who has given her child to a wet nurse cannot love this child; a man who accumulates and saves his money cannot love.

"He who says he is in the light, and hates his brother, is in darkness until now. He who loves his brother abides in the light, and there is no temptation within him. But he who hates his brother is in darkness, and does not know where he is going, because the darkness has blinded his eyes ... Let us not love in word or in tongue, but in deed and in truth. And by this we know that we are of the truth, and shall assure our hearts ... Love has been perfected among us in this: that we may have boldness in the day of judgment; because as he does, so do we in this world."[2]

Only this love gives true life to people.

"You shall love the Lord your God with all your heart, with all your soul, and with all your awareness. This is the first and great commandment."[3]

And the second, similar commandment: "You shall love your neighbor as yourself," said the pettifogger to Christ. And to this Christ responded, "You have answered correctly, now do so"—that is, love God and your neighbor—"and *you shall live*."[4]

True love is life itself. Christ's disciple says, "We know that we have traversed death back to life because we love our neighbors." "He who does not love his brother abides in death."[5] Only he who loves is alive.

In Christ's teaching, love is life itself, but not unreasonable life, which is beset by suffering and is ruinous, but life that is blessed and infinite. We all know this. Love is not a reasonable conclusion, not a consequence of a certain activity; it is instead the joyous activity of life itself, which surrounds us on all sides and which we know in ourselves, beginning with our first childhood memories until the time when the false teaching of this world stains this memory in our soul and renders us incapable of experiencing it.

Love is not a preference for those things that increase a person's temporary individual happiness, such as love for certain individuals or objects. Love is the pursuit of a happiness that exists outside a person, something that remains with him after he has renounced the happiness of his animal individuality.

Who among the living does not know that blessed feeling, even if it is experienced just once and most likely in very earliest childhood, when the soul was not littered with the falsehood that stifles life within us, that blessed feeling of tender serenity when you want to love everyone: those near and dear, father, mother, brothers, but also wicked people, enemies, a dog, a horse, a blade of grass? You want one thing: that everyone feel good, that everyone be glad. What you want even more is that you be the one who makes this happen, who makes everyone well; you want to devote yourself, your whole life, so that everyone will always be well and joyous. This is it, this is that same love where the life of man resides.[6]

This love that alone contains life manifests itself in the soul of man as a barely noticeable, gentle sprout among all the crude shoots of weeds that look like it, those various human lusts that we call love. At first it seems to everyone, including the man himself, that this sprout—the one that will grow into a tree where birds will find shelter—and the other shoots are all the same. People at first prefer the weed shoot, for it grows faster, and the single sprout of life is choked and weakened. Worse yet and more often, people hear that among these shoots there is a single true, vigorous sprout called love, and they begin mistakenly tending a shoot of weed, calling it love, all the while trampling on the real thing. Still worse, people yank out the sprout with their uncouth hands and shout, "Here it is, we have found it, we know it now, and we will raise it. Love! Love! Supreme feeling, here it is!" So they transplant it, try to make it right, and smother it, manhandling it so that the shoot dies before blooming. Those same people or others then say, All this is nonsense, a trifle, sentimentality. When this sprout of love first appears, it is tender and cannot tolerate being touched. It is mighty only once it has reached its full size. Whatever people might do for it will only do it harm. It needs one thing—that nothing block the sun of reason, which alone causes it to grow.[7]

CHAPTER 26

The Effort of People Directed at the Impossible Improvement of Their Existence Deprives Them of the Possibility of Their Only True Life

The only way to attain happiness is by recognizing the illusory, treacherous nature of animal existence, and by liberating from within oneself that one true life of love. What do people do for the attainment of this happiness? People whose existence consists of a slow destruction of their individuality and the approach of the ineluctable death of that individuality, who cannot help realizing this fact, trying everything possible and occupied with nothing else, spend their entire existence affirming this perishing individuality, feeding its lusts and thereby depriving themselves of the singular happiness of life: love.

People who do not understand life direct their activity toward the battle for their existence, trying to procure pleasures, rid themselves of suffering, and postpone their inevitable death.

However, increasing pleasure intensifies the struggle and one's susceptibility to suffering. It brings death nearer. There is but one means one can use to obscure the approach of death: increasing pleasures even more. But the increase of pleasure eventually reaches a limit, pleasures cannot be further increased, and they turn into suffering. Only sensitivity to suffering remains, along with terror mingled with the suffering of impending death. A vicious cycle occurs: each causes the other, and each intensifies the other. For people who do not understand life, the main horror of life lies in what they consider pleasure. The pleasures of the rich life are such that they cannot be equally distributed among all people and must be taken away from others, must be acquired through violence and by evil means. This destroys the possibility of goodwill toward people, from which love sprouts. Pleasure is thus always opposed to love, and the stronger it is, the more it is love's antithesis. Thus, the stronger and the more intense the activity that obtains pleasure, the more unobtainable becomes the only happiness available to man—love.

We do not understand life in the same way that our reasonable consciousness is aware of it: we do not understand it as that invisible but certain obedience, at every present moment, of one's animal [self] to the law of reason, which liberates the goodwill toward all, an obedience that is natural for us and the loving activity that stems from it. Instead, we understand life only as the existence in the flesh during a certain period, in the certain self-defined conditions arranged by us, precluding the possibility of goodwill toward all people.

For people who accept the teaching of this world, who have directed their reason toward arranging certain conditions of their existence, it seems that to increase life's happiness one must improve the external arrangement of existence. But this improvement in the external arrangement of their existence depends upon greater violence against people, something directly opposed to love. So the better arranged life is, the less love remains, and the less possible becomes life.

Having failed to use their reason to understand that for all people the happiness of their animal existence is equal to zero, they have taken zero for a value that can be increased or decreased. On this temporary increase, this multiplication by zero, they have used up all their reason, with no remainder left over.

People do not see that this nothing, this zero, no matter what value you multiply it by, remains the same for everyone—zero. They do not see that the existence of the animal individuality in every man is equally miserable and that no matter the external circumstances, this life cannot be made happy. People do not want to see that no existence, as an existence in the flesh, can be made more favorable than another, but it is a law, much as it is a law that you cannot raise the level of water in a lake higher than its general level. People who have corrupted their reason cannot see this, so they use their corrupted reason on a task as impossible as trying to raise the level of water at different spots on the surface of the lake, just like the game that children play while swimming called brewing beer. They expend their entire existence on this.

It seems to them that human existences can be more or less good and fortunate. The existence of a poor worker or a sick man is a bad, unfortunate one, they say; the existence of a wealthy man or a healthy man is a good and fortunate one. They devote every force of their reason to avoiding the bad, unfortunate, poor, and sickly existence and arranging for themselves a good, wealthy, healthy, and fortunate one.

For generations, we have worked out ways of arranging and maintaining these various, most fortunate lives. Programs for these imagined better lives, as they call their animal existence, get passed on as an inheritance. Vying with one another, people seek to maintain this fortunate life that they have inherited thanks to their parents' arrangements, or they try to create a new, even more fortunate life. It seems to people that, by maintaining their inherited mode of existence, or by arranging a new and better one as they understand it, they are doing something.

By supporting one another in this deception, people are sincerely convinced that this insane "milling of water" is life, something that is clearly insane even to them. Yet they grow so convinced that they contemptuously turn away from the call of true life, a call they never stop hearing—in the teaching of truth, in the examples of the lives of living people, and in their own sputtering heart, where the voice of reason and love is never completely stifled.

An astonishing thing takes place. People, an enormous number of people, who have the chance for a reasonable and loving life, find themselves in the position of sheep that are being dragged out of a burning house but that imagine they are being thrown into the fire and use all their strength to struggle with those who are trying to help them.

Out of a fear of death, people do not want to escape death. Out of a fear of suffering, people torment themselves and deprive themselves of the happiness and life that are alone available for them.

CHAPTER 27

Fear of Death Is Only the Consciousness of the Unresolved Contradiction of Life

"There is no death," the voice of truth tells people. "I am the resurrection and the life; he who believes in Me, though he may die, he shall live again. And whoever lives and believes in Me shall never die. Do you believe this?"[1]

"There is no death," all the great teachers of the world have said and continue to say, and millions of people who have understood the meaning of life bear witness. Every living man, during moments when his consciousness clears, also experiences the same thing in his soul. But people who have not comprehended life cannot keep from fearing death. They can see it, and they believe in it.

"What do you mean there is no death?," these people shout with indignation and rancor. "This is sophistry! Death faces us; it has cut down millions with its scythe and will cut us down, too. No matter how long you go on saying that it does not exist, it will nonetheless remain. Here it is!" And they can see what they are talking about in the same way that a mentally ill man sees a ghost that terrifies him. He cannot touch this ghost, it has never before touched him; he knows nothing of its intentions, but he is so afraid, and suffers so from this imaginary ghost, that he loses the possibility of living. It is the same with death. Man does not know his death and can never fully comprehend it. It has never before touched him, he knows nothing of its intention. So why is he afraid?

"It has not snatched me yet, but it will, I know that for certain—it will grab me and destroy me. And that is terrible." So say the people who do not comprehend life.

Were people with a false understanding of life able to reason calmly, and were they to think correctly on the basis of these ideas that they hold about life, they would come to the conclusion that in one's existence in the flesh, a change shall take place, the same change one can see happening without pause in all creatures, which one calls death, and there is nothing unpleasant or terrible in it.

I shall die. What is so terrible about that? After all, many changes have taken place and continue to take place in the existence of my flesh, and did I fear them? So why am I afraid of this change, which has not even taken place? There is nothing contrary to my reason and experience in it. It is so clear, familiar, and natural for me that all my life I have been making, and continue to make, assumptions that I have found acceptable and often enjoyable that involve the deaths of animals and people. What is so terrible about it?

There are only two strictly logical views on life. One incorrectly understands life as the visible changes that occur in my body from birth to death. The other correctly understands life as that invisible consciousness that I bear within myself. One view is false, the other true, but both are logical. People may hold one or the other, but fear of death is impossible for either.

The first and false view, which understands life as those visible phenomena in the body from birth to death, is as ancient as the world itself. This is not, as many think, the view worked out by the materialist science and philosophy of our time. Science and philosophy of today have only taken this view to its extreme, and the incompatibility of this view with the basic demands of human nature have only become more apparent than before. It is actually a timeworn, primordial view of people who stood on the bottom step of their development: it has been expressed by the Chinese, the Buddhists, the Hebrews, in the book of Job, and by the saying, "Dust thou art, and unto dust shalt thou return."

In its present form this view is expressed in this way: Life is an accidental play of forces within matter made manifest in space and time. Whatever we call our consciousness is not life but a certain trick of the senses that makes it seem that life is contained within this consciousness. Consciousness is a spark that catches under certain material conditions. This spark catches fire, produces flames, dims down, and then goes out completely. For a certain period between two temporal infinities, matter undergoes this spark of consciousness, which is nothing. Though this consciousness contemplates itself and the whole infinite world, and judges itself and the whole infinite world, and sees the whole play of contingencies in this world, and—*the main thing*—in contradistinction to something that is not conditional, it calls this play conditional, this consciousness is itself merely a product of inanimate matter, a phantom that originates and then disappears without remainder or meaning. All this is a product of matter that changes infinitely. What they call life is just a certain condition of inanimate matter.

This is one, perfectly logical view of life. According to this view, the reasonable consciousness of man is a mere accident that accompanies certain conditions of matter; therefore, what we call life in our consciousness is a phantom. Only the inanimate exists. What we call life is a game of death. According to this view, not only death should be feared but also life should be feared—as something unnatural and unreasonable, as it is by the Buddhists and the new pessimists, Schopenhauer and Hartmann.

The other view of life is this: Life is only what I am conscious of within myself. I am aware of my life not as I used to be, or as I will be (this is how I reason about my life), but I am aware of my life as I am now. Never and nowhere do I begin, and never and nowhere do I end. The concept of time and space is incommensurate with the consciousness of my life. My life becomes manifest in time and space, but this is just its manifestation. Life as I am aware of it is realized outside time and space. This view of life leads to an opposite conclusion: It is not the consciousness of life that is a phantom; rather, all that is temporal and spatial is phantasmagoric. The temporal and spatial cessation of existence in the flesh bears no consequence for what is real given this view and therefore can neither stop nor violate my true life. There is no death according to this view.

Neither the first nor the second view admits a fear of death, so long as one strictly adheres to one or the other.

Neither as an animal nor as a reasonable creature can a person fear death. Without a consciousness of life, an animal does not see death; a reasonable creature, having a consciousness of life, cannot see in animal death anything but the natural and ceaseless movement of matter. If man is afraid, he is not afraid of death, which he does not know, but of life, which alone is known to his animal and reasonable being. The feeling that people call the fear of death is nothing more than the realization of an inner contradiction of life; likewise, the fear of ghosts is only the awareness of a morbid mental condition.

"I will cease to be—I will die, and everything that I stake my life on will also die," says one voice to man. "I am," says the other voice, "I cannot and ought not die. I ought not die, and yet I am dying." Our fear stems not from death but from this contradiction that seizes a person when he thinks of death in the flesh. The horror that possesses man at the thought of death is not caused by death but by this very contradiction: the fear of death does not arise from man's fear that his animal existence will cease but because something seems to be dying that cannot and should not die. The thought of future death is merely the transference into the future of something that is taking place in the present. That the ghost of future death makes an appearance does not indicate that the thought of death has stirred, but the opposite—that a thought of life has stirred, which one ought to have but does not. This feeling is akin to what a person ought to undergo when he comes back to life in his casket underground. There is life, but I am dead, and here it is, death! It seems that what is, and what ought to be, is being destroyed. And man's mind goes wild, is terrified. The best proof that the fear of death is not the fear of death but is instead false life is that people often kill themselves out of fear of death.

People are terrified of the idea of death in the flesh not because they fear that their life will end with it but because death in the flesh demonstrates to them the absolute need of true life, which they lack. Thus, people who do not comprehend life do not like to remember death. Remembering death is the same as admitting that they do not live according to the demands of their reasonable consciousness.

People who are afraid of death are afraid of it not because it appears to them as a dark void. They see the void and the darkness because they do not see life.

CHAPTER 28

Death in the Flesh Destroys Spatial and Temporal Consciousness, but It Cannot Destroy What Constitutes the Basis of Life: Every Creature's Unique Relationship toward the World

Even those who do not see life, if only they were to get closer to the ghosts that terrify them and touch them, they would see that the ghost is a ghost and not something real.

The fear of death always occurs in people because they fear losing, upon their death in the flesh; their unique *I*, which—so they feel—constitutes their life. I will die, my body will decay, and my *I* will be destroyed. This I of mine is what has lived within my body for however many years.

People treasure this *I* of theirs; and since they believe that this *I* coincides with their corporeal life, they conclude that it will be destroyed upon the destruction of their corporeal life.

This conclusion is a most ordinary one, and it rarely occurs to anyone to question it. It is, all the same, completely arbitrary. People—those who consider themselves materialists and those who consider themselves spiritualists—are so used to the idea that their *I* is that consciousness of their body that has lived for however many years that it never crosses their mind to check the truth of such an assertion.

I have lived fifty-nine years, and during this time I have been conscious of myself, as myself, within my own body. It seems to me that this consciousness of myself as myself has been my life. But this only seems to be so. I have not been living for fifty-nine years, or for fifty-nine thousand years, or for fifty-nine seconds. Neither my body nor the time of its existence has in the least defined the life of my I. If at every second of my life I were to ask myself, within my consciousness, what am I? I would answer, Something that thinks and that feels—that is, something that bears its own quite particular relationship toward the world; I am aware of this alone as my I, and nothing else. When and where I was born, when and where I started to feel and think the way I think and feel now—I am decidedly unconscious of such things. My consciousness tells me only this: I am. I am, with the certain relationship toward the world in which I presently find myself. I often remember nothing about my birth, my childhood, about many periods of my youth and middle years, and about very recent periods. If I remember, or if I am reminded, of a certain something from my past, then I remember and recall it almost as if it were a story about other people. So, on what grounds do I assert that during the entire time of my existence I have been all the while this *one I*? There has never been and there is not a single body that is mine: My body has been and is matter that flows ceaselessly through something else immaterial and invisible, a something that recognizes the body that flows through it as its own. My whole body has changed a dozen times, nothing of the old thing remains: muscle, internal organs, bones, and the brain—all of this has changed.

My body is singular only because there is something immaterial that recognizes this changing body as one, and as its own. This immaterial thing is what we call consciousness: it alone holds the whole body together and recognizes it as one and as its own. Without this consciousness of my being separate from everything else, I would know nothing of my life or of any other life. It therefore seems initially that consciousness—this basis of everything—should be constant. But this, too, is untrue: consciousness is likewise inconstant. Throughout my life and presently, the phenomenon of sleep seems to us very simple since we all sleep every day. It is, however, decidedly incomprehensible when we recognize something that we cannot help recognizing: consciousness completely ceases during sleep.

Every day, while we are fast asleep, we lose consciousness and then regain it. This consciousness meanwhile is the only thing that holds the body together and recognizes it as its own. It would seem that during the cessation of consciousness, the body should fall apart and lose its singularity; but this does not happen during natural or induced sleep.

This consciousness that holds the body together not only periodically breaks off without the body falling apart but also changes like the body. There is nothing in common between the matter that now makes up my body and the way it was ten years ago: just as there has never been one body, so there has never been one consciousness within me. My consciousness as a three-year-old child and my present consciousness are as different as the matter of my body now and thirty years ago.

The consciousness that holds the whole body together and recognizes it as its own is thus not singular but is instead intermittent and varying. No singular consciousness exists in man, as we usually imagine, just as there is no single body. We lack a single body. Nor is there anything that separates this body from everything else—there is no constant consciousness of one person, singular throughout his whole life; there is instead nothing more than a series of successive consciousnesses linked together by something. Yet man still experiences himself as a self.

Our body is not singular, and what recognizes this changing body as one and as ours is also not stable over time but is instead merely a series of varying consciousnesses. Many times we have lost our body and lost these consciousnesses; we lose our body constantly and we lose our consciousness every day when we fall asleep, and every day and at every hour we feel within us the changes in this consciousness, and we are not in the least afraid. Hence, if there really is something like our I, which we fear losing at death, then this I ought not be located in that body that we call ours and not in that consciousness that we call ours at a particular time but in something else that links the whole series of successive consciousnesses into one.

What, then, is this something that unifies all the successive consciousnesses through time? What is this most cardinal and unique thing, my *I* that is composed neither of my body nor of the series of consciousnesses that occur in this body but that fundamental *I*, that shaft onto which our various successive consciousnesses, one after another, are strung? This question seems very profound and wise, but there is no child who would not know the answer, who does not announce the answer twenty times a day. "Well, *I* love this, but *I* do not love that." While very simple, these words offer the answer to the question of that particular I that links all the consciousnesses into one. It is the very *I* that loves this but does not love that. No one knows why one might love this but not love that, but in the meantime this is the very thing that constitutes the basis of life for every person; it unites all the temporally diverse stages of every person's consciousness. The external world affects all people identically, but people's impressions of these identical conditions are infinitely different, in part because of the number of these impressions, in part because of the infinite ways one might break down these impressions, and in part because the impressions differ in their intensity. These impressions produce a series of successive consciousnesses for each person. These successive consciousnesses are linked only because at any given moment certain impressions affect the consciousness, while others do not. And whether or not certain impressions affect a person depends on whether he loves this thing more or less but does not love that thing.

One particular series of consciousnesses arises, rather than another, as a result of this greater or lesser degree of preference. Thus, the tendency to love something more or less and not to love something else constitutes that unique and fundamental I of a person in which all the scattered and intermittent consciousnesses are united. Although it continues to develop during our life, we introduced this tendency into life as something ready-made, from some past that remains invisible and unknowable to us.

This particular quality of a person to love one thing to a greater or lesser degree and not to love another is commonly known as character. We often understand this word to indicate the particular characteristics of each distinct person that forms because of certain conditions of place and time. This is untrue. The main quality of man to love one thing more or less and not to love another does not derive from spatial or temporal conditions, but, on the contrary, spatial and temporal conditions affect or do not affect a person only because, upon entering the world, a person already possesses a certain capacity to love one thing and to not love another. For this reason, people who were born and raised under completely identical spatial and temporal conditions often offer the sharpest disparity in their inner *I*.

Something quite definite unites the disparate consciousnesses that are, in turn, united in our single body, although it is independent of spatial and temporal conditions. It is introduced by us into the world from a sphere that is beyond space and beyond time; this very *something*, which consists of my certain and exclusive relationship toward the world, is my real and genuine *I*. I understand myself as this fundamental quality. Likewise, if I know others, I know them only as some particular relationship toward the world. Of course, when entering into a serious and spiritual interaction with people, none of us is governed by their external features. We all instead attempt to penetrate into their essence—that is, we try to learn what kind of relationship they have toward the world, what they love, and to what extent, and what they do not love.[1]

Every single animal—a horse, a dog, a cow—if I know them and have a serious spiritual interaction with them, I know them not by their distinctive external marks but by that distinct relationship toward the world in which each is situated—by what each of them loves and to what degree or what each does not love.[2] If I know certain distinct and diverse animal species, then strictly speaking I know them not so much because of their external features but because of the special relationship each has toward the world—whether it's a lion, a fish, or a spider. All lions in general love one thing, while all fishes love another, and all spiders love a third thing. They remain separate in my imagination as different living creatures solely because they love different things.

The fact that I do not as yet distinguish in each of these creatures their distinct relationship toward the world is no proof that it does not exist; it is proof merely that this distinct attitude to the world that constitutes the life of each spider is remote from that relationship toward the world where I abide, and therefore I have not yet understood it the way Silvio Pellico understood his particular spider.[3]

I base everything I know about myself and about the whole world on that particular relation to the world where I abide; that is the basis on which I regard all other creatures that abide in their own particular attitude to the world. My particular relationship toward the world was not established in this life, nor did it originate with my body, nor in the series of successive consciousnesses in time.

My body, tied up into a single thing by my temporal consciousness, may therefore be destroyed, my very temporal consciousness may be destroyed, but my special relationship toward the world, which constitutes my distinct I and from which everything was created that exists for me, cannot be destroyed. It cannot be destroyed because it alone exists. If it did not exist, I would not know the series of my successive consciousnesses, would not know my body, would not know any other life. And therefore the destruction of the body and consciousness cannot signal the destruction of my distinct attitude to the world, which did not originate or emerge in this life.

The Fear of Death Originates from the Fact That People Accept as Life What Is Really Just the Small Part of Life That Their False Notions Permit Them

With our death in the flesh, we fear losing our distinct *I*, which unites the body and the series of consciousnesses that manifest themselves in time. This unique *I* did not begin with my birth, and therefore a cessation of a certain temporal consciousness cannot destroy what unites all temporal consciousnesses.[1]

Death in the flesh indeed destroys what holds the body together—the consciousness of temporal life. But this happens to us continuously and every day when we fall asleep. The question is instead whether death in the flesh destroys what unites all the successive consciousnesses into one—that is, my unique relationship toward the world. To assert this, one must first prove that this unique relationship toward the world that unifies all the successive consciousnesses was born simultaneously with my existence in the flesh and therefore will die with it. And there is no such thing.

When I deliberate using my consciousness, I see that whatever unified all my consciousnesses into one—a certain susceptibility toward one thing and coldness toward another, the result of which is that one thing remains within me while the other disappears, that is to say the degree of my love of what is good and hatred of what is evil, my particular relationship toward the world that constitutes precisely me, the distinct me—is not a product of some external cause but is the main cause of all other phenomena in my life.

Then, when I deliberate based on observation, at first it seems to me that the causes for the particularity of my *I* reside in the particularity of my parents and the conditions that have exerted an influence over me and over them; but, reasoning in such a way, I cannot help seeing that if my particular I lies in the particularity of my parents and those conditions that had influence over them, then it also resides in the particularity of all my ancestors and the conditions of their existences—into infinity; that is, outside space and time. My particular *I* thus originated outside space and time—that is, the same thing of which I am already conscious.

In this and only this foundation, beyond time and space, of my particular relationship toward the world, the thing that unites all the consciousnesses available to my memory, as well as all the consciousnesses that precede my memory of life (as Plato has said and as we all can feel from within)—in this foundation, in my particular relationship toward the world, is that particular *I* that we fear will be destroyed with death in the flesh.

What unites all consciousnesses into one, what this particular I of a person is, exists outside time—it is and has always been. What is intermittent is merely the series of consciousnesses from a certain period. If you bear this in mind, it becomes clear that the destruction of the finite consciousness during death in the flesh can do as little harm to the genuine, human *I* as daily sleep. No one fears falling asleep, though in fact what happens when you fall asleep is the same thing as what happens when you die—namely, your temporal consciousness ceases. Although the destruction of consciousness is precisely the same as upon death, not a single person fears falling asleep because he knows that he has fallen asleep and awakened many times previously and will therefore awaken again next time. (This theorizing is wrong: he could have awakened a thousand times and not awaken the thousand and first time.) Nobody thinks this way, and this theory could not put him at ease. Instead, he does not fear falling asleep because he knows that his genuine *I* lives outside time and that therefore the temporary cessation of his consciousness cannot disrupt his life.

If a person slept for thousands of years, as in a fairy tale, he would fall asleep as serenely as he does when he sleeps for two hours. For a consciousness of life that is not temporal but genuine, a million-year break and an eight-hour one are the same, for time does not exist for such life.

If the body is destroyed, that day's consciousness is destroyed.

But by now a person should have grown used to changes in his body and the replacement of some temporal consciousnesses by others. These changes date back for as long as a person can remember himself, and they have kept happening without pause. One does not fear these changes taking place in his body; he is not only not terrified but also frequently only desires to facilitate these changes, desires to grow up, mature, or be cured. A person used to be a red piece of meat, and his whole consciousness consisted of the demands of his stomach; now he is a bearded reasonable man, or a woman who loves her grown children. There is nothing[2] in common between these states, neither in the body nor in the consciousness, yet he was never horrified at the changes that brought him to his current condition; he welcomed them. What is so terrifying in the change to come? Destruction? The place where all these changes take place—that particular relationship toward the world—that which makes up the consciousness of true life, did not begin with the body but began outside the body and outside time. So how can any kind of temporal and spatial alteration destroy what is outside it? Someone fixes his eyes on a tiny piece of his life, does not want to see the whole of life, and just trembles lest this little piece of his delight disappear from view. This reminds me of an anecdote about a madman who imagined that he was made of glass. When he was dropped he said, "Crack!" and died instantly. To have life, one must take it all rather than the small part made manifest in space and time. He who accepts the whole of life will receive it in excess, but he who takes a part of it will be deprived of what he has.

CHAPTER 30

Life Is a Relationship toward the World. The Movement of Life Is the Establishment of a New, Higher Relationship. Death Is Therefore Entrance into a New Relationship

We cannot understand life otherwise than as a certain relationship toward the world: this is how we understand life within ourselves and how we understand it in other creatures.

But within ourselves we understand life not only as a relationship with life given once and for all but also as the establishment of a new relationship toward the world through greater and greater obedience of the animal individuality to reason and through the manifestation of a greater measure of love. The inevitable destruction of our existence in the flesh that we witness within ourselves demonstrates to us that the relationship toward the world where we find ourselves is inconstant. We must begin to establish another one. What destroys the notion of death is the establishment of this new relationship—that is, the movement of life. Death seems to exist only to someone who, having not admitted that his life is the establishment of a reasonable relationship toward the world and manifestation of this relationship through more and more love, has remained in the former relationship, that is to say that he has remained in a relationship with the same degree of love toward one thing and lack of love toward another that he had when he entered into existence.

Life is an incessant movement. By remaining in the same old relationship with the world, by remaining with the same degree of love that he had upon entering into existence, he feels the halting of life, and death appears to him.

Death is visible and terrible only to such a person. His whole existence is incessant death. Death is visible and terrible to him not only in the future but also in the present, at every sign of his diminishing animal life, from the dawn of his days to his old age, because the movement of existence from childhood to maturity seems merely a temporary increase in strength; it is essentially the same as his limbs growing stiff, his loss of vitality—things that take place from birth until death. This person constantly sees death ahead, and nothing can save him from it. Every day and hour, the condition of such a man gets worse and worse, and nothing can improve it. His particular relationship toward the world, his love of one thing and lack of it for another, appears to this man to be just one of the conditions of his existence. His life's only mission—establishing a new relationship toward the world, the increase of love—seems to be unnecessary. His whole life is passed doing the impossible: avoiding the inevitable diminution of life, avoiding its hardening, enervation, aging, and death.

This is not how it is for someone who understands life. This person knows that he has introduced into his current life his own particular relationship toward the world (his love for one thing and lack of it for another) from a hidden past. He knows that this love for one thing and lack of it for another, brought by him into this existence, is the very essence of his life, that this is not an accidental quality of his life but that it alone possesses the movement of life. He stakes his life in that movement alone, in the increase of love.

As he looks back at his past life he sees, judging by the series of his consciousnesses that he can recall, that his relationship toward the world has been changing, that his obedience to the law of reason has been increasing, and that the sphere of love has also been ceaselessly increasing, which allows him a greater and greater happiness that is independent from, and at times directly and proportionately opposed to, a decrease in his individual existence.

Such a person, by accepting his life from the past invisible to him and realizing its constant and uninterruptible growth, transfers, not only calmly but also with joy, this life into the invisible future.

It is said: the destruction of consciousness and of life comes from illness, old age, decrepitude—our second childhood. For whom is this true? I think of John the Theologian, who, according to legend, entered his second childhood in old age. According to legend, John kept repeating, "Brothers, love one another!" This nearly immobile centenarian, with teary eyes, burbles just three words over and over: "Love one another!" In this man, the animal existence barely glimmers—it has been completely consumed by a new relationship toward the world, the new living creature that can no longer fit inside the existence in the flesh of man.[1]

For someone who understands life for what it really is, to speak about the diminution of life during illness and old age and to despair about it would be like a man who, when approaching a light, grieves that his shadow gets thinner and thinner the closer he gets to the light. Believing that his life is destroyed when his body is destroyed is no different from believing that the destruction of an object's shadow under full light signals the destruction of the object itself. Such a conclusion is possible only for someone who has stared at the shadow for so long that he has begun to imagine that the shadow is the object itself.

For someone who knows himself not by his reflection in his spatial and temporal existence but by his increased loving relationship toward the world, the destruction of the shadow of spatial and temporal conditions is rather a proof of the greater amount of light. For the man who understands his life as a certain particular relationship toward the world with which he entered into existence, and which has been growing as his love has been growing, for this man to believe in his destruction is the same as someone who knows the laws of the world through its visible external phenomena and believes that his mother found him under cabbage leaves and that his body will fly off somewhere, leaving no trace.

CHAPTER 31

Life of the Deceased Does Not Cease in This World

The superstition of death becomes even clearer when we look at it—not "from another angle" but instead when we look at the very essence of life as if we are aware of it. My friend, my brother, used to live the way I did, and now he has stopped living as I am living. His life was his consciousness, and it took place in the conditions of his bodily existence; that is to say, there is no place and time for the manifestation of his consciousness, and he does not exist for me. My brother at one time lived, I interacted with him, and now he is no more, and I will never know where he is.

"All ties have been severed between him and us. He is no more for us, and we, too, shall be no more for those who remain. What is this if not death itself?" So say people who do not comprehend life. In the cessation of external interaction these people see an indubitable proof of a real death. Meanwhile, there is no clearer and more obvious a basis for dispelling the illusory character of this idea of death than the cessation of my existence in the flesh. My brother has died, so what happened? What happened is that his relationship toward the world, which was once available for my observation in space and time, disappeared from my view and nothing remains.

"Nothing remains" is what a chrysalis, a cocoon that has not yet released a butterfly, would say upon observing that a nearby cocoon remains empty.[1] If it could think and speak, a cocoon would say this because after losing its neighbor, the cocoon would indeed be unable to sense it. This situation is not so with man. My brother died, and, true, his cocoon has stayed empty. I do not see him in the same form that I used to, but his disappearance from view did not destroy my relationship toward him. What remains with me, as we put it, is a recollection of him.

The recollection remains—not as a recollection of his hands, face, eyes but of his spiritual image.

What is this recollection? It seems to be such a clear and simple word. The forms of crystals and animals will disappear, and no recollection is left among such beings. However, I have a recollection of my friend and brother. This recollection is livelier in proportion to the degree that the life of my friend and brother conformed to the law of reason, the more his life was expressed through love. This recollection is not merely an idea, it is something that has an effect on me, the same effect that my brother's life had on me during his lifetime on earth. This recollection is his invisible and immaterial atmosphere that surrounded his life and affected me and others during his existence in the flesh, and it continues to affect me now, after his death. This recollection makes demands upon me in the same ways that it did during his life. Moreover, this recollection has become more binding on me after his death than it used to be during his life. That force of life that was once in my brother not only did not disappear or diminish, nor, too, did it stay the same: it increased, and it affects me now more powerfully than before.[2]

The force of his life after his death in the flesh affects me as powerfully or even more powerfully than before his death, and it affects me like all truly living things do. How, then, can I say that my deceased brother no longer has life when I feel that force of life on myself, precisely as I felt it during his existence in the flesh? I feel his relationship toward the world, which clarifies for me my own relationship toward the world. That he has left behind that inferior relationship toward the world he had while he was an animal, the one I am still in—that is all I can say. I can say that I do not see the center of the new relationship toward the world where he now is. I cannot deny his life, because I can feel its force on me now. On a reflective surface, I once saw someone holding me; that reflective surface has now grown dim. I can no longer see how he holds me, but I can feel with my whole essence that he is still holding me. Therefore he exists.

This life of my brother, invisible to me, not only affects me but also enters into me. His unique living *I*, his relationship toward the world, becomes my relationship. It is as though the way that he has built his relationship toward the world had elevated me to the level where he had ascended. To me, to my unique living *I*, the next step up that he has taken becomes clearer, though he has vanished, beckoning me to follow after him. In such a way, I comprehend the life of my brother, and therefore I cannot doubt this life. By watching the effects of this life on the world, I become even more indubitably convinced of the reality of this now-vanished life. A man has died, but his relationship toward the world continues to affect people, not in the same way as during his lifetime but far more strongly, and this effect increases and grows proportionate to its reasonableness and lovingness like everything that lives, never ceasing and never knowing pause.

Christ died very long ago, and His life in the flesh was brief. We have no clear idea about His individuality in the flesh, but the force of His reason-loving life, His relationship toward the world, like that of no one else, even now keeps affecting millions of people who have accepted His relationship toward the world and live by it. What causes this? What is this thing that was once connected with Christ's existence in the flesh and that now makes up the continuation and growth of His same life? We say that this is not the life of Christ but its consequence. By saying these words that mean nothing, it seems to us that we have uttered something clearer and more definite than the fact that this force is the living Christ himself. This is precisely what ants might say while poking around an acorn that has taken root and grown up into an oak tree. The acorn took root and became an oak tree and tears the soil apart with its roots, sheds dry twigs, leaves, and new acorns, gives shelter from the sun and rain, and alters everything that lived around it. "This is not the life of the acorn," the ants would say, "but consequences of its life, which ended when we hauled that acorn away and tossed it in a little hole."

My brother died yesterday or a thousand years ago, and that force of his life that produced effects during his life in the flesh continues to produce effects within me and in hundreds, thousands, millions of people more strongly now, despite the fact that the center of this force of his existence in the flesh, once visible to me, has now disappeared. What does this mean? I saw the light of grass burning before me. The grass no longer burns, but the light has grown stronger. I no longer see the reason for this light, and I do not know what is burning, but I can conclude that this is the same fire that was burning the grass and now is burning some distant forest or something that I cannot see. This light is such that not only can I see it now but also it alone guides me and gives me life. I live by this light. How can I deny it? I may think that the force of this life now has a different, invisible center. But I cannot deny it, for I can experience it, am moved by it, and live by it. What this center is like, what this life is in and of itself, I cannot know—I can guess if I like fortune-telling and am not afraid of erring. If I am seeking a reasonable comprehension of life, however, I will be satisfied by what is clear and indubitable, and I would not want to spoil what is clear and the indubitable by mixing in dim and unreliable fortune-telling. It suffices to know that what I live by has been composed from the lives of the people who have lived before me and died long ago, and that therefore every man who has fulfilled the law of life and put his animal person in obedience to reason, and who has demonstrated the force of love, lived, and continues to live in other people after the disappearance of his existence in the flesh. The absurd and terrible superstition of death will never trouble me again.

Based on these people who leave behind them a force that continues to produce effects, we can observe also why these people, in having subjected their individuality to reason and by giving themselves over to the life of love, could never doubt and never did doubt the impossibility of the destruction of life.

In the life of such people we can also find the foundation of their faith in an uninterrupted life, and then, having looked deep within ourselves, we can find the same foundation. Christ used to say that He would live after the phantom of life has disappeared. He said this because during his existence in the flesh He had already entered into that true life that cannot end. During his existence in the flesh He lived in the rays of light that issued from that other center of life where he was headed. He could see during life that the rays of that light already illuminated people around Him. Any person can see this when he gives up his individuality to live a reasonable and loving life.

However narrow the range of someone's activity—be he Christ, or Socrates, a kind, unknown, self-sacrificial old man, a youth, or a woman—if he lives, renouncing his individuality for the happiness of others, then in this life, here, he already enters into a new relationship toward the world where there is no death. For everyone, the main work of this life lies in establishing this relationship.

A person who has staked his life in obedience to reason and the manifestation of love can see already in this life, from one direction, the rays of light issuing from that new center of life where he is headed; from the other direction he sees the effect that this light, passing through him, has had on those around him. This gives him faith in the irreducibility of life, in its imperishability and eternal intensification. One cannot receive faith in immortality from anyone, nor can one convince oneself of immortality. To have faith in immortality that immortality must exist, and for it to exist, you must understand your life as immortal inasmuch as it is immortal. Only he who has completed his life's work—only he who has established that new relationship toward the world, a relationship that exceeds him—can believe in a future life.

The Superstition of Death Comes to Pass Because Man Confuses His Various Relationships toward the World

Yes, once you regard life in its true meaning, it becomes difficult to understand how this strange superstition of death persists.

Just as once you have figured out what frightened you in the dark you cannot again make yourself afraid of the phantom.

We fear losing the only thing that really exists because life appears to a person not only in that single invisible yet particular relationship of his reasonable consciousness toward the world but also in two other relationships that are unknown yet visible to him: the relationships of his animal consciousness and his body to the world. Everything that exists appears to man as (1) the relationship of his reasonable consciousness toward the world, (2) the relationship of his animal consciousness toward the world, and (3) the relationship of his body toward the world. When he does not comprehend that the relationship of his reasonable consciousness toward the world constitutes his sole life, man imagines his life also in the visible relationship of his animal consciousness and his material being with the world. He fears losing the particular relationship of his reasonable consciousness toward the world when the previous relationship of the animal and the material in his individuality, a relationship that constitutes him, is violated.

It seems to such a person that he originates from the movement of matter that then passes into a level of animal consciousness. It seems that this animal consciousness passes into a reasonable consciousness, and that this reasonable consciousness grows weaker and then passes back into animal consciousness, and then, in the end, this animal [self] grows weak and passes back into the inanimate matter from which it had come. In this view, the relationship of his reasonable consciousness toward the world appears to him as something accidental, useless, and perishable. Given this view, it turns out that the relationship of his animal consciousness toward the world cannot be destroyed: the animal self-perpetuates in its species. The relationship of matter toward the world can in no way be destroyed and is eternal. The most precious thing—his reasonable consciousness—is not only not eternal but also only a flash of something useless and redundant.

A person feels that this cannot be so. This is the source of the fear of death. To save themselves from this fear, people want to assure themselves that their animal consciousness is itself their reasonable consciousness, and that the undying nature of animal man—his species, his progeny—satisfies the need of the reasonable consciousness, borne within him, for something undying. Others would like to assure themselves that a life that had not previously existed, by suddenly appearing in fleshly form and then by disappearing from that form, will be resurrected in the flesh and will live again. It is, however, impossible for people to believe either of these so long as they do not stake their life in the relationship of their reasonable consciousness toward the world. It is obvious for them that the continuation of the human race does not satisfy the demand for eternity that comes from the unique *I* of the self, which never tires of advancing it; and the concept of resurrected life includes within itself the notion that life has ended; but if life has not existed previously, has not always existed, then it cannot exist afterward.

For both groups, earthly life is a wave. Individuality is distilled from inanimate matter; reasonable consciousness, the crest of the wave, is distilled from individuality; having reached its crest, the wave—reasonable consciousness and individuality—fall back down to where they originated and are destroyed. For both groups, human life is visible life. A person has grown, matured, died, and there can be nothing else for him after death; whatever remains after him, his progeny or even his deeds, cannot satisfy him. He pities *himself* and is afraid of the end of *his* life. That this life of his, which began here on earth within his body and ended here as well, that it will be resurrected—in this he cannot believe.

A person knows that if he was not around before and that if he emerged out of nothing and died, then his self, his particular self, will no longer be and cannot be. He comes to comprehend that he will not die only when he comprehends that he was never born and had always been, is, and will be. He will believe in his immortality only when he understands that his life is not a wave but is that eternal movement that in this life finds its expression as merely a wave.

I imagine that I will die and that my life will end, and that thought torments and terrifies me because I feel sorry for myself. But what will die?
Why do I feel sorry? What am I, from the most ordinary standpoint? I am
above all flesh. So what? This is what I fear, why I feel sorry for myself?
No, not this, it seems: The body, matter, can nowhere and never disappear, not a single particle. And thus this part of me has been guaranteed, I
have nothing to fear for this part. All will be intact. But no, they say, that
is not why we feel sorry for ourselves. We feel sorry for Lev Nikolaevich,
Ivan Semenovich . . .[1] But none of us is the same as we were twenty years
ago, and every single day we are something new. Which of these selves do
I feel sorry for? No, they say, we do not feel sorry for ourselves because of
that. It is the consciousness of me, of my I that I feel sorry for.

Of course, this consciousness of yours has never been consistently one
thing. There have been various ones: A year ago there was something different, and ten years ago something even more different, and previously
there was something altogether different. For as long as you can recall,
it has gone on changing. Why have you grown so fond of your present
consciousness, the one you pity losing? Were it one and the same thing for
all time this would make sense, but all along it has done only one thing,
which is to change. You do not see its beginning, and you cannot find it,
and suddenly you want it to have no end, so that the consciousness that is
presently within you should remain the same forever. For as long as you
can remember yourself, you have kept on going. You arrived in this life
not knowing the way, but you know that you arrived as that particular I
that you are. You then walked on and on, and you made it to the middle.
And suddenly, not entirely overjoyed nor entirely frightened, you go and
balk and refuse to budge. You will not continue walking forward because
you cannot see what lies ahead. But after all, you cannot see where you
came from, yet you have made it this far. You have walked into the entry-
way and now refuse to walk out the exit.[2]

Your whole life has been progress through your existence in the flesh:
you walked, made haste to go on, and now suddenly you feel sorry for
yourself because you are doing what you have always been doing. You are
terrified by the great change in your situation upon death in the flesh. Yet,
was there not a great change at your birth, and not only did nothing bad
come out of that—on the contrary, that change turned out to be so nice
that you do not want to part with it.

What makes you afraid? You say that you feel sorry for that you, the
one with its present feelings, thoughts, and views on the world, the one
with your present relationship toward the world.

You are afraid of losing your relationship toward the world. What is this relationship? What does it consist of?

If it is in how you eat, drink, multiply, build dwellings, dress, and treat other people and animals this way or that, then this relationship toward life is the one held by every person as a thinking animal, and this relationship can in no way disappear. There have been, are, and will be millions of others like it, and their species will be preserved as surely as every particle of matter is preserved. Animals are so powerfully endowed with this instinct for preservation of the species that it is assured—you have no need to fear for it. If you are an animal, you have nothing to fear; if you are matter, you are guaranteed better still in your eternity.

If you are afraid of losing what is not animal, then you are afraid of losing your particular reasonable relationship toward the world—the one with which you entered into this existence. But you know, after all, that it did not arise when you were born: it exists independent of the animal [self] that was born, and therefore it cannot hinge on its death.[3]

CHAPTER 33

Life That Is Visible Is Part of the Infinite Movement of Life

Earthly life and the life of all other people appear to me in this way:

I and every living person—we find ourselves in this world with a certain, definite relationship toward the world, with a certain degree of love. It seems to us initially that our life begins from this relationship that we have to the world, but self-observation and observing others demonstrate that this relationship toward the world, the degree of love we each possess, did not begin with this life; they were instead introduced by us into life from a past that our birth in the flesh hides from us. Moreover, we see that the whole course of our life here is nothing but an incessant growth and intensification of our love that never stops but only becomes hidden from us by our death in the body.

Our visible life appears to me as a slice of a cone, the tip and base of which are hidden from my mental vision.[1] The narrowest part of the cone is my relationship toward the world through which I first become aware of myself; the broadest part is that highest relationship toward life that I have now reached. The beginning of this cone—its tip—is hidden from me in time by my birth, while the extent of the cone is hidden from me by the future, which is equally unknowable both in my existence in the flesh and in my death in the flesh. I can see neither the tip of the cone nor its base, but judging by the part of it where my visible life has passed, the part of it that is memorable to me, I undoubtedly recognize its qualities. It seems to me at first that this segment of the cone is my whole life, but in proportion to the movement of my true life, I see, on the one hand, that what constitutes the foundation of my life is situated behind and beyond it: as life proceeds, I feel with more vigor and clarity my connection with the invisible past. On the other hand, I see that what makes up the foundation rests upon a future that remains invisible to me, and I feel my connection with this future with greater clarity and vigor. I conclude that the life visible to me, my earthly life, is only the smaller part of my whole life on either end—before birth and after death—which indubitably exists

164

but is hidden from my present process of knowing. And therefore the fact that life is no longer visible after death in the flesh, much the same way as it is invisible before birth, does not deprive me of the certain knowledge of its existence before birth and after death. I enter life with certain predetermined qualities of love toward the world outside me; my existence in the flesh–brief or long–is spent increasing this love that I introduced into life, and therefore I conclude without doubt that I was alive before I was born and that I will live, after this moment in the present in which I, making this judgment, find myself now, as well as after any other moment in time before or after my death in the flesh. Looking about myself at the beginnings and ends of the existence in the flesh of other people (or even other creatures in general) I can see that one life seems longer, while another seems shorter; one is revealed earlier and continues to be visible to me for a longer period; another takes longer to be revealed and then very soon again becomes hidden from me. In every case, I see the manifestation of one and the same law of any true life–love increases, as though the rays of life are growing broader. Sooner or later, the curtain that will conceal from me the temporal course of human life will fall. The life of all people is one and the same, and like each and every life, it has neither beginning nor end. That a person has lived longer or shorter within the conditions of this visible existence makes no difference where his true life is concerned. That one man took a longer time to pass across my field of vision while another passed quickly across it in no way means I should ascribe more real life to the former and less to the latter. If someone passes by my window, regardless of how quickly or slowly he does so, I know that this person existed prior to the time when I saw him and that he continues to exist when he disappears from my view.

Why do some pass quickly while others pass slowly? Why should an old man, withered, morally ossified, and incapable, according to our view, of fulfilling life's law–the increase of love–live, while a child, a youth, a young maiden, or a man devoted to his spiritual work dies, leaves the conditions of that life in the body where, according to our view, he had just begun to establish within himself the correct relationships toward life?

The deaths of Pascal or Gogol I can somehow understand; but what of Chénier, Lermontov, and the thousands of other people whose inner work had just started? If they had had but the chance to accomplish it, would it not have been so good?[2]

It only seems this way. None of us knows anything about the foundations of life brought into this world by others, or about the movement of life that has been accomplished within this world. None of us knows about those obstacles to life's movement that existed in that creature and, chiefly, about those other possible conditions of life that remain invisible to us, conditions in which the life of this person could be placed in another existence.

It seems to us when we watch a blacksmith's work that the horseshoe is ready—it takes only a couple of strikes—but he breaks it and throws it into the fire, knowing that it has not been properly made.

We cannot know whether or not the work of true life is being accomplished in a person. We can know this only about ourselves. It seems that a person is dying when he does not need to, but that cannot be. A person dies only when it is necessary for his happiness, just as a person grows and matures only when he needs it for his happiness.

Indeed, if by life we understand life and not its mere appearance, if true life is the basis of all, this basis cannot depend on what it produces, the cause cannot proceed from [its own] consequence. The flow of true life cannot be broken by a change in its manifestation. The movement of man's life in this world, begun and not finished, cannot be interrupted because he has gotten a boil, or he comes down with some bacterial infection, or if someone shoots him with a pistol.

A person dies only because the happiness of his true life can no longer increase, and not because his lungs hurt, or he has cancer, or they shot him or dropped a bomb. We usually think that living in the flesh is natural, and that it is unnatural to perish from fire, water, cold, lightning, diseases, a pistol, or bomb. But one need only think seriously, looking at life from a detached perspective, to be convinced of the opposite: It is perfectly unnatural for someone to live a life in the flesh amid these fatal conditions, amid these pervasive and for the most part murderous and innumerable bacteria. It is natural for him to perish. In a material sense, therefore, life in the flesh is the most unnatural thing amid these lethal conditions. We are alive not because we take care of ourselves but because we do life's work. The work of life is finished, and nothing can stop the unrelenting death of man's animal life—this death happens, and one of its nearest causes, out of all the causes that surround us, appears to us to be its exclusive cause.

Our true life exists, we know it alone, from it alone we have knowledge of the animal life, and therefore, if life's semblance is subject to invariable laws, how can it [life]—that is, what produces this semblance—not also be subject to laws?

What bothers us is that we cannot see the causes and effects of our true life in the same way that we see the causes and effects of external phenomena: We don't know why one person enters life with certain qualities of his I, and another person enters with others, why the life of one man is cut short while another's continues. We ask ourselves, What were the causes that existed prior to my birth that caused me to be born the way that I am? And what will be the consequences, after my death, that I have lived this way or that? We regret that we do not receive answers to these questions.

But regretting that I cannot learn now what exactly was in existence before my life or what will be after my death is the same as regretting that I cannot see something outside the field of my vision. If I saw things outside my field of vision, I would not see what is within it. And for me, for the happiness of my animal [self], it is most necessary to see what is around me.

The same is true for my reason, which is how I comprehend things. If I could see what is beyond the limits of my reason, I would not see what is within its limits. For the happiness of my true life, it is most necessary for me to know what I ought to make my animal individuality obey here and now, so that I can achieve the happiness of life. And reason reveals this to me—reveals to me, in this life, the sole path upon which I can see no end to my own happiness.[3]

Reason indubitably indicates that this life did not begin with birth but that it existed previously and will always exist. It shows that the happiness of life grows and increases here, reaches limits that can no longer contain it, and only then does it exceed those conditions that limit its increase and transcend into another existence.

Reason puts man onto that single path of life that, like a widening conical tunnel, reveals to him in the distance, amid walls hemming him in on every side, the indubitable infinitude of life and its happiness.

The Inexplicability of Suffering in Earthly Existence Proves to Man Most Conclusively That His Life Is Not the Life of His Individuality, Which Begins with His Birth and Ends with His Death

Even if a person could not fear or not think about death, the sufferings to which he is subject—terrible, purposeless, unjustifiable, and impossible to avoid—would be enough to destroy every reasonable meaning ascribed to life.

I am busy doing something good, undoubtedly useful for others, and suddenly I am seized by a disease that cuts my business short; it oppresses and torments me without any sense or meaning. A pin in the rails rusts, and on the very day when it pops out, on that train, in that car, a kind woman and mother is traveling, and her children are crushed before her very eyes. An earthquake causes a landslide precisely where Lisbon or Vernyi stand, and perfectly innocent people are buried alive and die in terrible torment. What meaning can this have? Why, what is the use of these and thousands of other senseless, terrible, and accidental sufferings that afflict people?[1]

Rational explanations explain nothing. Rational explanations of all such phenomena always evade the very essence of the question and prove more convincingly that the question is unsolvable. I fell ill because certain microbes infected my body, or the children got crushed before their mother's eyes because dampness affects iron in such and such a way; or the town of Vernyi fell because certain geological laws exist. The issue at stake is why precisely these people were subjected to precisely these terrible sufferings, and how can I be rid of these accidents of suffering?

There is no answer. Reflection shows that, on the contrary, there is no law and cannot be any law that explains why these accidents happen to certain people and not to others. It shows that there are countless numbers of such accidents, and that therefore whatever I do, my life is subject, at any given moment, to countless accidents that might lead to terrible suffering.

If people drew only those conclusions that follow inevitably from their worldview, understanding their lives as individual existence, they would not remain alive another minute. Just as no worker would stay with a master who, at the moment of hiring, proclaims his right to roast the worker alive over a slow fire whenever it crosses his mind, or skin him alive, or stretch him out on a rack—who perpetrates all these horrors on his workers with no explanation or reason in the very presence of the person being hired. If people really understood their life in quite the way they say they do, not one person would remain alive in this world out of sheer terror of all those tormenting sufferings that are inexplicable by anything that he sees around him—sufferings he may fall prey to at any second.

Despite the fact that they all know various easy methods of killing themselves, of exiting this life suffused with cruel and senseless suffering, people live. They whine, complain about suffering, and continue to live.

You cannot possibly say this happens because there are more pleasures in this life than sufferings, because, first, both simple reasoning and philosophical investigation demonstrate clearly that all earthly life is a series of sufferings that are by no means redeemed by pleasure; and second, we all know on our own, and from the example of others, that, faced with a series of intensifying torments with no chance for recovery, people still do not kill themselves and cling to life.

There is only one explanation for this strange contradiction: in the depths of their souls, people know that every torment is always needed, necessary for the happiness of their life, and for this reason alone they continue to live, knowing in advance that they will suffer. They clamor against suffering because, under the false view of life that demands individual happiness, the violation of this happiness—when it does not lead to some other obvious happiness—must appear as something incomprehensible and therefore outrageous.

People are terrified by the sight of suffering, surprised as though it were something unexpected and incomprehensible. All the while, every person is brought up on suffering; every person's life is a series of sufferings. By now it would seem that he should have gotten used to suffering, would not be terrified at its sight, and would no longer ask himself why he suffers, or what the use of suffering is. If he just thinks about it for a moment, every man will see that all pleasure is purchased at the expense of the suffering of other creatures, that all his suffering is necessary for his own enjoyment, that there is no enjoyment without suffering, that enjoyment and suffering are the opposite poles of one condition, that one causes the other, and that both are mutually necessary. So what do these questions mean? Why do we suffer? What is the use of suffering? Why should someone who knows that suffering is tied to pleasure ask himself, Why? What is the use? Why not instead ask ourselves, Why do I experience pleasure? What is the use?

All animal life, and the life of man as animal, is an uninterrupted chain of sufferings. An animal's activity, and man's activity as an animal, is caused by suffering alone. Suffering is a painful sensation that brings about activity aimed at getting rid of this painful sensation and producing a state of pleasure. Not only does suffering not disrupt an animal's life, and the life of man as an animal, but life is itself only made real by suffering. Suffering is the very thing that gives movement to life, and it must therefore exist."

So why does man ask, Why do I suffer? What is the use of suffering? No animal asks this.[2]

When a perch torments a minnow out of hunger, or a spider torments a fly, or a wolf torments a sheep—they know that they are doing what should be done. Therefore, when the perch, the spider, and the wolf suffer the same torment from more powerful creatures, they know—as they flee, fight back, and are torn apart—that everything is as it should be, and therefore they can have no doubt that what is happening should happen. But a person whose only preoccupation is getting his legs healed after they have been mangled on the field of battle where he had once mangled the legs of others; or someone preoccupied with getting the most out of his solitary confinement after he has, one way or another, sent others to prison; or someone whose only care is beating back the wolves that are tearing him apart and getting away, the same person who has himself slaughtered and eaten thousands of living creatures—in all these cases, a person cannot think that what is happening to him should happen. He cannot admit that what is happening to him is what should happen because, when subjected to these sufferings, he has not done everything that he should have done. Not having done what he should have done, it seems to him that what is happening to him should not happen.

But what else, aside from fleeing and fighting back the wolves as he is being torn apart, should someone do? He should do what is natural for a reasonable man as a reasonable creature: he should be aware of that sin that has caused his suffering, repent, and comprehend the truth.

An animal suffers only in the present, and therefore the activity caused by the animal's suffering is directed at the creature itself in the present moment. The activity entirely satisfies the creature. A person, on the other hand, does not suffer exclusively in the present but suffers also in the past and in the future. Therefore, the activity caused by man's suffering and directed only at his own animal [self] in the present moment cannot satisfy him. Only an activity directed at the cause and the consequence of suffering—at the past and future—satisfies a person who is suffering.

An animal is locked up and tries to break out of its cage, or its leg is broken and it licks the sore spot, or it is being devoured by another animal or tries to fight back against it: the law of its life is violated from without, and the animal directs its activity at the restoration of the law. What happens is what should be. Consider a person—myself or someone close to me—who is in prison, or me or someone close to me who has lost a limb in battle, or me or someone close to me who is being torn apart by wolves: In such cases, the activity (breaking out of prison, fixing my leg, fighting back against the wolves) does not satisfy me because the confinement, the pain in my leg, the torment from the wolves all constitute only a tiny bit of my suffering. I see the causes of my suffering in the past, in my own errors and those of others, and if my activity is not directed at the cause of my suffering, at the error, and if I make no effort to be rid of it, then I do not do what I should, and suffering therefore appears as something that should not exist. The suffering grows, not only in reality but also in my imagination, until it reaches terrible proportions that preclude the possibility of life.

The cause of suffering for an animal is the violation of the law of animal life, and this violation is expressed by the consciousness of pain, while the activity caused by the violation of the law is directed at being rid of the pain. For the reasonable consciousness, the cause of suffering is the violation of the law of the life of reasonable consciousness; this violation is expressed in the consciousness of error and sin. The activity caused by the violation of the law is directed at being rid of the error—directed at the sin. Just as the animal's suffering produces an activity directed at the pain, and this activity relieves the suffering of its misery, so, too, the suffering of a reasonable creature produces an activity directed at the error, and this activity relieves the suffering of its misery.

Why? What is the use? These questions arise in a person's soul upon experiencing or imagining suffering, and they demonstrate only that this person has not comprehended the activity that should have been produced in him by this suffering, the activity that could have relieved the suffering of its misery. Indeed, for someone who stakes his life in his animal existence, there can be no activity that relieves the suffering of its misery, and such an understanding is all the less likely depending on how narrowly someone understands his own life.

When someone who stakes his life in personal existence finds the cause of his personal suffering in his personal error, when he understands that he has fallen ill because he has consumed something harmful, or that he has been beaten up because he picked a fight, or that he is hungry and naked because he has avoided work—he discovers that he is suffering *for having done* what he should not have. And *so as not to* do whatever he should not have done, he directs his activity at the destruction of the error, not rebelling against his suffering but bearing it lightly and often joyously. But when suffering that transcends the visible connection between suffering and error is visited upon such a person—for instance, when he suffers for reasons that do not stem from his personal activity—it seems to him that something has been visited upon him that should not have been. He asks himself, Why? What is the use? Finding nothing at which he might direct his activity, he rises up in anger against suffering, and his suffering becomes a terrible torment. The majority of human suffering has always been like this—its cause and consequence, or sometimes just one or the other, are hidden from someone in space and time, whether it's hereditary illness, accidents, poor crops, train derailments, fires, earthquakes, or similar things that end in death.[3]

Explanations to the effect that this is necessary because it teaches people in the future not to give into passions that will result in hereditary illnesses, or that we need to do better in designing our trains, or that we ought to treat fire with caution—all these explanations offer no answer so far as I am concerned. I cannot take the meaning of my life to be some illustration of carelessness for other people; my life is my life, with my pursuit of happiness, and not an illustration of life for others. These explanations are useful for chitchat, but they do not alleviate the horror before the meaninglessness of suffering that threatens me and precludes the possibility of life.

Were it somehow possible to understand that since others suffer because of my errors, then I suffer for the errors of others—even were it possible to understand in some vague way that suffering is an indication of some error that must be corrected by people in this life, there remains a vast series of sufferings that is completely inexplicable. Someone alone in the woods is torn asunder by wolves, someone drowns, or freezes to death, or is burned alive, or simply has caught an illness and dies alone—nobody will ever know how such a person has suffered, and there are thousands of such cases. Who will derive any kind of benefit from that?

For someone who understands his life as an animal existence, there is no answer and none can exist, because for him the connection between suffering and error exists only in visible phenomena; this connection slips his mind during his deathbed agonies.

A person has two alternatives: either not to acknowledge the connection between the suffering he experiences and his life, and to go on enduring the majority of his sufferings as utterly meaningless, or to acknowledge that my errors, and the deeds I commit as a consequence, are my sins, whatever they are, that cause my sufferings, whatever these may be, and that my sufferings are deliverance and expiation for my sins and the sins of others, whoever they may be.[4]

These two attitudes toward suffering are the only ones possible: that suffering is something that should not be since I can see no external meaning in them, or that suffering is what must be since I know its inner meaning for my true life. The first stems from acknowledging as happiness the happiness of my individual life taken discretely. The second stems from acknowledging as happiness the happiness of my whole past and future life in its inextricable connection with the happiness of other people and creatures. Under the first view, suffering has no explanation and it does not cause any activity other than constantly mounting despair and anger that cannot be assuaged by anything; under the second view, suffering causes the very activity that constitutes the movement of true life—consciousness of sin, liberation from error, and making oneself obedient to reason.

If it is not a person's reason that does it, then the misery of suffering brings man to acknowledge unwillingly that his life cannot fit into his individuality, that his individuality is only the visible part of his life, and that the external connection between cause and effect revealed through his individuality to him does not coincide with the internal connection between cause and effect that is always known to someone from his reasonable consciousness.

The connection between error and suffering, visible to an animal only in its spatial and temporal conditions, is always visible beyond space and time to someone from within his consciousness. Someone becomes conscious of suffering, whatever it may be, as a consequence of his sin, whatever that may be, and he understands repentance for this sin as his liberation from suffering and as the attainment of happiness.

After all, from earliest childhood, a person's whole life consists only of becoming conscious of his sin through suffering and of liberating himself from error. I know that I arrived in this life with a particular knowledge of truth, and that the more errors I made, the more the sufferings for me and for others. The more I was rid of errors, the less the sufferings for me and others and the greater the happiness I could achieve.

The misery of suffering is experienced only by someone who, having separated himself from the life of the world—and, failing to perceive those sins through which he has introduced suffering into the world—considers himself innocent and therefore rails against the suffering that he endures for the sins of the world.

Amazingly, the very thing that is clear to reason, mentally, is confirmed in the sole true activity of life: love. Reason says that someone who acknowledges the connection between his own sin and sufferings with the sin and sufferings of the world rids himself of the torment of suffering. Love proves this in deed.

Half of every man's life is passed in sufferings that he does not even consider to be tormenting but goes so far as to disregard, considering it his happiness only because they are borne as the result of error and as a means to ease the suffering of those he loves. So the less love there is in a person, the more a person is prone to the torment of suffering; the more love there is, the less is the torment of suffering. A life is entirely reasonable when its activity is made manifest through love alone, precluding the possibility of any suffering. The torment of suffering is only the pain that people experience when they attempt to disrupt the chain of love, toward their ancestors, their heirs, or their contemporaries, the love that unites human life with the life of the world.

CHAPTER 35

Bodily Suffering Is the Necessary Condition of Life and Human Happiness

"Ouch, I am in physical pain. Why is there this pain?" "Because not only is it necessary for us but also we cannot live without having some pain every once in a while," whoever caused us the pain might answer. And he has made it only as painful as necessary while making the happiness of this "ouch" to be as great as it can be. Everyone knows that the initial sensation of pain that we experience is the first and foremost means of preserving our body and continuing our animal life. Were it not for this pain, as children we would have set our bodies on fire and cut ourselves all over just for fun. Bodily pain protects the animal individuality. When this pain is serving to protect someone in childhood, pain cannot be the terrifying torment we experience once we are possessed of reasonable consciousness, when we resist it, considering it to be something that should not exist. In animals and children, pain is very specific and small in size; it never reaches so tormenting a degree as the reasonable consciousness accords it. We see that a child cries when bitten by a flea as plaintively as from a pain that happens when his internal organs are being destroyed. The pain of an unreasonable creature leaves no trace in memory. Let any one try to remember his childish sufferings from pain, and he will see that he not only lacks a memory of them but also is powerless even to imagine them. The impression made on us at the sight of suffering children and animals is more our own suffering than theirs. The way unreasonable creatures express suffering is immeasurably greater than the suffering itself and therefore provokes our compassion to an immeasurably greater degree, as one can observe when considering illnesses of the brain, delirium, typhus, and the pain of dying.

During the times when reasonable consciousness is not yet awake and pain serves only to set limits on the individual, it is not tormenting; at those moments when there is a possibility of reasonable consciousness in man, it is a means to make animal personality obedient to reason, and it becomes less and less tormenting the more this consciousness is awake.

In essence, only when we fully possess reasonable consciousness can we also speak about suffering, because life and those states of life that we call suffering begin from this condition. In this state, the sensation of pain can range from very great to very negligible amounts. Indeed, even without having to study physiology, we all know that our sensitivity has limits, and that when pain increases to a certain point, we stop feeling it—we faint, fall into a stupor, have a fever—or death arrives. Pain, then, can increase only to a certain amount and cannot transcend its limits. But our sensitivity to it, on the other hand, can increase depending on our attitude: it can increase to infinity, just as it can decrease to an infinitesimal amount.

We all know that one can, by resigning oneself to pain and recognizing it for what it must be, reduce it to the point where it is no longer felt, even to the point that one can experience joy while enduring it. I am not talking about the martyrs or about Hus, who sang on his pyre—but there are simple people who, just to demonstrate their valor, endure without a cry or a twitch what are considered the most tormenting of operations.[1] There is a maximum limit to the increase of pain, but there is no limit to the diminishment of its sensation.

The torments of pain are truly terrible for those who have invested their life in the life of the flesh. How can these torments be otherwise when the force of the reason that is given man to destroy the torment of suffering is instead directed only at increasing it?

There is a myth in Plato that God initially set the length of human life at seventy years but then, after realizing that people were the worse for it, changed it to what it is now,—that is, he made it so that people do not know the hour of their death.[2] One could equally imagine the reasonableness of a myth that people were first created without sensitivity to pain but that later, for their happiness, things were made as they are now.

If the gods had created people with no sensitivity to pain, people would very soon have begun to beg for it. A woman without labor pains would give birth to children in such conditions that few of them would remain alive; children and the young would do significant damage to their bodies. Adults would know neither the errors of others who lived before or of those now alive, nor would they know, most important, their own errors. They would not know what to do in this life, would not have a reasonable purpose for their activity, and would never come to terms with the idea that death awaits them. They would have no love.

For the man who understands life as obedience of his individuality to the law of reason, pain is not only not evil but also the necessary condition of both his animal and reasonable life. If it were not for pain, the animal individuality would have no indication of when it transgresses its law; if reasonable consciousness did not experience suffering, man would never learn the truth, would never learn his law.

But you are speaking about your own suffering, they will say in response, yet how can you deny the suffering of others?[3] The sight of this suffering—here is the most excruciating suffering, people would say not entirely sincerely. The sufferings of others? But the sufferings of others—or what you call suffering—has never ceased and does not cease. The whole world of people and animals is suffering and has never stopped suffering. Can it be that we just discovered this? Wounds, disabling injuries, hunger, cold, illnesses, all kinds of unhappy accidents, and labor pains most of all, without which not one of us would have made it into the world—are not all these necessary conditions of existence? This is the very thing—or the decrease of it, helping out with it—that constitutes the reasonable life of people, the very thing that the genuine activity of life is aimed at—that is, understanding personal suffering and the causes of human error in order to decrease them. This is, after all, the business of human life. After all, that is why I am a man—an individuality—so that I can understand the suffering of other persons. After all, that is why I am a reasonable consciousness, so that I perceive, in the suffering of every single person, the common cause of all suffering—errors—so I can destroy that cause within me and in others. How can the material of his work be the suffering for the worker? It is as if a plowman would say that virgin soil is his suffering. Virgin soil can be suffering only for someone who would rather see the field tilled but does not consider it the business of his life to till it.[4]

The activity that is aimed at direct and loving service to those who suffer and aimed at the destruction of the general cause of suffering—delusions—is that very singular and joyous work that faces man and grants him that inalienable happiness that constitutes his life.

There is just one suffering for man, and it is the suffering that forces him to yield himself, like it or not, to that life where there is only one happiness in store for him.

This suffering is the consciousness of the contradiction between one's own sinfulness and the sinfulness of the whole world; it is not just the possibility for but also the duty of realizing—and not by anyone else but by me alone—the whole truth in my own life and in the life of the whole world. This suffering cannot be assuaged—not by participating in the sin of the world while not seeing one's own sin, nor even less by no longer believing in not merely the possibility but also the duty of realizing, not by anyone else but by me alone, the whole truth in my life and the life of the world. The former only increases my suffering; the latter deprives me of the force of life. Only the consciousness and activity of true life that destroy the incommensurability existing between personal life and the conscious goal of life can assuage this suffering. Whether he wants to or not, a person has to admit that his life is not limited by his individuality from birth to death and that the conscious goal is an attainable one; that the whole business of life, indivisible from the life of the whole world, consists, has consisted, and always will consist of pursuing this goal—in the greater and greater consciousness of his sinfulness and in the greater and greater accomplishment of the whole truth in his life and in the life of the world. If it is not reasonable consciousness, then it is suffering caused by errors in his understanding of life that, whether he wants it or not, drives a man onto that sole path of life on which there are no obstacles, no evil, where there is nothing but this single indestructible and always-increasing happiness, which has no beginning and can never come to an end.

Conclusion

A person's life is the pursuit of happiness, and what he pursues will be given to him.

Evil in the guise of death and suffering is apparent to a person only when he accepts the law of his fleshly, animal existence as the law of his life. Only when he, as a human, descends to the level of an animal–only then does he notice death and suffering. Death and suffering, these twin specters, howl at him from all around and drive him onto the single path open to human life, which is obedience to its law of reason and which is expressed in love. Death and suffering are merely a person's transgressions against the law of his life. For a person living according to the law of his life, there is no death and no suffering.

"Come to Me, all you who labor and are heavy laden, and I will give you rest."[1]

"Take My yoke upon you and learn from Me, for I am gentle and lowly in heart, and you will find rest for your souls."[2]

"For My yoke is good and My burden is light" (Matthew: chapter 11).[3]

Man's life is striving for happiness; what he strives for will be given to him: life, which cannot be death, and happiness, which cannot be evil.

APPENDIX I

It is often said that we study life not using a consciousness of our own life but instead as something general, entirely outside ourselves. That is the same as saying that we examine objects not with our eyes but as something general, entirely outside ourselves.

We see objects as something outside ourselves because we see them with our own eyes, and we know life as something outside ourselves only because we know it from within. We see objects only as they appear in our eyes, and we define life as something outside ourselves only because we know it within ourselves. And we know life within ourselves as a pursuit of happiness. Therefore, without a definition of life as a pursuit of happiness it would be impossible not only to observe life but also even to see it.

The first and main act of our cognition of living creatures is that we include many various objects under the notion of a single living creature, and we differentiate this living creature from everything else. Both these things we do based solely on a definition of life that we are all aware of—a pursuit of one's own happiness as a creature separate from the whole world.

We learn that a man on a horse is neither a multitude of creatures nor a single creature, not because we observe all the parts that make up the man and the horse but because neither in the head, nor in the legs, nor in the other parts of the man and the horse do we see the kind of separate pursuit of happiness that we know within ourselves. And we figure out that the man on the horse is not a single creature but two creatures because we recognize in them two separate pursuits of happiness, while within ourselves we know only one.

It is only in this way that we learn that there is life in the combination of the horseman and horse, that there is life in a team of horses, that there is life in birds, insects, trees, and grass. If we did not know that the horse desires its own happiness, while the man desires his own, and that every single horse in the team desires the same, that the same happiness is desired by every bird, every bug, tree, grass, we would not see the separateness of creatures, and not seeing this separateness, we would never be able to understand anything that is alive: the cavalry regiment, the team of horses, the birds, the insects, and the plants—all of these would be like waves in the sea, and the whole world would be merged for us into one undifferentiated movement where we would never be able to find life.

If I know that the horse, the dog, and the tick sitting on it are all living creatures, and I can observe them, it is only because the horse, the dog, and the tick all have their separate aims—the aim of each is its own happiness. I know this because I know myself just as such a creature—one pursuing happiness.

All cognition of life is based on this pursuit of happiness. Without acknowledging that this pursuit of happiness that a person feels within himself is life, and the sign of every life, any study of life is impossible, any observation of life is impossible. Therefore, observation begins when life is already known, and no observation of the manifestations of life (as the false science presumes) can define life itself.

People do not allow that the definition of life consists of a pursuit of happiness, something they find in their own consciousness; they allow instead the possibility of knowing this pursuit in a tick, and on the basis of this unfounded presumption of knowing the happiness that the tick is pursuing, they make their observations and even draw conclusions about the essence of life itself.

Every single concept of external life is based on my being aware of my pursuit of happiness. And therefore, once I know what my happiness and my life are like, I will be in a state where I can know the happiness and life of other creatures. Without having comprehended my own happiness, there is no way I can understand the happiness and the life of others.

Observations of other creatures that pursue aims that are unknown to me, aims that bear a resemblance to the happiness I know, within myself, that I am pursuing—such observations are not only powerless to clarify anything for me but also can surely conceal from me the true cognition of life.

To study the life in other creatures without having defined your own life amounts to drawing a circle without knowing its center. Only by establishing one unshakable point as the center can one draw a circle. Whatever geometrical figures we draw, without a center we will not have a circle.

APPENDIX II

False science, by studying the phenomena that accompany life, all the while claiming to study life itself, distorts the concept of life. The longer, therefore, that it studies the phenomenon, the thing that it calls life, the further it departs from the concept of life that it wants to study.

At first, mammals are studied, then the vertebrates, fishes, plants, corals, little cells, microscopic organisms, and eventually one loses the distinction between animate and inanimate, the limits between organic and inorganic, the limits between one organism and another. Eventually it gets to the point that we imagine that the most important object of study and observation is something that is already beyond observation. We imagine that the mystery of life and the explanation of everything rest in decimal points, in spermatozoa, in something that is beyond observation, something we can only surmise, something that we discover today and forget tomorrow. The explanation of everything is assumed to be in creatures that are contained within microscopic creatures and in creatures that are themselves contained within these creatures, which are contained within others . . . and so on, ad infinitum, as if infinite divisibility of some small quantity is not the same kind of infinity as the infinity of great quantity. The mystery will then be unveiled only when the whole infinity of smaller values has been discovered—that is, never. People cannot see that the idea that the issue will be solved only in some infinitely small quantity is doubtless proof that the question has not been correctly posed. And this final stage of insanity, the one that certainly demonstrates complete loss of meaning on the part of the investigators—this very stage is touted as the triumph of science; the final stage of blindness is seen as the utmost degree of clarity. People have run into a dead end, and thereby they have exposed the falsity of the route they have taken. Yet there is no end here to their adulation. Let us improve our microscopes just a little and we shall understand how the inorganic becomes organic, and the organic becomes psychological, and the whole mystery of life will be revealed to us.

By studying shadows instead of objects, people have completely forgotten the object whose shadow they are studying. They have been delving deeper and deeper into the shadow and have now reached complete darkness, and they rejoice that the shadow has now fallen into pitch-darkness.

The meaning of life is revealed in the consciousness of man as a pursuit of happiness. An elaboration of this happiness, defining it more and more precisely, makes up the main goal and work of the life of all humanity; because this work is laborious, not a piece of cake but work, people decide that the definition of what happiness is cannot be found where it was placed—that is, in a person's reasonable consciousness—and that therefore one should seek it everywhere, only not where it has been revealed.

This is something like a man who receives a piece of paper with precise instructions for what he needs to do but who, because he cannot read it, tosses this paper away and goes about asking every passer-by whether they know what he needs. The definition of life is inscribed in indelible letters on the soul of man as his pursuit of happiness, which people look for everywhere but within their own consciousness. This is all the more strange because all humanity, in the guise of its wisest representatives, beginning with the Greek maxim "Know thyself," has said and continues to say quite the contrary. All religious teachings are nothing more than definitions of life as a pursuit of a real, undeceitful happiness available to man.

APPENDIX III

We hear the voice of reason more and more clearly; we heed its voice more and more frequently, and the time is coming, and has already come, when this voice is stronger than the voice calling for individual happiness and false duty. It becomes clearer and clearer, on the one hand, that individual life and its snares cannot provide happiness; and, on the other hand, it becomes clearer that fulfilling every duty that people demand is a deception that prevents us from fulfilling our one obligation to the reasonable and happy beginning from which we emerge. The ancient sham that demands faith in what has no reasonable explanation has been worn out, and we cannot return to it.

Once it was said, Do not reason but believe in the duty that we set down. Your reason will deceive you. Only faith will reveal life's true happiness. And man has tried to believe, and has believed, but his interactions with other people have shown him that other people believe something quite different, and they say that this other thing produces more happiness. We must answer the question about which faith, out of many, is truest. Reason alone is capable of answering it.

A person knows everything through reason, not faith. You could deceive him by asserting that he knows things through faith and not through reason; but as soon as he gets to know two faiths and sees people professing a different faith just as he professes his own, he is inevitably forced to resolve the matter through reason. Having become cognizant of the Muhammadan faith, a Buddhist, should he remain a Buddhist, will stay a Buddhist through reason, not faith. As soon as he encounters another faith, the question arises whether he should discard his own faith or the proselytized one; the issue is decided inevitably through reason. If he, having known Muhammadanism, stays a Buddhist, his formerly blind faith in Buddha now rests on reasonable foundations.

In our time, attempts to funnel spiritual content into man through faith in a way that bypasses reason is the same as attempts to try to feed someone in a way that bypasses his mouth.

Human communication has demonstrated to people the universal basis for cognition, and people cannot retreat to their former delusions—the time will come, and it has already come, when the dead will hear the voice of the Son of Man and those who hear will come back to life.[1]

It is impossible to muffle this voice because this is not one person's solitary voice but the voice of the whole reasonable consciousness of humanity, which makes itself heard in every single person, in the best people of humankind, and now in the majority of people as well.

Editor's Notes

Epigraphs to *On Life*

Tolstoy's epigraphs from Pascal and Kant are in the original French and German, with minor modifications of punctuation. Additionally, there is a short concision in the Pascal text and a substantial contraction of the quotation from Kant. My translations follow:

"Man is nothing but a reed, the weakest in nature, but he is a thinking reed. The entire universe does not require taking up arms to destroy him: a vapor, a droplet of water suffices to slay him. Even if the universe were to destroy him, man would still have more dignity than his slayer, because he knows that he is dying and he knows of the advantage that the universe has over him. But the universe knows nothing about this. And thus our whole dignity lies in thinking. It is through thinking that we should elevate ourselves, and not through space and duration. Let us then act on thinking well: in this consists the moral principle." See fragment 200/347 in Blaise Pascal, *Oeuvres completes*, ed. Louis Lafuma (Paris: L'Integrale / Seuil, 1963), 528.

"Two things fill the soul with ever new and increasing wonderment and awe, the more frequently and attentively our contemplation engages with them: the starry skies above me and the moral law within me . . . The former begins with that point that I occupy in the external world of perception, and it broadens the connection wherein I stand to an unbounded measure with worlds upon worlds and systems upon systems; and moreover expands their temporal motions, their beginning and continuation, into boundless times. The latter begins with my invisible 'I,' my individuality, and projects me into the world, which has true endlessness and is traceable only in the understanding through which I recognize myself not just as an accidental, but as a universal and necessary connection." See Immanuel Kant, *Kritik der praktischen Vernunft*, ed. J. H. Kirchmann (Berlin: Gebrueder Grunert, 18–?), 194.

Tolstoy omits a whole phrase from Pascal in the sentence "C'est de là qu'il faut nous relever, non de l'espace et de la durée, que nous ne saurions remplir" [It is through thinking that we should elevate ourselves, and not through space and duration, which we would not know how to satiate]. See Pascal,

Oeuvres completes, 528. By ending the sentence with the word *durée,* Tolstoy commits a not-all-that-innocent alteration, which illustrates his disagreement with Pascal's geometrical reason with its respect for space and time.

Tolstoy omits the following passage from his quotation of Kant: "Beide darf ich nicht als in Dunkelheiten verhüllt, oder im Überschwenglichen, außer meinem Gesichtskreise, suchen und bloß vermuten; ich sehe sie vor mir und verknüpfe sie unmittelbar mit dem Bewußtsein meiner Existenz" [I do not need to search for, or merely presuppose either as if they were wrapped in darkness or were in the realm transcending my circle of vision; I can see them before me and connect them directly to the consciousness of my existence].

Tolstoy provides his reference in the abbreviated German "*Kant. (Krit. der pract. Vern. Beschluss)*" just as it appears at the beginning of *On Life.*

Tolstoy quotes from the first paragraph of the conclusion to Kant's *Critique of Practical Reason.* When reading the work in the copy that was preserved in his personal library at Yasnaya Polyana, Tolstoy made many approving notations in the margins of the above-mentioned edition produced by J. H. Kirchmann. I gratefully acknowledge the assistance of the directorship of the Tolstoy Museum Estate at Yasnaya Polyana for permission to examine this copy from Tolstoy's library. In my translation, I have taken into account the markings and marginalia during Tolstoy's reading of Kant's text. For the standard and widely used English translation of this passage, see Immanuel Kant, *Critique of Practical Reason,* trans. T. K. Abbott (Amherst, N.Y.: Prometheus Books, 1991), 191.

In the text of *On Life,* Tolstoy makes good use of the ambiguity present in Kant's text: the nouns *die Welt* (the world) and *die Persönlichkeit* (personality or individuality) are of feminine gender, and the qualification present in the sentence may relate equally to both, with *die* in German being not only the definite article in the feminine but also the qualifying indicative adjectival pronoun in the feminine. The ambiguity is one example of how Tolstoy takes freedom (or poetic license) in reinterpreting Kant's idea of "personality" as if extending the possibility of its endlessness. This practice continues throughout the text of *On Life.* Tolstoy imagines Kant's "allgemeine und notwendige Verknüpfung" (a universal and necessary connection) to be a kind of harnessing relationship that dialectically unites individual freedom with universal laws and with the eternal, which is unbounded by space and time.

Tolstoy's quote of John 13:34 (12:34 in the Russian original is erroneous) is provided in the standard Russian vernacular translation of the Gospels. Tolstoy would use the same verse from John in a great number of his best-known and most penetrating works. John's Gospel will be his key reference text; it is subjected to some of his most radical revisions throughout *On Life.*

Introduction

1. Tolstoy refers to two apocryphal characters emblematic of opposite types of behavior, Kifa Mokievich (the long-winded idealistic father) and Mokii Kifovich (his unthinking, thuggish son), from chapter 11 of Gogol's *Dead Souls*. One problem that torments Kifa Mokievich during his unstoppable bouts of daydreaming and paradoxical philosophizing is why animals are born naked and why mammals can't hatch out of eggs like birds. Mokii Kifovich, Kifa's progeny and his very opposite, incurs torrents of complaints from neighbors. As he considers whether or not he should restrain his son, whom complaining neighbors identify with an enraged elephant, Kifa Mokievich goes on a tangent and begins to consider whether an artillery gun would be necessary to help a baby elephant out of an eggshell—should we presume that elephants hatch from eggs. "Kifamokievism" was a term in Tolstoy's time used to describe this sort of vapid and aimless thinking. Tolstoy is emphasizing the importance of an individual's conscious, deliberate approach toward thinking and life. In this same paragraph, he introduces a concept of a responsive and responsible relationship toward life that is a highly conscious and aware stance, a position of selfless, compassionate activity. The outward movement implied by "toward" would be most appropriate to describe the above existential relationship. At the same time, the phrases "relationship toward the world" and "relationship toward life" might sound a bit unusual in English. This is the whole point. While it would be more natural in everyday parlance to say "relationship with the world" and "with life," or "relation to the world" and "relation to life," they convey the kind of passivity that Tolstoy is calling on us to drop, and would do injustice to his meaning. The Russian phrase that he uses is "otnoshenie k." Used as well in common spoken and written Russian, the phrase would normally be rendered as "relation to," only to remain unnoticed. "Relationship toward" is a fuller, more expressive phrase that implies a more intentional, more emotional connection than its synonym, the word "relation." We have opted therefore for "relationship toward" throughout the translation to indicate the consistency of Tolstoy's concept of an intentional relationship. As Tolstoy wittily observes in the chapters of *On Life*, to experience discomfort at the mention of the need and duty for establishing an active relationship toward life and the world is a symptomatic of the resistant, deluded consciousness, which is a relative of "Kifamokievism." Tolstoy develops his concepts of true, reasonable consciousness, and of false, deluded consciousness, in the chapters that follow.

2. Tolstoy attempts to convince the reader that the miller's thinking is idle and futile by playing with the otherwise neutral Russian word *rassuzhdeniia*, which can be translated as "theorizing," "inference making," or "deliberating"

but which, in nineteenth-century Russian, meant something more like "day-dreaming," "dolled-up thought," or "idle thought." The miller's cogitative stalemate reminds one strongly of Tolstoy's Konstantin Levin, one of the main characters in *Anna Karenina* (1873–78). Levin struggles to find the meaning of life while keeping busy managing his estate. Once he focuses on the work per se, it all goes well, but whenever he engages in philosophizing about why and how various forces (manpower, industrial mechanisms, and agricultural tools) function in concert and individually, everything falls into a state of disrepair. Interestingly, Levin does not support the idea of "reinventing the mill." He is on the side of those who believe that the old-fashioned Russian horse-driven mill (*rossiiskii topchanok*) can only be made worse by Western technological "improvement" (see part 3, chapter 27, of *Anna Karenina*; 18:351). Tolstoy's interest in the parable of the mill goes back to his earlier years when he would make compilations of didactic stories for *Russkie knigi dlia chteniia* ["Russian Readers"]. A total of four "Russian Readers" were published by Tolstoy between 1874 and 1875. Along with two editions of alphabet books for peasant children that had come out in 1871 and 1874, which were likewise selected, edited, and written in parts by Tolstoy, "Russian Readers" were intended to provide both basic education and wholesome moral instruction to illiterate learners. In the second "Russian Reader," we find a parable about a peasant who invents a self-rotating mill and spends the bonus that financed his enterprise, only to realize that his mill would not rotate (see "Samokrutka (Byl')" [A Self-Rotating Mill (A True Story)]; 21:150–51]). It might be interesting for readers to know that in the early drafts of *On Life*, the mill was activated by horses walking in a circle, not by water.

3. By "theorizers," Tolstoy means the same kind of idle thinkers whom he has been lampooning through Gogol's Kifa Mokievich. In this paragraph, Tolstoy continues to attack *rassuzhdeniia* (deliberations and vague, idle talk) and its perpetrators, the theorizers for whom he even invents a special word that doesn't exist in standard Russian, *rassuditeli*, which, translated literally, is something like "judgment-mongers."

4. Tolstoy most likely refers to "Povest' o Feodore Khristianine i ego druge Abrame zhidovine" (The Tale about Theodore the Christian and His Friend, Abraham the Hebrew), one of the parables on tolerance in *Prolog* [*The Prologue*], a collection of Russian hagiographic narratives and didactic instructions patterned on Menology and told in the form of vitae, religious legends, and fables, where readings are arranged by the month following the calendar of saints. Tolstoy owned a richly decorated oversize edition of *Prolog* in four volumes and used it frequently in his writings after 1880. In 1886 the writer Nikolai Leskov (1831–1895), with whom Tolstoy stayed in close

contact discussing these legends, employed his famed storytelling technique by retelling this very same tale in contemporary stylized Russian.

5. "Life is the ensemble of functions that resist death. Life is the ensemble of phenomena that succeed in the organized being during a given time." Tolstoy provides this unattributed quotation in French. It is very reminiscent of the language and arguments summarized by a well-known experimental physiologist, Claude Bernard (1813–78), in his feature "Définition de la vie" [A Definition of Life] for issue 9 of *Revue de Deux Mondes*, published in 1875, the same year that parts 1 and 2 of *Anna Karenina* appeared in print in installments. One of the benign idle thinkers in the book is Stiva Oblonsky. Oblonsky loves reading fashionable journals with a slightly liberal bent and may well be imagined reading precisely such an essay that allows his mind to wander away from unpleasant trains of thought about his infidelity to his wife, Dolly, or about the tragedies in the life of his sister Anna. Stiva's body functions with the sort of natural unanimity that Bernard describes, guaranteeing that his life is a very agreeable and happy journey that cannot be derailed by tragic impasses. Similar flighty thoughts about happiness are entertained by Ivan Ilyich in the 1886 story, prior to the beginning of his illness. Unlike Nikolenka Irteniev in the other example (see note 2 to chapter 5), it is not the precariousness of the representative powers of our inwardness but the story of his wandering kidney that catches Ivan off guard and puts him face-to-face with the emptiness of the *néant*. The question asked by Ivan is this: "So what will there be when I am not?"

Tolstoy subscribed to *Revue de Deux Mondes* for many decades and mentions its authors and essays numerously—for example, in the drafts of *War and Peace*, in his last novel, *Resurrection*, in various unfinished philosophical fragments, as well as in his diaries, letters, and pamphlets. He also records his familiarity with Bernard and fellow "physiological materialists," as he calls them, in particular Emil du Bois–Reymond (1818–96) and Gustav Theodor Fechner (1801–87), in many diary entries, one of the most important of which is found in Tolstoy's entry for December 19, 1900 (54:73). Fechner's *Das Büchlein vom Leben nach dem Tode* [A little book on life after death, 1836] was very popular in Russia and admired by Wilhelm Wundt. See Tolstoy's letter to Strakhov of February 14, 1895, in which he speaks of his knowledge of Bernard's views: "Of Claude Bernard, I'd known the main idea more or less" (*PTS*, 2:984; 68:32–33).

6. This unattributed quotation is in Russian. It is typical of the evolutionary views of life prevalent among the physiologists, pathologists, and natural scientists engaged in the medical and biological research of the time. These views were widely popularized in the print media in Russia.

7. One of the first uses by Tolstoy of the polysemantic Russian word *blago* (happiness) occurs when he confronts the postulates of cell theory. Developed in the 1830s, the theory claimed cells to be the common units of all living tissues and organs.

8. Please note that Tolstoy does not say "about the mill as if it were a river"; he says "about the river as if it were a mill." His usage confirms a point he makes a little earlier about the order in which thoughts should unfold. This order is confused by the miller in Tolstoy's opening parable.

9. Throughout this paragraph, the word "what" is italicized in keeping with the pattern of italics that Tolstoy applies to the corresponding Russian pronoun *chto*.

10. In the three preceding paragraphs that describe the dangers of succumbing to received opinion, we can see that Tolstoy vacillates between "they" and "we." He also uses phrases such as "I am being told" (*mne govoriat*). Most likely he does so to underscore in his discussion how important it is to be mindful of our critical autonomy in thinking. By paying close attention to pronouns, he emphasizes the nuances of referencing and addressing ideas in our thinking. Tolstoy's exposition of the dangers inherent in regurgitating the opinions of the impersonal collective plural and in echoing the dicta of "they say that" anticipates Heidegger's preoccupation with the tyranny over the capacity for critical thought that questions the position and orientation of our individual being (Dasein) by the impersonal collective "das Mann" [*sic*] (usually translated as "the they") (see especially section §27 in chap. 4 of division 1 of Martin Heidegger, *Being and Time*, trans. Joan Stambaugh [Albany: SUNY Press, 2010], 122–26). As is well known, Heidegger was especially impressed by Tolstoy's doing away with the idea of the impersonal "man dies." In a famous footnote that he added to §51 of division 2 of *Being and Time*, Heidegger writes, "L. N. Tolstoy in his story 'The Death of Ivan Ilyich' has portrayed the phenomenon of the disruption and collapse of this 'one dies'" (244n12). Throughout the course of *On Life,* Tolstoy continues to object—and very inventively—to other instances of "they say." See Medzhibovskaya, "Tolstoy and Heidegger," 64–72, for details.

11. The original line runs, "We do not say that in the cell there is a gush [*bryzn'*], we say that there is life [*zhizn'*]." *Bryzn'* rhymes with the Russian word *zhizn'*. It is the (hypothetical) imperative form of *bryznut'* (to gush, to spurt). It sounds something like a command to effuse, be plentiful, and break through a limit. We therefore came up with the rhymed "life" and "jive" to convey this sense of Tolstoy's playful exuberance.

12. It is hardly coincidental that in his use of "according to our concept of life" (*po nashemu poniatiiu zhizni*) Tolstoy blurs the boundary between "according

to my meaning of life" and "according to our common or consensual meaning of life" as reasonable human beings.

13. The first artificial international language, Volapük, owes its appearance, in around 1880, to Johann Martin Schleyer, a Catholic priest from southern Germany. Consisting mainly of Germanic vocabulary intermixed with French and based on the simplest grammar culled from major European languages, Volapük initially enjoyed an enthusiastic following. By 1887, the time of Tolstoy's treatise, the second international congress of Volapük linguists was taking place. Because in Russian it inspires very unflattering auditory associations, the name of the new international language very quickly became a derogatory tag denoting any sort of nonsensical jargon, and Tolstoy makes fun of the word's sound, hinting that the new linguistic fashion is devoid of meaning. It should be noted that in the same year, 1887, Volapük suddenly acquired a more powerful rival. On July 26, 1887, Ludwik Zamenhof (1859–1917) published, in Russian, the first manual of Esperanto, *Unua Libro* (*Mezhdunarodnyi iazyk: Predislovie i polnyi uchebnik* [Warsaw: Kelter, 1887]). Tolstoy was not yet acquainted with Zamenhof's book during his work on *On Life*. The acquaintance would occur soon enough: on September 13, 1889, the writer thanked a young translator and Esperanto aficionado Vladimir Mainov for sending the second edition of *Mezhdunarodnyi iazyk* (1888) to him. He shared with Mainov his conviction that a universal language was necessary but doubted, however, whether the language was universal rather than simply trans-European. As such, it could not yet serve at once the needs of India, China, and Africa. Tolstoy recommended, as a first step, that all Europeans should master the language. He added that he did not know Volapük enough to judge the advantage of one universal language over the other (64:304–5). Tolstoy's interest in Esperanto continued in later years.

14. Tolstoy ridicules the term "monera" by using the word *shtuka*, which is best rendered in contemporary parlance as "this whatchamacallit." However, Tolstoy's aristocratic contempt for neologisms like "monera" is not captured by "whatchamacallit," "thingamabob," and the like. "Whatsit" (which was in use circa 1882) captures Tolstoy's meaning and was, moreover, a word of his day. The category of "monera" referring to single-cell organisms was introduced into biological science around 1866 by Ernst Haeckel (1834–1919), a promoter of Darwin and one of the chief developers of recapitulation theory (the assumption that the ontogeny of individual organisms encapsulates the development of species [phylogeny]). Haeckel was a pioneer of stem-cell research and creator of a genealogical map of life-forms and their ecology. Haeckel sparked a number of racial and embryonic-research controversies.

He discussed loose single-cell organisms at length in *Monera* (1870). Tolstoy's ridicule of Haeckel continued in years to come. For a recent account of Haeckel's career, see Robert J. Richards, *The Tragic Sense of Life: Ernst Haeckel and the Struggle over Evolutionary Thought* (Chicago: University of Chicago Press, 2008).

15. In his essay on life, Bernard operates with the same terms in the discussion of animism and vitalism that Tolstoy uses here as he launches into his polemic.

16. By means of this multiple repetition of the word "easy" (*legko*) Tolstoy makes a pun on the difference between the self-serving tasks of life that are "easy" and the worthy tasks of life that require hard work and are not achievable by shortcuts.

Chapter 2

1. Tolstoy wittily translates the Judaic notion of "receiving happiness" or becoming ethically content (also with another's success), which corresponds to the notion of the receipt of happiness as a necessary human satisfaction (the Yiddish *naches* derives from the Hebrew *nakhát*). Without the receipt of happiness man feels deprived and—literally—"un-happy." Tolstoy's interest in Judaism dates to the early 1880s; he began studying Hebrew and the Holy Books in 1883 with the Moscow Rabbi Solomon Minor.

2. The listing of Confucius, the Brahmins, Buddha, Laozi, the Judaic Prophets, Greek philosophers, the Stoics, and Christ as opposed to the official agents of major religions who administer rituals and stand on guard of their sacrosanct dogmas, whom Tolstoy calls "Pharisees" in his discussion elsewhere in *On Life*, was one of the reasons why this work was banned by Synodic censorship and condemned by the prelates in the Russian Orthodox hierarchy. But it was quite typical of Tolstoy to place Socrates, Epictetus, Confucius, Jesus, Buddha, Marcus Aurelius, and Pascal in the same lineage of the great teachers of life. The sayings of the thinkers above alongside selections from the Talmud, the Bible, the Vedas, and the Zend-Avesta are an important part of Tolstoy's calendars published in his later years, *The Cycle of Reading* (1904–8), *Thoughts for Every Day* (1907–10), and *The Path of Life* (1910), which were widely read and known internationally. Tolstoy's first compilations of wise thoughts from the religious writings of great teachers and sages of all times developed out of the copious notes he took during his intense religious studies of the late 1870s. Almost immediately, he started organizing these notes with a view to making them accessible to a wide readership, and pilot publications of this sort became easier with the establishment of the Posrednik firm (see page 7 in the editor's introduction). At the end of October 1886,

when he was still recovering from his injury, Tolstoy was selecting peasant sayings that could be paired with Gospel verses and organized so as to be read every day of the month. Eventually, the compilation grew into *A Calendar with Proverbs for 1887* [*Kalendar' s poslovitsami na 1887*]. The calendar was published by Ivan Sytin in mid-January 1887 as *The Calendar with Proverbs for Every Day* [*Kalendar' s poslovitsami na kazhdyi den*]. One of these proverbs in the manuscript finished by Tolstoy on March 11, 1887, three days before his talk at MPS, put it, quite in the spirit of *On Life*, as follows: "Fast by your spirit, not by your belly" (40:476).

Chapter 3

1. Tolstoy's eclectic group of true teachings on life discussed in the previous endnote for chapter 2 returns in chapter 3, where it is now juxtaposed with the "insignificant teachings" of Aristotle, Francis Bacon, and August Comte, which are trailed a few sentences later in the same chapter by the mention of the teachings of Herbert Spencer and Hermann von Helmholtz. The evil group of false prophesies about life is no less eclectic than the good list above, but it is important to note that, like the previous group, the latter one is not composed randomly. The Aristotelian concept of the multidisciplinary system of knowledge about life; Bacon's materialism; Comte's and Spencer's positivist solutions (the methodology of happiness and social statistics) as scientific foundations for understanding life and its teleological destinations; and Helmholtz's scientific cocktail of physiology, psychology, aesthetic (sense) empiricism, and electro- and thermodynamics organized into a unified system of research directed at preserving the energy of life all violate Tolstoy's preference for a different starting point and a different endpoint for the question of meaning within the scope of human life that he explains in his introduction. Here, the question of the priority of meaning is substituted with controlled theories of knowledge, and consequently, in the context of Tolstoy's argument, Aristotle, Bacon, Comte, Spencer, and Helmholtz are the modern versions of the Scribes. This comparison is extended in the next chapter. Tolstoy's initial word choice for "insignificant teachings" was "meaningless" (*nichtozhnyi*). Only after a long fight would he agree to Grot's compromising substitute.

Chapter 4

1. Tolstoy surely means Helmholtz's preoccupation with finding patterns through which the laws governing reality are reflected in the world of symbols produced in the physiological and aesthetic activity of the senses. Helmholtz

publicized his experiments in the fields of nerve physiology, ophthalmic optics, and sensory acoustics through demonstrations and lectures. The works of Helmholtz that are important for us here are *Über das Sehen des Menschen* [On Human Eyesight, 1855], *Die Lehre von den Tonempfindungen* [A Teaching Concerning the Sensations of Tone, 1863], and *Die Tatsachen in der Wahrnehmung* [Facts in Perception, 1879]. Helmholtz's popularity in Russia stems from the fact that the latter two works were published in Russian in 1875 and 1880, respectively. Tolstoy, who had a near-native command of German from childhood, was not dependent on translations to read Helmholtz. The derogatory distortions that Tolstoy describes in his paragraph resemble the ideas found in many of Helmholtz's works. It is also noteworthy that Tolstoy uses his key term "reasonable consciousness" for the first time in the text of *On Life* precisely at the conclusion of chapter 4, in which Helmholtz and the "false science" that he symbolizes are debunked.

Chapter 5

1. Speaking of the "pointless struggle for existence" that "my children will continue," Tolstoy switches into the mode of thought of an individual in doubt. We hear the interior voice of this individual. Tolstoy does not mean *his* children, the children of Lev Nikolaevich Tolstoy, but he makes the conflation between "my children" and the children of others on purpose to bring home the idea that the struggle for existence concerns us and those who continue after us personally. For this reason, the phrase cannot be rendered through something like "one's children" or "their children." This is also Tolstoy's voice contradicting a famous postulate of Aristotle in *The Nicomachean Ethics* claiming that we cannot regard ourselves as happy unless we die a good and easy death and our surviving progeny are happy in their own lives.

2. By not capitalizing in this instance his mention of the story of Genesis and the world's creation, Tolstoy demonstrates his lack of respect for creationism. He also objects to the Pharisees of all organized religions who insist that the roots of evil are not to be sought in human error and delusion, but rather in the remotest past, in the accepted versions of original sin.

3. Tolstoy undoubtedly refers to Pascal's famous wager (*pari*), his own long-term sustainer in searches for faith. (If God exists, the one believing in Him is saved; if God does not exist, one has nothing to lose since everything is already lost in that case.). See fragment 418 in Pascal, *Oeuvres complètes*, 550–51. Pascal posited the possibility of a dialogue with God from His hiddenness and His silence. Tolstoy greatly admired Pascal's type of spirituality,

but this form of spirituality was far from common in Russia at the time. All the more important is Tolstoy's rebellion against this tendency. His love of Pascal and the poet of self-consciousness, Friedrich Schelling, is introduced in a humorous description of the struggles for faith raging in his adolescent character Nikolenka Irteniev, the hero of his strongly autobiographical trilogy *Childhood, Boyhood, Youth* (1852–57). In an earlier version of chapter 19 of *Boyhood*, Nikolenka does not know what to make of Pascal's "order of the heart" (*l'ordre du coeur*) and his wager. Nikolenka gives Pascal's wager a try after his fiascoes with Epicureanism—for which he lacked adequate funds. He demands of Pascal a proof of God's existence in the form of making Nikolenka a better person. Arriving at a pantheist idea, he becomes preoccupied with the question of what he had been before becoming a man—a horse, a dog, or a cow. This thought, in turn, was replaced by another idea, Pascal's idea, more precisely, "that even if all that religion teaches us were untrue, we would lose nothing by following it; by not following it, on the other hand, we risk receiving eternal damnation instead of eternal bliss" (2:287). Since eternal bliss is a long shot, Nikolenka consoles himself by eating gingerbread cakes. In the final version of chapter 19, Nikolenka struggles to rely on "inalienable attributes of the mind" that he senses in himself independently of knowing "of the existence of the philosophical theories." In the end, Nikolenka comes to the conclusion that objects do not exist; only his relationship toward them exists. And yet he hopes to "catch the emptiness [*néant*] off guard" by identifying the space where he was not (2:57). The transcendental idealism attributed here to a fanciful, but still immature mind that posits that "objects do not exist but only my relationship toward them exists," is a major theme in *On Life* where finding one's own unique relationship toward life guided by reasonable consciousness becomes the main commitment of a mature mind, rather than fanciful, idle searching. In chapter 4 of *On Life*, the Schellingian quest for making plausible a pursuit of infinity in a finite lifetime, which is more typical of the Romantic era, gives way to investigations and critique of what Tolstoy describes as Helmholtz's experimental shenanigans (see also the note to chapter 3, note 1 to chapter 4, and note 6 to chapter 25).

4. Here, Tolstoy must mean the ancient Chinese custom of lighting candles to show respect for living parents or to commemorate deceased ancestors. These candles are set on specially designated plaques on the important dates of the lunar calendar. Tolstoy could also be referring to the Qingming Festival, a memorial celebration for deceased parents that takes place every year during the third lunar month, when great numbers of commemorative candles are

lit during ancestor worship rituals. I am grateful to Dr. Michelle Wang, a cultural anthropologist and specialist in Buddhism and traditional Chinese religious practices, and to Peter Lee, for their generous help explaining this otherwise unclear reference in Tolstoy's text.

Aylmer Maude added the following footnote to Tolstoy's mention of dueling in chapter 5: "Duels were still in vogue in Russia when this was written" (Leo Tolstoy, *"On Life" and "Essays on Religion,"* trans. Aylmer Maude [Oxford: Oxford University Press, 1934], 33). Although Alexander III (1881–94) sought to restore the dueling honor code in the Imperial Army, Maude's comment is somewhat inaccurate. Duels had been in vogue in Russia through the end of the 1840s, but by the latter half of the 1870s, they already belonged to the realm of legend, in practice only among the elite officer corps. The poet Mikhail Lermontov, whose death is mentioned later in the text of *On Life*, did die in a duel fought in the mountainous outskirts of the town of Pyatigorsk in the North Caucasus after a trifling dispute with an officer by the name of Martynov (1841), and his *A Hero of Our Time* (1838–40) describes a famous duel between Pechorin and Grushnitsky at a gorge in the Caucasus. But note that in the Caucasus near the Black Sea in Chekhov's "The Duel" (1891), von Koren, a zoologist and hardened social Darwinist, who swears by Spencer, fails to exterminate Laevsky, a superfluous man, who constantly compares himself to Tolstoy's characters and measures his thoughts by Tolstoy's dicta. As they approach the site, von Koren asks, laughing, if someone remembers Lermontov's description or at least Bazarov's parodic duel with Kirsanov in Turgenev's *Fathers and Sons* (1862). The problem is that duels are "literature." For a definitive treatment of duels and dueling in Russia, see Irina Reyfman, *Ritualized Violence Russian Style: The Duel in Russian Culture and Literature* (Stanford, Calif.: Stanford University Press, 1999).

Tolstoy's mentions of duels and dueling are always ironic or negative. Duels and suicide were intended to be a topic of a much broader discussion in an earlier version of chapter 11. At a later stage of his work, Tolstoy excluded the draft. In the draft, which was not discovered until later and had not been known to A. I. Nikiforov, Tolstoy writes, "*O zhizni*. What does this astonishing phenomenon called suicide mean? The animal, that creature whose entire activity is to preserve and enhance its life, kills its own self. The killing of self with the pistol is only one of the cases when the death of the animal coincides with the dying of reasonable consciousness. And in this sense, death at war, in a brawl, and in a duel is in no way different from suicide" (90:161).

5. This is likely a hint that there are other, true doors of life, or the doors that lead to true life. Note an allusion here to variations on this theme in chapter 10 of John (e.g., John: 10:7–9).

Chapter 6

1. Tolstoy is faithful to the modern Russian version of John 5:25.

2. Maude provides a footnote to this passage in *On Life*: "The time comes when rational consciousness outgrows the false doctrines, and man halts in the midst of life and demands an explanation" (Tolstoy, *"On Life" and "Essays on Religion,"* appendix 3, 36). Maude had no theory about "rational consciousness" versus "reasonable consciousness" and used both terms interchangeably.

3. Tolstoy's phrase in the Russian original, "prosypaiutsia liudi . . . ozhivaiut v grobakh svoikh" (26:339), is a polemical rendition of a long line of biblical imagery connected with the themes of the end of time, Last Judgment, and Resurrection, beginning with Ezekiel 37:12, Daniel 12:2, Matthew 25:46, John 5:28–29 and 11:24, Acts 24:15, and ending with Revelation 20:12. His controversial rendition makes it possible for reasonable consciousness to be the sole agent of salvation. When their reasonable consciousness wakes up, people come back to life in their graves. Tolstoy has "caskets" (*groby*), the traditional Russian way to render this thought from Revelation. The use of the image of the casket in the context of Tolstoy's theory of reasonable consciousness sets the stage for the embrace of the idea of the resurrection of spiritual life in the mortal frame (casket) of one's perishable body.

4. See, in the historical supplement, the earlier evocations of the same idea in Tolstoy's diary for 1886–87.

Chapter 9

1. The idea and image of the sprout appear in Tolstoy's letter to Diterikhs and in the text of his presentation at MPS on March 14, 1887.

2. Tolstoy introduces here the word *otnoshenie* (relationship), one of the key descriptions of the emerging active stance toward the chief aims of human life.

3. Just above (and throughout the book), Tolstoy employs the verbal usage of "stake in" that may seem a little unusual. This is because Tolstoy merges here on purpose several meanings of the Russian word *"polagat'"*: to suppose or surmise; to posit; and to stake at risk of winning or losing something that other playing-it-safe punters would be reluctant to gamble on. The resulting meaning is that of a radical choice that Tolstoy invites us to make between safe conduct and inertia in hopes of securing personal and selfishly understood well-being on the one hand, and on the other hand, a heterodox turn away from the possessive understanding of happiness toward the embrace of reasonable consciousness that would lead us through our new, selfless life. Throughout the book, the deluded consciousness objects to reasonable consciousness by saying that it is too risky to place its stakes *on* the tasks of selfless

existence and active love. The deluded consciousness tends to speak as a very timid gambler would.

Chapter 10

1. Tolstoy capitalizes the terms he employs in order to answer the question that he poses, "But then what is reasonable consciousness?" (*No chto zhe takoe eto razumnoe soznanie?*) (26:347). Neither in Tolstoy's time nor nowadays do these terms require capitalization. While he is frequently reluctant to capitalize the words "God" and "Genesis" (see elsewhere in this book), Tolstoy is punctilious about capitalizing the terms that he uses to construct the notion of reasonable consciousness. For making his construct work, he relies on such terms in Russian as *Logos-Razum*, *Mudrost'*, and *Slovo*.

Chapter 12

1. Tolstoy's parenthetical "the less comprehensible it is for man" (*menee poniaten cheloveku*) clarifies the relationship of reasonable consciousness to reason (*ratio*) proper. Tolstoy thinks it imprecise to conflate the issue of comprehension with that of cognition and hence his "the less it renders itself to human cognition" (*menee poznavaem dlia cheloveka*).

Chapter 13

1. *Zakon organizma* (the law of its organism) is an amateurish invention of Tolstoy's, which does not pertain to any specific law of organic life. Tolstoy suggests a hierarchy of life in which all these completely unreasonable cells, as he understands them, would be closest to the inanimate realm. He relegates cells to the more impersonal, lower reaches of life, such as dead matter. In Tolstoy's scheme of things, as individualities, animal and human, we should have less business relating to these unreasonable spheres, for the sake of the health of our true relationship toward life.

Chapter 14

1. In terms of temporality, here is what Tolstoy achieves in this chapter: After the reign of reasonable consciousness sets in, there is no death, since the constraints of space and time have been overcome. Time stops, in a way, as its meaning remains the same. This is an Augustinian type of time arising after

Augustine's conversion, described in book 11 of *Confessions*, chapters 13–15. Augustine describes the period of prolonged delusion before his conversion in the first nine books. He describes eternity in the four remaining books. The Augustinian scheme above resembles the long life of spiritual sleep or inauthentic life that characterizes the being and judgments of the deluded consciousness described by Tolstoy in *On Life*. Examining the types of underlining in Tolstoy's copy of the French edition of Augustine's *Confessions*, most of which occurs in books 10, 11, and 12, allows one to deduce that Tolstoy evinced the most interest in the question of spiritual time and its elongation and in timing things in the process of spiritual search (see Aurelius Augustinus, *Les confessions de Saint Augustin*, trans. Arnauld d'Andilly [Paris: Garnier, 1861], 374–75, 471, 473). The same pattern of stabilized intellectual time as we find in Augustine occurs in John Stuart Mill's *Autobiography* (1873), which Tolstoy knew and esteemed. Mill describes the process of a conscious self-reorientation that he achieved after 1845 by turning away from his crippling personal suffering to focus on the concerns for achieving universal utilitarian happiness. His suffering was henceforth over. Both Augustine's *Confessions* and Mill's *Autobiography* supplied Tolstoy with the necessary parameters to present his own searches for eternal time, overcoming temporality. The ways that Tolstoy deals with temporality and the confession genre are discussed in detail in Medzhibovskaya, *Tolstoy and the Religious Culture of His Time*, 236–44, 248, 295–337.

Chapter 16

1. Matthew 10:39. In his quote of Matthew, Tolstoy capitalizes the pronoun, "for My sake" (*radi Menia*).

Chapter 17

1. Tolstoy's liberal interpretation of Christ's parables was one of the causes of the banning of *On Life*.

Chapter 19

1. In this section of the chapter, the long tirades of reasonable consciousness against the feeble and lame objections of the deluded consciousness are introduced by Tolstoy with the help of long dashes (so-called typographic em-dashes). By contrast, the objections of the deluded consciousness are set

off only by quotation marks. Tolstoy represents in this case alternations in the mind of a human being struggling for comprehension between reasonable consciousness and divided (deluded) consciousness. The blurring together of paragraphs and of which consciousness speaks taking turns, and in what order, is purposeful.

Chapter 21

1. Tolstoy first mentions nirvana, the desirable result of self-renunciation of all life's desires, in chapter 2 of *On Life*. That Tolstoy does not support Buddha's precepts for countering unhappiness with the negation of our individuality becomes clear when the word "nirvana" reappears in an imagined objection uttered by one of the hypothetical opponents to Tolstoy's theory of reasonable consciousness in chapter 21: "'Yes, but what is this? It's nothing but Buddhism!' This is how people of our time usually respond. 'This is Nirvana, it is standing on a pole!'" By using this example of the Western misappropriation of the notion of nirvana and happiness and unhappiness, Tolstoy is preparing his assault, in the next chapter, on Schopenhauer's and Hartmann's pessimism.

2. Roburite is a powerful explosive; its potency exceeds that of dynamite by about 25 percent.

3. The Russian word *Indeets* (the Indian) referred in Tolstoy's time to both a denizen of India and a Native American; Tolstoy means the former.

4. Tolstoy refers to the legendary words (*Eppur si muove*) that Galileo allegedly uttered almost soundlessly after the High Court of Papal Inquisition forced him, in 1632, to recant his position in support of the heliocentric view.

5. Tolstoy's mention of Galileo and Copernicus is an example of how science and the laws that it studies can be "good." *On Life* culminates previous conversations that Tolstoy used to have with himself on this score. The names of Galileo and Copernicus, as well as those of Isaac Newton, Johannes Kepler, and the Russian scientist Ivan Sechenov, appear in the drafts and—to a lesser degree—in the finished sections of *War and Peace* and its two philosophical epilogues. In Tolstoy's searches of the late 1860s, we observe the contours of what would become reasonable consciousness. He does not yet use the term but is already actively looking for a force that unifies reason and consciousness, necessity and freedom, God and man. In the examples that he culls in various fragments of *War and Peace* from the philosophy of history and science, Tolstoy seeks to apprehend how human mind and human actions can serve consciously, and with prodigious understanding, the aims of Reason or the

Absolute. Mulling over the results of the physiologist Sechenov's study of the reflexes of the brain, Tolstoy writes in the draft notes for *War and Peace* that "the highest rung of science is to acknowedge its lack of knowing [*neznanie*]" (fragment 314 [ms 101 EII/ch. 8–9; 15:229–31]). In his *Reflexes of the Brain* (1863–66), Sechenov disallows the existence of free will. Tolstoy all but dismisses his views alongside similar denial of free will in the theories of modern psychology, statistics, and zoology, which focus on the dependence of one on the many rather than of the many on one: "If me, *my I*, can step outside of the conditions of time, *this I* would possess absolute freedom. The *I* is free, but only beyond time. Within time, it is but an infinitely small moment" (ibid., page 231). Tolstoy moves on toward embracing the view that is close to Schelling's idea of life potencies that link individual consciousness and its *unknowable remainder* with infinity, which would thus allow the connection of the future, present, and past with "each individual consciousness . . . by means of innumerable linkages." See F. W. J. Schelling, *System of Transcendental Idealism*, trans. Peter Heath (Charlottesville: University Press of Virginia, 1997), 201.

Tolstoy argues in the finished version of the second epilogue of *War and Peace* that, having arrived at a colossal number of infinitely small integers, each of which holds an undisclosed link to the reason of reasons and causality, such reformers of science as Copernicus and Newton were able to explain life without questioning God's authority yet were brave enough to oppose the grave resistance of old theology in their newly discovered universal laws (the heliocentric model and the law of gravity). The new history should do the same, instantiating "the law of necessity in history" for the maintenance of the whole edifice of life and paying no heed to theological resistance in fear of the collapse of its foundations (E2/12; 7:354–55). Such was Tolstoy's proposal of a Copernican revolution for historical science in 1869.

Now, in 1886–87, he is creating a new science of life. Prefaced as it is by selections from Pascal's *Pensées* [Thoughts], the conclusion of Kant's second *Critique*, and by John's precept of love, Tolstoy is ready to move forward toward proposing his next Copernican revolution, the transfiguration of life by way of love-bearing reasonable consciousness. In sum, whereas previously Tolstoy was struggling to decide whether human freedom could translate into acts of a conscious choice between good and evil, in *On Life* he is more than determined to answer these questions in the affirmative. By resorting yet again to the examples of Galileo and Copernicus, *On Life* shames newer generations of scientists whose theories, tools, terms, and explorations do not bear out the essential foregrounding in the eternal meanings of our connection to the divine.

Chapter 22

1. Tolstoy accuses Schopenhauer and Hartmann, his student in pessimism, of dishonesty (*nedobrosovestnost'*) not only in this chapter but also in chapter 27. *On Life* is a platform for Tolstoy to renounce pessimism, his temporary inspiration, as a nonproductive worldview. An admiration for Kant sounds strongly in comparison with a near contempt for Schopenhauer in Tolstoy's letters written on October 11, 12, and 13, 1887, to Grot and Biriukov (64:102, 103). After years of studying Schopenhauer, of admiring him and arguing with him, Tolstoy announces his final rejection of him in a letter to Strakhov of October 16, 1887, written when *On Life* was already at the printer's but when its galleys were undergoing endless corrections. In the letter to Strakhov, Kant's *Critique of Practical Reason* is said to manifest that "the center of gravity is not in negation," but Schopenhauer, for whom negation of the will to live is central, is called "a talented scribbler" (*talantlivyi pachkun*) (*PTS*, 2:753; 64:105).

Eduard von Hartmann (1842–1906) was a well-established presence in Russian intellectual thought in the 1880s. His speculative inductive method elaborated in *Philosophie des Unbewussten* [The Philosophy of the Unknown, 1869], *Das Unbewusste vom Standpunkt der Physiologie und Deszendenztheorie* [The Unconscious from the Standpoint of Physiology and Descent Theory, 1872], *Die Selbstsetzung der Zukunft* [Self-Determination of the Future, 1874; often published in English as *The Religion of the Future*], and his two-volume *Aesthetik* (1887) were all readily included in discussions by the Russian philosophical community. Hartmann fared somewhat worse than Tolstoy when both candidatures were brought up for promotion to distinguished members of the Moscow Psychological Society on January 24, 1894. In a vote of twenty-five *for* and five *against*, Tolstoy was promoted to the distinguished rank of membership in the society. Twenty-four voted for Hartmann and six against him. Pessimism did not prevent Hartmann from feeling optimistic about the study of "little cells" (see *Das Problem des Lebens: Biologische Studien* [The Problem of Life: Biological Studies, 1906]).

Chapter 23

1. Tolstoy quotes these poetic lines in the original Russian (*Liubit'... no kogo zhe?.. / Na vremia ne stoit truda, / A vechno liubit' nevozmozhno...*). They come from a well-known manifesto of Romantic dejection, "I skuchno i grustno . . ." (Feeling bored and sad . . .), by Mikhail Lermontov. The poem was written in 1840, the year before Lermontov died in a complicated duel with Martynov, in which inflated pride played no small part. He was twenty-six. Allegedly, the duel was caused by the poet's mockery of his pompous rival, more fortunate

in drawing the attention of a provincial society in the Caucasus. The poem complains of the inability to love, of the unavailability of those worthy of love, and delivers a damning blow of disbelief to the capacity for feeling compassion. Tolstoy's layout of Lermontov's lines, which are the first two lines taken by Tolstoy from the second of the three amphibrach quatrains of the poem, and Tolstoy's punctuation differ from Lermontov's original that has it thus: "*Liubit'* . . . *no kogo zhe?.. na vremia—ne stoit truda, / A vechno liubit' nevozmozhno.*"

2. We have added the word "supposedly," implied in the original but not conveyed by a lone standing adverb in the Russian.

3. Tolstoy refers to Luke 10:29.

4. See Matthew 6:23.

5. Tolstoy's phrasing in the subjunctive of nineteenth-century Russian is somewhat misleading and may be misinterpreted to mean its opposite: "If there were nothing in man but love for himself and his children, ninety-nine percent of the evil we find among people today would cease."

Chapter 24

1. In this instance, Tolstoy allows himself a nonlegitimate paraphrase of the Gospels.

2. Note that in this sentence Tolstoy uses the plural of the word *blago*, which is not the same as "gifts of life," according to the Old Testament, but is rather closer to "goods," even "commodity goods," that cater to the selfish appetites of animal individuality, as Tolstoy sees them. The plural "goods" has been chosen to render the idea in this instance.

Chapter 25

1. See Matthew 20:28 and Mark 10:45.

2. See John 2:9 and 2:10.

3. In using his signature word "awareness" (*razumenie*) in place of the traditional word "mind," "You shall love the Lord . . . with all your awareness," Tolstoy paraphrases Matthew 22:37–38.

4. The retelling occurs in Matthew 19:18–19.

5. The two quotations are summaries and paraphrases of various verses from John and the First Epistle of John.

6. These very animals are named in the aforementioned chapter 19 of Tolstoy's *Adolescence*, when Nikolenka Irteniev is contemplating the possibility of metempsychosis by imagining a ladder of beings. Nikolenka needs this faith in eternal life and in love for a happy life. The list of animals and the

ladder of beings reappear in a number of Tolstoy's later works where younger protagonists think or speak about eternity—for example, in chapter 10, part 4, book 2 of *War and Peace*. See also note 2 to chapter 5.

7. Like Diogenes, Tolstoy's sprout hates everything that stands between it and its sun.

Chapter 27

1. See John 11:25.

Chapter 28

1. Tolstoy is saying here that our perception of people should be governed by the intuition of their internal rather than external features.

2. In this sentence Tolstoy plays with the variations of meaning afforded by the Russian verb for "to love," which can also mean simply "to be fond of" or "to like." Tolstoy engages all these possibilities.

3. Tolstoy refers to the episode in Silvio Pellico's (1789–1854) autobiographical book *Le mie prigioni* [My Prisons] in which the author describes his friendship with a spider in his cell during the first year of his solitary confinement as one of the leading Carbonari sentenced by Austrian authorities in 1820. Prior to his arrest, Pellico had been known as the author of a well-received tragedy, *Francesca da Rimini* (1818). In the years following his liberation in 1828, he quickly regained literary fame by releasing *Le mie prigioni* (1832) and then publishing another celebrated meditation, *Dei doveri degli uomini* [On the Duties of Men, 1834]. Alexander Pushkin was one of Pellico's earliest advocates in Russia, and his writings would eventually become well known within Russia's educated circles.

Chapter 29

1. Tolstoy again speaks about memory in terms of its atemporal (*vnevremennoe*) and supraspatial (*neprostranstvennoe*) aspects. We can again include Augustine as a reference point to this conversation. See the note to chapter 14. However, Tolstoy's use of the terms in this instance invokes the "memorable memory" of consciousness, the memory of the preceding life (*predshestvuiushchaia pamiatnaia mne zhizn'*) before birth—which brings to mind Plato's concept of παρουσία (*parousia*), the perception of the presence of an idea in things, which is distinct from simple recollection as discussed in *Phaedrus* 275A. Especially important in the connection of memory with eternity are Tolstoy's

echoes of *Meno* 81B, 85C, *Phaedo* 72E–76A, and of the imagining of the happy life discussed in *Laws* 12, 945D.

2. The stark contrasts found in this paragraph are in the original. They sound as odd and uncomfortable in Russian as they do in English. Tolstoy surely intends to shock readers by presenting to them these glimpses of our progress through life stages.

Chapter 30

1. Tolstoy means Saint John the Theologian and Apostle (Ioann Bogoslov, in Russian), one of the twelve disciples, who was the author of the Gospel of John, the Epistles, and the Book of Revelation. Ioann Bogoslov is celebrated on May 21, according to the Eastern Orthodox calendar.

Chapter 31

1. Tolstoy's phrase *nichego ne ostalos'* may be a hidden reference to famous lines in Shelley's sonnet "Ozymandias" (1818). It is quite possible that his very title *On Life* is borrowed from Shelley's short meditative essay of the same name, written in 1819 and published in 1832. Tolstoy rarely liked poetry, but Shelley was one of his favorite poets. Concerning Russian sources, one might also note the equally famous lines written by the influential democratic critic Vissarion Belinsky (1811–48) to his friend and critic Vladimir Botkin on the occasion of the death of a young star of Russian philosophical Romanticism, man of letters, and critic, Nikolai Stankiewicz (1813–40): "Nothing, Botkin! Nothing remains . . . Only death is immortal" (letter of August 12, 1840, in V. G. Belinsky, *Sobranie sochinenii v deviati tomakh* [Collected Works in Nine Volumes], 9 vols. [Moscow: Khudozhestvennaia Literatura, 1982], 9:389–91). An admirer of Schelling, Stankiewicz was one of the first to use *razumenie* and other such terms for "reasonable consciousness" in Russian, terms which were translations into Russian of the synthesis of German Romantic "observing reason" and "conscious freedom."

2. Tolstoy refers to the death in his early thirties of his beloved elder brother Nikolai (Nikolenka) Tolstoy in early October 1860 at Hyères, France. After becoming orphaned at age nine (his mother, Maria Nikolaevna, née Volkonsky, died in 1830, and his father, Nikolai Ilyich Tolstoy, died in 1837), Tolstoy lost two of his older brothers—Dmitry Nikolaevich Tolstoy (1827–56) and Nikolai Nikolaevich Tolstoy (1823–60). Both brothers died of tuberculosis. Tolstoy was much closer to Nikolai, whom he nursed in his final days and hours. When Nikolai died, Tolstoy's world was only a little short of

collapsing. In a letter to a friend, the poet Afanasy Fet, Tolstoy confessed his shocked witnessing of "this absorption of self into nothingness." He continues, "You can't influence the stone to fall up instead of down, where it is being drawn . . . This state into which we have been placed by someone is the most terrible lie and evildoing, for which we (we the liberals) would find no words if it were a man who placed another man in such a situation . . . I do take life as it is, as the most vulgar, repellent, and false condition" (60:357). Note that Tolstoy does not mention the very recent death of his son Aleksey in January 1886 (b. 1881).

Chapter 32

1. "Lev Nikolaevich" is indeed a common first name and patronymic in Russian. For any educated Russian, nonetheless, the mention of Lev Nikolaevich would immediately evoke Tolstoy. Someone bearing the name Lev Nikolaevich, would be congratulated for being Tolstoy's namesake. By referring to himself as he would to any other "Lev Nikolaevich," along with an "Ivan Semenovich," of whom there are hundreds of thousands, Tolstoy is promoting his point about fame being no factor for a chance to encounter eternity.

2. This is again a reference to the true door of life; see page 76 at the end of chapter 5.

3. Tolstoy may yet again be hinting at the hinges of the door opening up into true life. See page 162 in this chapter.

Chapter 33

1. For the evolution of this image of the cone, please see Tolstoy's diary for August 28, 1886, in the historical supplement section of this book where we also find Tolstoy's drawing representing the cone.

2. Pascal (1623–62) died aged thirty-nine of stomach cancer, and Gogol (1809–52) died a little short of turning forty-three of a mysterious ailment, taking to his bed and refusing to eat or drink. Both men achieved a sort of equanimous peace with their torments by embracing faith in their final years and writing about their religious conversions. As Tolstoy explains elsewhere in *On Life*, Lermontov's bitterness about life, coupled with his untimely death in a duel at twenty-six, and his lack of a firm religious conviction at the time of his death save a poetic one, was harder for Tolstoy to make his peace with. On Lermontov, see also the notes to chapters 5 and 23.

André-Marie de Chénier (1762–94), author of *Iambes*, was arguably the greatest French poet of the eighteenth century. Imprisoned for four months at Saint-Lazare, he was guillotined in July 1794 in the final hours of the Reign of Terror. (His *iambes* were smuggled out of prison in a laundry basket.) Chénier was a well-known subject of Romantic worship. His glorification in Chateaubriand's *Le génie du christianisme* [The Genius of Christianity], Saint-Beuve's *Joseph Delorme*, and Alfred de Vigny's *Stello* in the Romantic era was continued in Umberto Giordano's *Andrea Chenier*, which was finished in 1886. The most famous Russian contribution to Chénier's cult was Alexander Pushkin's "Andrei Shenie" (1825), a warning to the international coalition of tyrants prefaced with lines from Chénier's poem "La jeune captive" [The Young Captive Maiden] from his "Dernières poèsies"[Last Poems]: "Ainsi, triste et captif, ma lyre toutefois s'éveillant" [And so, though sorrowful and a captive, my lyre was still awakening].

Maude adds sentence-long biographies of Pascal, Gogol, Chénier, and Lermontov in a footnote to this portion of the translation: Tolstoy, *"On Life" and "Essays on Religion,"* 142.

Tolstoy wrote a chapter titled "Pascal" for the July portion of weekly readings of his *Cicyle of Reading* (1904–8). The chapter on Pascal, a short biographical summary of his life and beliefs, was written in 1905. It has never been translated into English and can be found in *The Jubilee*, 41:477–84. Tolstoy calls Pascal's *Pensées* a "prophetic book" (*prorocheskaia kniga*) that demonstrates to people that to live without God is to live like an animal, and that to believe that they know (*qui croyent savoir*) life—a characteristic of people who live without God—is to entertain one's mad delusions (41:483). One of the remarkable features of Tolstoy's note on Pascal is the constant invocation of Gogol (41:477–78, 482). Tolstoy finds their cases of a later-in-life conversion to faith to be of the same order and to be at the base of their neglect by the educated world. What brings these two thinkers together is their shared view that "man needs two faiths for his happiness [*blago*]: one is to believe that there *is* an explanation of the meaning of life and, second, faith in finding this best explanation of life" (41:481). At the time of writing *On Life*, Tolstoy was at work on a short essay on Gogol, which paid special attention to Gogol's employment of the term "reasonable consciousness." See Medzhibovskaya, *Tolstoy and the Religious Culture of His Time*, 338, 352–53.

3. Tolstoy is clearly playing with Kant's notion of rational boundaries, most notably as expressed in his *Die Religion innerhalb der Grenzen des bloßen Vernunft* (*Religion within the Limits of Reason Alone*, 1793).

Chapter 34

1. The Lisbon earthquake inspired Leibniz to devise his theodicy theory and Voltaire to parody the efficacy of Leibniz's optimism in his philosophical tale *Candide, or Optimism*. Tolstoy makes a powerful connection between the dawn of the theodicy argument and recent catastrophes that had just made headlines. He refers to the earthquake at the military outpost of Vernyi in the region of the Kazakh Alatau on June 9 (May 29, according to the Julian ["old style"] Russian calendar), 1887, in which an estimated eight hundred people died. (Vernyi was then not far from Lake Issyk-Kul', later known as Alma-Ata [Almaty], which was for many years the capital of Soviet Kazakhstan.) The disaster of 1887 was followed by two other powerful earthquakes in the region: the first of these two took place in July 1889, and the second took place in 1911. All three earthquakes served the first generation of seismographers as test cases for the formulation of disaster warnings and the organization of rescue operations. Following is Aylmer Maude's footnote to the same passage in chapter 34: "In the great Lisbon earthquake of 1755 over 50,000 people were swallowed up. Vernyi in Asiatic Russia, near the borders of China, has frequently suffered from earthquakes. A particularly severe one occurred not long before *On Life* was written, a peculiarity of which was that the earth opened wide, swallowing all that was within range" (Tolstoy, *"On Life" and "Essays on Religion,"* 145).

2. According to Robin Feuer Miller, "Tolstoy's Peaceable Kingdom," in *Anniversary Essays on Tolstoy*, ed. Donna Tussing Orwin (Cambridge: Cambridge University Press, 2010), 73, "Tolstoy's animals are not burdened by their creator's perennial questions, 'How shall I live?' 'How shall I die?'"

3. The writing of this paragraph listing natural disasters and home accidents may have been motivated by the death in a fire in March 1887 of the sister of Miss Martha, the English governess living with the Tolstoy family.

4. Tolstoy's switches from "he" and "his" to "I" and "my" in this instance are conflations of the same order as were his flights from "they say" toward the critically and lovingly minded individual with his unique relationship toward the world, which were explained in note 9 to Tolstoy's Introduction chapter to *On Life*. Unlike the previous flight from "they" toward the individual ("he"), we have here the interchangeability of one's personal individuality ("I" and "my") and the individuality of one's neighbor—the results of an embrace of reasonable consciousness and love.

Chapter 35

1. Tolstoy is referring to the heroic behavior of the Bohemian preacher Jan Hus (John Huss; circa 1371–1415), a supporter of John Wycliffe and director

of the Bethlehem Chapel in Prague. Excommunicated in 1412 for his condemnation of clerical exploitation of Christian miracles and papal simony, he was burned at the stake on July 5, 1415, refusing to recant.

2. Plato's discussions of the length of life and life stages are numerous and can be found as early as in *Apology*, continuing in *Phaedo, Phaedrus, Republic, Statesman,* and *Timaeus.*

3. Regarding the use of the collective pronoun "they" and other impersonal pronouns, see note 10 to Tolstoy's "Introduction" to *On Life.*

4. In the paragraphs above, Tolstoy's use of emphatic particles and parts of speech is conspicuous. We have rendered his multiple repetitions of the Russian words "ved'" and then "zatem" and "zatem-to" with the help of "after all."

Conclusion
1. Matthew 11:28.
2. Matthew 11:29.
3. This is Tolstoy's own reference in the text. The Russian New Testament has the adjectival form of the word *blago* (happy, good) in place of the adjective "easy" in this concluding verse of Matthew 11:30: *Ibo igo Moe blago, i bremia Moe legko* (For My yoke is easy and My burden is light).

Appendix III
1. Tolstoy's paraphrase of John 5:25.

Historical Supplement

**Selected, translated, and annotated
by Inessa Medzhibovskaya**

Tolstoy's Diary

(May 1886–February 1887)

May 25, 1886

Sleep death. What will it be like after death? Why fear death? How not to fear death? What use to live better if death will come?

Death sleep. Why fear sleep? Because I have not finished what has been started. How not to fear sleep? Why fear it when it is rest, a change in life? Why live better now if I shall fall asleep? But you will wake up tomorrow. And that death is sleep, this is without doubt. We see how everything is falling asleep and waking up. And we fall asleep and wake up. And we remember the waking and are looking forward to falling asleep.

May 26, 1886

At first God created man to be eternal. He was growing while asleep. And then he came to know past life and the immediate life in the future. He became lazy. And then he became mortal, lonely and knowing nothing about his former and past life. He became angry.[1] He put infinite life within man and showed to him whence he came and wither he will go and that he is All and out of All. And he started to work and to love.

June 19, 1886

The world is alive. Life is in the world. Life is a mystery for all people. Some call it god;[2] others call it force. It is a mystery all the same. Life flows over everything. All lives together and all lives individually: so lives man and so lives a worm. (Science calls these individual lives organisms.) This is a silly word, an unclear one. What they call an organism is the force of life bounded by space and time, which is voicing the demands of universal life unreasonably on behalf of its individual separateness. This separation of life carries a contradiction within itself. It excludes all else. And all else excludes it. Besides that, it excludes itself. While it is striving after life, [the separation of] life is annihilating itself: every step, every act of living is dying.

This contradiction would be unresolvable were there no reason in the world. But there is reason in man. It is reason that annihilates the contradiction. A man would eat another man if he lacked reason. Reason shows to him what his happiness is: it is better for him to exist in love with another man and to kill beasts together with him for food. The same reason has shown to him that it is better for him not to kill beasts but to exist in love with them and to nourish himself with what they produce. The same reason will keep revealing more in the same direction and will annihilate the contradiction of egoism. [. . .]

[In] the whole enormous world of creatures that are consuming one another, only man is endowed with reason (and love); that should annihilate the whole contradiction of egoism. It seems so little for such an enormous task. This is the same as to say that one spark is too little to burn a forest. If the spark [of] fire *is* the combustible material, then no matter how small it would be it would suffice.[3] It is only the combustible material that is needed, that it should be and would not be annihilated. And it exists in the world of contradictory egoism. In the world of creatures' contradictory egoism, in order for them not to get annihilated they are endowed with egoistic drives—drives for florescence, insemination (which in man is the sexual drive for intercourse). And the world lives and does not represent in itself a perishing material upon which reason could act: love annihilates the contradiction of the creatures' egoism. The world may wait; the material will never be annihilated—it will always be; and the real spark of fire is there. God or nature acts always in the same manner.[4] It or he never creates the ready-made, but they make possible the process of accomplishing—not a tree but a seed.

Time does not exist for God and nature. When there is a possibility of anything, what must be already is. The same is true with the process of annihilating the contradictions of the egoism of creatures by means of the activity of reason. There is a possibility and therefore there is the accomplishment, there is what the prophet had spoken about: that the lion will lie with the lamb.[5] One could say more: that not a single beast will trample down an insect or a plant. For a man who has not grown aware of his reasonable nature, there is complete satisfaction in the life of egoistic contradiction. He does not notice it at that stage. He is following the lower law of God or nature; but as soon as he has become aware of his reasonable nature, the inner contradiction of his life poisons it for him. He cannot live by it and gives himself over to another law of reason: love, which has as its goal the annihilation of the contradiction. And by having given himself over to this new law, he receives the same complete satisfaction. For a reasonable creature there is no other life than the activity that has as its goal the annihilation of contradiction. This activity leads it out of its personality and forces it to resign itself; it leads it toward common life, toward serving that God or that nature for which there is no time.

The task of man in this life is to renounce everything contradictory within himself, the personal, the egoistical, that is, for the sake of the possibility to serve reason, for annihilating the inherent contradiction of life. In this task alone does he find full satisfaction—devoid of danger and fear—and calm before death. If he fails to complete this task he remains in [the grip of] the contradictions of personal life and annihilates himself in the same way as any contradiction annihilates itself.

They talk about future life, about immortality. Only that which is not I is immortal. Reason-love-God-nature.

August 28, 1886[6]
The main contradiction of human life is that it seems to each person individually that his director in life is his striving for pleasure and aversion to suffering. And a human being submits to this director unguided, on his own: he seeks pleasures and avoids suffering and posits the aim and meaning of life in this. But man cannot forever live pleasurably, as he cannot avoid suffering. And so, the meaning of life is not in this. And if it were in this, then what nonsense it would be: pleasures are the aim, but they are not available and cannot be available. And if they were there, the end of life—death—is always in conjunction with suffering. If a mariner were to decide that his aim is to steer clear of wave surges, where would he get? The aim of life is beyond pleasures and sufferings. It is achieved by passing through them.[7]

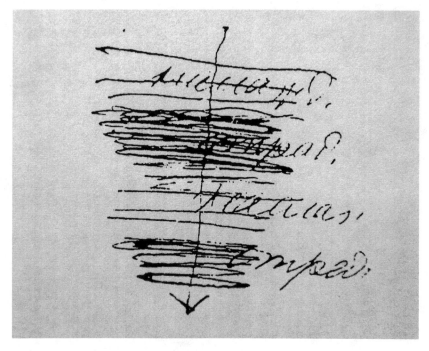

Tolstoy's text repeated from top to bottom: "pleas[ures] suffer[ing] pleas[ures] suffer[ing]." *The Jubilee,* 49:129.

Pleasures and suffering are the breath of life: inhalation and exhalation, the food of life and its procession.

To posit one's aim in pleasure and in the avoidance of suffering is to lose the path that runs across them.

The aim of life is universal or spiritual. Unification. Only . . . *I don't know what there is further to say, tired.*

October 18, 1886

How strange and improbable that it would seem at first that my future life were only in the entire activity carried out by my life and not only in the souls of men but also in the world in general. It would seem as strange and improbable to an embryo that its future life will be that of the complex activity of my body.[8]

February 3, 1887[9]

Man employs his reason in order to inquire, what for? and why?—and he applies his questions to his life and the life of the world. And the same reason demonstrates to him that there are no answers. These questions trigger something like nausea and vertigo. To the question, why? Indians respond, Maya seduced Brahma, who used to exist through his self-interiority, so that he could create the world. And to the question, what for? they do not even care to think up a similarly silly answer. No religion has thought it up, and the mind of man cannot think up answers to these questions.

What does it mean then?

It means that reason has not been granted to man to answer these questions and that the very asking of such questions suggests the delusion of reason.[10] Reason resolves only the main question "how?" What is this *how?* How to live? How then to live? Blessedly.[11]

This is needed by everything that is alive and by me. And the possibility of this is given to everything that is alive and to me. And this solution makes redundant the questions "why?" and "what for?"

But why and what for is it that blessed happiness is not found at once? It is the error of reason again. Happiness [*blazhènstvo*] is the making of one's happy-stances [*blazhènstva*]; there is no other happiness.[12]

Notes

These selections from Tolstoy's diary before and after the injury are taken from The Jubilee, *49:126–30.*

1. Uppercase "He" refers to God, lowercase "he" to man.

2. Tolstoy uses lowercase "god."

3. Tolstoy most literally is asking this: If the spark of fire *is* indeed the combustible material, then no matter how small it is it would suffice to set everything on fire. He must mean that, as a particle of fire, the spark renders combustible everything with which it is comes into contact.

4. Tolstoy must be referring to Spinoza's postulate "Deus sive natura." Tolstoy uses lowercase "god" again when referring to God and nature interchangeably in the sentence that follows: "It or he never creates the ready-made . . ." etc.

5. Tolstoy is paraphrasing Isaiah 11:6–8, using a common substitution of "lion" for the "wolf" and the "leopard" in the verses of biblical prophecy.

6. Tolstoy turned fifty-eight on this day; he was ill and bedridden when he made the entry.

7. The drawing in Tolstoy's diary entry for August 28 occurs next to the lines describing the passage to truth from pleasures through suffering. The word "pleasures" (*naslazhd[eniia]*) is followed by "suffering" (*strad[aniia]*) in the direction of the arrow. Both words are written twice in the same order in abbreviated form.

8. Here Tolstoy means that an embryo has no concept of ownership of its future body.

9. This is the sole diary entry for the entire year. It is especially precious to us because of its timing during Tolstoy's conversations with Grot about the possibility of making his presentation. Only five weeks remain before Tolstoy's talk at MPS on March 14, 1887.

10. Note that in this instance Tolstoy uses *um* (mind) and *razum* (reason) interchangeably.

11. *Blazhenno* is a derivative of *blago*, which here implies the highest ecstasy, happiness saturated with divine grace.

12. The stressed syllable in both words is indicated by the diacritic.

Tolstoy's Letter to
A. K. Diterikhs

(September–October 1886)

I will try to respond to your letter—for which I am very grateful to you—point by point.

1. My health is very good. I am still bedridden, the leg is healing little by little, and I am able to think and write a little.[1]

2. On life and death[2] [is] what I have been thinking so much and so intensely about of late and what you, as I can see, have been thinking about and are thinking about. At a certain point in his life an astonishing and terrifying inner contradiction of his personal life and reason appears at first to man—and to you and to me. "I, only I, everything is for me, and everything outside me is dead: only I am interesting, important, and dear to me, and I do not believe in my annihilation, I want to live eternally, I cannot imagine life without myself." At the same time, this terrible reason that is united with my "I" tells me clearly and indubitably that, first, I am not alone and that there is an innumerable quantity of others like me who are putting forth similar demands about their exceptionality; that a struggle against these "I's" is inevitable for me as is my perishing in this struggle. Second, it tells me that the strivings of my *I* are not in agreement but are directly in contradiction with the common life that comes into touch with me. Third, it tells me that, after me, the so-treasured "I" who wishes to live eternally and who lives driven only by this feeling of his, there will remain at best only a fertilizer for future alien lives of others, or nothing at all.[3] This contradiction, which seems terrifying when one becomes fully conscious of it, in the meantime lies dormant in the soul of every man, child and even constitutes the necessary condition for the life of man as a reasonable creature. This contradiction would be terrible if one stopped living and acting and just kept staring at it. But this contradiction grows out of life itself and accompanies life, and keeps changing form as life goes on. This contradiction cannot be resolved for man by way of

words because it's the foundation of the life of man; it is resolved for man only by way of living—through the activity of life, which is *liberating* man from this contradiction.

One must live because otherwise the contradiction will tear life asunder, as will a malfunctioning steam engine. And really all people live and get liberated from this contradiction when its germination begins. [. . .]

Reason is not another new force, but it is born out of the same force of life, and is its blossom. The energy of life infused with reason produces a new job for life using the same tools. Reason has blossomed, the contradiction has arisen, but one must live—that is, life demands activity as would a wheel falling under a horse's legs.[4] One must live with reason, which produces the contradiction, and the struggle ensues. [. . .] We call this a contradiction when it is represented to us clearly for the first time and so it is felt by us.[5] But is it really a contradiction? Can what is for man the universal law of his life be a contradiction for him? If so, then there is a contradiction for a rotting germ that by way of rotting shoots up a sprout.

And indeed, what is the contradiction for me when I am bedridden and aching, and I want to move around and be joyous or even, when not sick, I want to eat and enjoy myself? There is no contradiction in the fact that *I want* to enjoy myself, but reason demonstrates to me that there is no life in this, no contradiction but a clarification of life, should I only believe reason.[6] [. . .] When the shell of the germ—after the germ has broken through it—wishes to assert its life, what we call a contradiction is only the painful birth into new life. What is needed is only to avoid resisting the inevitable annihilation of personal life by reasonable consciousness and instead to surrender to this reasonable consciousness, and then new life opens up as if to a born-again Christian.[7] Whoever has not been born is not aware of what has been causing his suffering,[8] but the one who has been born recognizes his freedom. Only the one who has been born becomes aware reasonably of that from which he has been saved by his birth and becomes aware of the happiness of being born.[9] [. . .] Personal life is struggle; reasonable life is unification. Personal life is discord, resistance to the life of the world; reasonable life is all in accord with the life of the world. [. . .]

Notes

The letter is dated the end of September through the beginning of October 1886 and was sent from Yasnaya Polyana. The more finished sections of the letter to Diterikhs are translated here. Chertkov published the letter in volume 85 of The Jubilee *(392–96), which had come out a year before volume 26, containing* On Life.

1. *Ponemnogu,* translated here as "a little" and "little by little," is repeated in the sentence.

2. The phrase "on life and death" is written by Tolstoy as a plain phrase, not as a title of a work.

3. This thought is the leitmotif of the conclusion of Tolstoy's novella *The Strider* [*Kholstomer*, 1885].

4. Tolstoy writes "legs" rather than "hooves." The simile itself is both humble and inventive. Tolstoy means that a wheel comes off the axis of a broken horse-driven carriage and rolls underneath the legs of the horse that is pulling the carriage forward. The reader must imagine this situation and should attempt to try to guess why the wheel would want to break loose, or how the horse must react to adjust to the sudden malfunction, what the riders should do, etc.

5. I have corrected Tolstoy's use of the incorrect dative here with the correct instrumental case: Tolstoy writes *chuvstvuetsia nam,* which is clearly an unintended lapse.

6. Tolstoy does not say "believe in reason" but "believe reason," as if reason were a voice making arguments. This idea, of course, is put forward in many chapters of *On Life.*

7. Through an extended unfolding of this analogy in the long paragraph that follows, Tolstoy pays tribute to descriptions of the dawning of a new awareness of life that are commonly found in conversion narratives.

8. "What has been causing his suffering" (*chem on stradaet*) can also mean "what has been making him ill."

9. The word translated here as "happiness" is *blago.* For reasons of space only, I have omitted the section that shows signs of Tolstoy's dissatisfaction with this version and where he tells himself, "This is bad."

"The Concept of Life"

Tolstoy's Talk at the Moscow Psychological Society (March 14, 1887)

"Let us assume the impossible," said the count, "let us assume that everything that the science of life today wishes to know, all is clear as day! It is clear how organic matter is born through adaptation from inorganic matter; how forces are transformed into feelings, will, and thoughts; and all this is known not only to students at gymnasia but also to peasant children.[1]

It is known to me that such and such thoughts and feelings happen because of such and such movements. So what? Can I or can I not control these movements in such a way so as to excite in myself these and other thoughts? The question about the kinds of thoughts and feelings that I need to excite in myself and others remains not only unresolved but also even untouched.

But this question is the sole question about the central concept of life.

Science has chosen for its subject matter certain phenomena attendant to life, and having adopted a part for the whole has called these phenomena the totality of life . . .

The question that is inseparable for the concept of life is not the question "whence has life begun?" but the question about "how one should live." Only thanks to having started with this question is it possible to come to any sort of decision about what life is.

The answer to the question about how one should live appears so well known to man that it seems to him that it is not worth talking about it . . . To live is better. This seems at first very simple and known by all, but this is far from being either simple or known . . .

The concept of life appears as most simple and clear to man at first. First of all it seems to man that life is within him, in his body. I live in the body, and therefore life is in my body. But as soon as man begins looking for this life in a specific part of his body, complications emerge at once. There is no life in nails or hair, but neither is there life in a leg or in an arm, which can be amputated, none in the blood, none in the heart or in the brain.[2] Life is everywhere and nowhere. And it turns out that it cannot be located in the place of its domicile. Next, man looks for it within time, and at first it seems very simple also . . . But then, again, as soon as he begins looking for it within time, he sees that things are not simple here either. I have lived fifty-eight years; this is according to my birth certificate. But I know that I have slept twenty years of these fifty-eight. So did I live or did I not for these years? And then in my mother's womb, or when with my wet nurse, did I live or did I not? And then for the greater half of the remaining thirty-eight years, I was sleepwalking, and I don't know whether I was truly living or not.[3] I lived somewhat, and somewhat I did not; within time also it [life] is everywhere and nowhere. And then a question arrives involuntarily: whence does this life, which I can find nowhere, come [?][4] Here I am indeed going to find out . . . But here as well, it turns out, what had appeared to be so easy is not only difficult but also impossible. It turns out that I have been looking for something other than my life. It turns out that if you are bent on searching for it you should search neither in space nor in time and not as [if it were] consequence and cause but as something that I know in myself absolutely independently of space, time, and causality. And so should I study myself? How do I know life in myself?

This is how. I know, first of all, that I live and that I live wishing good things for myself, and I have been wishing this for myself ever since I can remember myself up until now, and I wish this morning through night. All that which lives outside me is important to me, but only insofar as it enables that which does me good. The world is important to me only because it brings me joys.

But with this knowledge of my life yet another piece of knowledge gets connected. Inseparably connected with this life that I feel within me is the knowledge that besides me there lives around me with the same consciousness of their exclusive life a whole world of living creatures, and that all these creatures live for their own aims, which are alien to me, and they don't know and don't want to know about my claims for exclusive life, and that all these creatures are ready, for the sake of attaining their aims, to annihilate me at any moment. And moreover, by watching the annihilation of other creatures similar to me, I also know that a very rapid and inevitable annihilation faces me, this precious me, in whom alone life appears to me . . .

It is as if there were two "I's" in man that do not seem to be able to get on with each other in life and that seem to fight with each other and exclude one another.

One "I" says, "Only 'I' live for real, all else only seems to live, and therefore the whole meaning of the world is my well-being."

The other "I" says, "The whole world is not for you but for its own aims, and it wants to know nothing about whether you are well or ill."

And life becomes terrifying. And it begins to be terrifying to live.

One "I" says, "I want my needs and desires to be satisfied. The desires and needs of animals are satisfied at the detriment of other animals, and therefore everything that is animal fights. You are an animal and must fight eternally. But however successfully you fight, all fighting creatures will sooner or later crush you."

Even worse. And it becomes ever-more terrifying.

And the most terrible thing that encompasses all the preceding:

One "I" says, "I want to live, to live eternally."

The other "I" says, "You will certainly die very soon, maybe now, and all those whom you love will die, and you and they are annihilating your life with your every movement and are on your way toward sufferings, death, the very same things that you hate and that you fear the most."

This is the worst of all . . .

It is impossible to change this situation. It is possible not to move, not to sleep, not to breathe even, but it's impossible not to think. You think, and every thought, every thought of mine poisons every step of my life as a person.[5]

As soon as man begins living consciously, [his] reasonable consciousness states the same thing over and over again to him: you can no longer live the life as you are experiencing it and as you see it in your past, the life that animals and many people live, and as that something that used to live out of which you became what you are now. If you attempt to walk away from the struggle with the whole world of creatures that live just as you do, for their personal aims, you will not succeed, and these creatures will inevitably destroy you.

[. . .]

We call the life of an animal a life, and the life of an organism a life . . . All this is no life but only a certain condition of life revealed to us.

But what is this reason—the demands of which preclude personal life and transfer the activity of man outside his self onto the condition that is recognized by us as the joyous condition of love?

What is reason? Whatever we define, we define only through reason. And therefore, with what can we define reason? . . .

If all that we have been defining we define through reason, we cannot define reason in the same way. But all of us know not only what reason is but also its nature alone without doubt and in the same way . . .

This is a law, the same as there is the law of life of every organism and plant, with the only difference being that we *see* that the reasonable law is fulfilling itself in the life of a plant. We cannot see the law of reason to which we are subject just as a tree is subject to its law, but we fulfill this law.

[. . .] Man's life is a striving for happiness, and what he is striving for is given to him. The light kindled in the soul of man is happiness and life, and this light cannot be darkness because there is truly for man only this light, which is burning in his soul.

Notes

L. V., "Soobshchenie gr. L. N. Tolstogo 'Poniatie zhizni'" [L. V., "Count L. N. Tolstoy's Presentation 'The Concept of Life'"], Novoe Vremia 3973 (March 23, 1887): 2–3. The text excerpted from Novoe Vremia in volume 26 has errors. I use the original newspaper version. Complete translated versions of all minutes of Tolstoy's talk that the editor was able to locate can be found in CG.

1. It was a customary practice for published talks and presentations in Russia, Europe, and America of the time to contain opening quotes at the beginning of a paragraph that would have no closing ones to go with them. Here, we reproduce the style of the quotations in the original.

2. See the editor's introduction, "Tolstoy's *On Life* and Its Times," for an explication of the origin of this phrase, "There is no life in nails or hair . . . ," etc.

3. This section develops the ideas of "dormant life" and lazy reason found in *A Confession* and *The Death of Ivan Ilytch*.

4. A question mark is missing in the newspaper summary.

5. In this phrase, Tolstoy shifts from the second-person pronoun to the first-person pronoun, a characteristic process central to his thought also observable in the main text of *On Life*.

Letters concerning *On Life*

Aleksandra Andreevna Tolstaya and Lev Tolstoy

A. A. Tolstaya to L. N. Tolstoy, August 8, 1887, from Tsarskoe Selo
[. . .] Truly and without any rhetorical flourish, I do speak with you in my dreams. How much remains unsaid! How many new questions stem from those touched upon by you! I am permeated with them to the point of its becoming morbid; it's like a thirst left unquenched. At this instant I stand undoubtedly closer to you than to my surrounding environment. Perhaps a whole system about the immortality of the soul could be constructed out of this. The soul is everywhere beyond space and time. *Vous voyez, mon cher Léon, que je n'oublie pas les expressions savants de votre opuscule. C'est maintenant que je le couve le loin et repasse dans mon esprit cet étrange amalgam de vérité et de ténèbres. Comme Dostoevsky, lorsqu'il a lu chez moi votre profession de foi, j'ai envie de m'écrier: ne to, ne to!*[1] In order to vanquish our sinful nature we are in need of something better, superior than Reason,[2] which plays the part of a hero in your new creation. This superior and better something has been burning for a long time in your heart, but you really seem to be afraid of giving it more leeway.

I am convinced that even the materialists would be jolted if a livelier word were uttered by you. Reason is their old chap or else their old manservant—a man of all work[3]—always ready to set off on any new commission.[4]

You see how untamed I am coming back full circle to the same thing. I was going to say only two words—of gratitude and love. [. . .][5]

Tolstoy's Response, around September 15, 1887, from Yasnaya Polyana
I am afraid that I will not have enough time to write at length to you, dear friend Alexandrine, but most of all I am afraid of leaving without answering your good letter, which is shot through with love. Your reproaches, dear friend, are really unfair. You are saying, do not affect others because your convictions may be erroneous and harmful. This argument is incorrect, but

primarily it can be directed against the Church teaching—and with greater legitimacy. If people consider the teaching of the Church to be false, how painful it must be for them to see the terrible network of false propaganda (in their view) into which simple and innocent people and infants get entrapped. When opinions differ one ought not speak of the consequences produced by false opinions; one ought to speak about opinions themselves. Falsity will always be falsity and will always be detrimental, too. I will only say in my defense that I very much ask you to accept and to take stock of these words in the same spirit of love in which you have been writing to me: I do not assert anything of what you would not admit to be true, and I derive joy from knowing that you are quite in agreement with me in everything I live by. But you also assert much of what I cannot accept, and you therefore derive sorrow from knowing that it is not only I but millions of people who do not agree with what you are asserting. [. . .] If it is true that in my life I practice only evil and am not becoming better even by a hair's breadth—that is, I am not beginning to practice evil even a little bit less—then I am lying for sure when I say that I *want to do good*. If a person wants to do good for sure—not for men but for God[6]—he is always moving ahead on the path of the good. This very movement—the process of getting closer to God (however small it is)—reinforces one on his way and gives hope and joy and the consciousness that one is doing at least a little of what God wills. [. . .] God is love. I cannot understand God otherwise than as all wise, omniscient, and, that which is the main thing, not only not resentful (and I am trying not to be resentful) but also merciful. How can I fear my weakness and sins in the face of such a judge? The whole of the Gospels is filled with direct and tributary indications of mercy, indications that sins before God do not exist for man who loves him. You are saying that God made this arrangement or performed this trick—I don't know how to put this—to forgive my sins, to redeem them through his son. (I cannot mention this sacrilege quietly. Please forgive me, for Christ's sake) [. . .][7]

Notes

The text of Tolstaya's letter is translated from PTAAT, *348–50. The letter was sent to Tolstoy a few days after the visit at Yasnaya Polyana and the reading of* On Life *at which she was present. This exchange covers the period closer to the end of Tolstoy's work on the text, when it was being sent on for printing and during the beginning of the proof stage. In preparing my translation of Tolstoy's response, I consulted the versions of the letter published in* PTAAT, *359–62, and* The Jubilee, *64:70–72.*

1. Tolstaya writes in French, adding the final two words in Russian: "You see, my dear Léon, that I have not forgotten the learned expressions of your little composition. Now that I am far away I am poring over it and am leafing mentally through this strange combination of truth and darkness. Just as Dostoevsky when he was reading your profession of faith, your confession, at my place, I am ready to exclaim, this is not it, not it!"

The words "this is not it, not it!" belong to Dostoevsky and were his end-of-life response to Tolstoy's religious views shared with Tolstaya during her visit. On this episode, and on A. A. Tolstaya's and L. N. Tolstoy's lifelong disagreements concerning faith and its place in life, see Medzhibovskaya, *Tolstoy and the Religious Culture of His Time*, 69–70, 74, 83–84, 138, 147, 168–69, 172, 201–2, 218–26, 264, 286, and 297.

2. The word *Razum* (Reason) is capitalized in Tolstaya's letter.

3. Tolstaya writes "a man of all work" in English.

4. Tolstaya makes a pun here based on the double meaning of the Russian word *posylki*, which means "assignments" and "commissions" on the one hand and "premises" and "starting points" of an inference on the other.

5. The letter continues with a detailed communiqué of society gossip and news of their family circle.

6. Tolstoy spells the word in uppercase, but *The Jubilee* changed the spelling to lowercase.

7. A lengthy omission occurs at this point and is indicated by a long series of dots in the 1911 publication, *PTAAT*, 360, but the excision is not flagged in *The Jubilee*, 64:71. While Tolstoy is not always consistent in using or not using capitals when he speaks of God and the divine, the inconsistency in volume 64 is also due to the rather indiscriminate and indeterminate rules for standardizing the spelling of these words in the Soviet publishing politics of the Stalin period.

Letter to Nikolai Grot, against Tolstoy and *On Life*

Archbishop Nikanor of Kherson and Odessa

Saint Petersburg, May 13, 1888[1]

Gracious and cordially respected Nikolai Iakovlevich,

Wishing you good health and peace of the soul. I celebrated the happy Easter as usual, in heavy toils to the point of exhaustion. But these toils and exhaustion for the sake of God on a holiday constitute the best delight of our monastic life. [. . .]

Yes, regarding Tolstoy, a harsh note sounded in your last but one letter. I did not take offense. And this is not the reason why I ceased corresponding but because any connections, even the closest ones, come apart because of long distances and time. I know this from experience as the old man that I am now already. [. . .] I hear that you are a persona grata at Count Tolstoy's. I hear (and know) that his creations are lying around on the desks of the highest dignitaries in Russia. I hear (and know) that distinguished ladies (excluding the Highest One) are bending over backward on Tolstoy's account. I hear and I am surprised. I am surprised at the incomprehensible thoughtlessness of some. I am surprised . . . at the audacity of your friend and idol. This is raised to the second and triple power: Rejoice, King of the Jews . . . Rejoice, Tsar of All Russia! And having given him a kiss . . . No, our century is strikingly immoral. No, we are rolling downward into the abyss of a cataclysm . . . On the one hand, a great mind, let it be the greatest mind, is committing such a grave sin . . . On the other hand, the simplest mind of a Russian moujik, the mind that up until now has been governed solely by the fear of God, is getting hired for a brass kopeck to commit murder . . . "N. N., can you finish off this tavern owner and send him to the other world?"—"Why not, we can do that. What are you paying?"—"This much."—"All right, give me a down payment."—"Here is a tenner for you."—"All right, I will come back to pick up the rest."[2]—And kill he did and came back for the rest! Here is what is terrible and unheard of in Russia. Rejoice, Count Lev Nikolaevich, rejoice that you are removing the final rein of religion from popular conscience, instructing all perfidiously that all this is but a fairy tale.

"Jupiter, you are angry, therefore you are wrong." A banal phrase—the Tolstoyan [dictum]: do not resist evil. Somebody slaps your mother in the face in front of your very eyes, rapes your wife, grabs your little son by the legs and squashes his skull against a corner of the wall . . . And you would not be right in the eyes of Tolstoy if you grew angry? No, you ought to have assisted your offender. —Come on: this is against nature. And I am not angry with Tolstoy. I cannot give him a bite. I only call things by their proper names. I had no patience to finish reading Tolstoy's *Karenina*, whereas I could not tear myself away from Dostoevsky's novels. What is this fawning before a man for? A genius, a great teacher. But I never heard Gogol or Lermontov called a genius by anyone. Goncharov and Turgenev did bring about mental upheaval. Pisarev, Dobroliubov, Chernyshevsky carried on with their destructive tendency in an honest way and turned up their heads exposing their foreheads. And when they could see that they had gotten tangled in lies one got drowned in the sea, another one was incinerated by a short-term consumption, and the third one went into hard labor . . .[3]

And why are Herzen, Dostoevsky not being called geniuses? And your idol, your count is accepting adulation . . . and from you . . . in his Moscow palace and making excuses that his Moscow house is not being run by him . . .

. . . Where do we go next? Can it be permitted to think that such a great sea, such a terrifying sea as our great Rus will not cause much destruction once it is stirred up? . . . And you are stirring it down to the bottom . . . And for starters it will get wet at the posh intelligential centers erected at the expense of the moneys the moujik have earned in sweat and blood. By the way, I have read Tolstoy's *Life*—at the Holy Synod; and I did not finish reading it. He is a wit, albeit a subtle, wily one, one could even say somewhat deep. But all of this is a concatenation of most . . . obvious sophisms.[4] It is remarkable that in Odessa Tolstoy was rebuked . . . as the most harmful antiscientific dreamer by none other than the great Mechnikov, who was foaming at the mouth.[5] [. . .] *Life* is condemned by the Moscow Committee on Spiritual Censorship. The Holy Synod only had to add its approval. [. . .] P.S. By the way: no joke, but we are going to pronounce an official anathema on Fofanov, his teacher Tolstoy, maybe on Pashkov, and others along the way.[6]

Notes

Archbishop Nikanor's letter to Nikolai Grot is from Nikolai Iakovlevich Grot v ocherkakh, vospominaniiakh i pis'makh tovarishchei i uchenikov, druzei i pochitatelei *[Nikolai Iakovlevich Grot in Essays, Reminiscences, and Letters by His Comrades, Students, Friends, and Admirers] (St. Petersburg: Tipografiia Ministerstva Putei Soobshcheniia / Tovarishchestvo I. N. Kushnerev, 1911), 329–31.*

1. By this time, *On Life* had been censored by the religious authorities.

2. Nikanor imagines that he is imitating the peasant speech in Tolstoy's popular tales of the 1880s (none, of course, excite murderous schemes of the kind described in Nikanor's dialogue).

3. Nikanor enumerates the previous generations of progressive thought in Russian letters, the predecessor enemies of the regime, who were more honest than Tolstoy, according to Nikanor: the democratic critics, or "men of the sixties"—all materialists and positivist by conviction—whom he names are Dmitry Pisarev (1840–68), who died in a drowning accident; Nikolai Dobroliubov (1836–61), who died of tuberculosis; and Nikolai Chernyshevsky (1828–89), who was still alive at that stage but who was no longer able to write after long years of hard labor and exile.

4. The expurgated segment must have contained what would have been unprintable in 1911.

5. The great physiologist Ivan Sechenov (see note 5 to chapter 21 of Tolstoy's *On Life*) had been forced out of St. Petersburg and moved to Odessa with his student and disciple, Ilya Mechnikov. With these forces onboard, the university in Odessa, where Grot, Mechnikov, and Sechenov were colleagues, was far from being an intellectual backwater. Growing repressions and a demand to conduct surveillance over students and faculty would force Mechnikov to resign in 1886 and open a bacteriological laboratory near his estate in Poltava. He would soon leave Russia to join Pasteur during the formation of a legendary institute, officially unveiled in 1888. Contrary to Nikanor's claims, Mechnikov made enlightened responses to *On Life*. On Mechnikov's responses to *On Life* directly, see my commentary in *CG*. On Mechnikov's interest in Tolstoy's views regarding longevity more generally, see Stephen Lovell, "Finitude at the Fin de Siècle: Il'ia Mechnikov and Lev Tolstoy on Death and Life," *Russian Review* 63, no. 2 (April 2004): 296–316.

6. This is a strange group of people, who were certainly not connected as conspiratorially as Nikanor presents them. Tolstoy never felt great sympathy for Pashkov's Evangelism, which he considered a high-society fashion, but he protested the prosecution of Pashkov followers. The religious poet Konstantin Fofanov (1862–1911) never concealed his admiration for Tolstoy, and Tolstoy likewise considered him the best living Russian poet (73:290–91).

"A Little Chronicle"

A Reader's Response to Critics of
On Life (1889)

Somebody with the last name Protopopov has been dragging poor Count L. N. Tolstoy through the coals in *Severnyi Vestnik*.[1] The stern critic likens the great writer to "senseless Pharisees and virtuous stuffed dummies" (page 23), saying that "Tolstoy's observations—and we say this while not standing on ceremony (for what kind of ceremony would that be!)—are very much senseless" (page 17). He calls Tolstoy "a greatly entertaining fellow and an amusing chap" and his sermonizing a "naughtiness of a bored baron who is over the hill and who is fed up with Gypsies and hunting with hounds, with card gambling and carousing at taverns" (page 31). Instead of arguments, in raising objections to Tolstoy's theory of nonresistance to evil the stern critic offers exclamations like, "This is disgusting, shameful, immoral—this is our argumentation" (page 33); and at the end of his "critique" he "hands over 'the great writer of the Russian land' (here quotation marks belong to the stern critic) to the just ire and indignation of all fathers and mothers . . . !" (page 34).[2]

In reading these frivolous remarks against Count Tolstoy in the ladies' journal—they are absurd in their substance and indecent in form—one asks oneself involuntarily, were the female editors of the journal intent on arousing a literary scandal on the eve of subscription season so as to draw the attention of the public? Incidentally, the matter can also be explained otherwise.[3] Mr. Protopopov, it turns out, simply did not understand some of Tolstoy's philosophical works, and he confesses as much. "About these ('Thoughts on Life' [Mysli o zhizni]) philosophical works by Tolstoy," writes Mr. Protopopov, "I have not spoken and will not speak for the simple reason: I don't understand them—that is, I understand each individual sentence in them, each particular thought, but the whole time that I have been reading I have been asking myself—like a character of Gleb Uspensky's—'What is the noise all about?'"[4]

It is frank of Mr. Protopopov, but not in the least lethal for Tolstoy, to admit that he "did not understand" Tolstoy's book. This provides justification for anyone to merely tell Mr. Protopopov, "You did not understand, so why don't you try to understand"—and so be in the right not to read him further.

Without claiming to write a critique of Mr. Protopopov's critique, I wished only to point it out as a certain literary curiosity, one that calls to mind Krylov's fable about the elephant and the lapdog.[5] Mr. Protopopov's critical essays can be compared to influenza—a literary kind, of course—since one can notice in them, just as in the true influenza, a high fever ("stuffed dummy," "naughtiness of a bored baron," "the indignation of fathers and mothers," etc.) and a partial loss of sensibility. In this case, these influenza-like symptoms are expressed through the absence of critical comprehension. By way of concluding his "critical essays," Mr. Protopopov says, "I can see clearly that I have not said even one-tenth of what one may and must say of Tolstoy."[6] This is perfectly true, Mr. Protopopov, but you have made up for your deficiency by saying much of what it seems one must not and should not say about Tolstoy. For all that—if not for your reader but for you—this is compensation.

Notes

Novoe Vremia *4951 (December 9, 1889): 3. Signed "A Petersburg Burgher" (Peterburzhets), this anonymous post defends Tolstoy against the right-wing attacks of Protopopov, specifically his long denunciations of Tolstoy's theory of life, which are discussed in the editor's introduction (see pages 25, 39).*

1. *Severnyi Vestnik* is hereafter referred to as *SV*.

2. The author quips about Protopopov's enclosing in quotation marks (as if they were undeserved) these farewell words from a dying Ivan Turgenev to Tolstoy in 1883. Turgenev sent Tolstoy his exhortations to stop dissipating his talent on sermonizing and moralizing and to return to fiction writing.

3. *SV* had been published by Antonina V. Sabashnikova and edited by Anna M. Evreinova since 1885. Yet the journal soon went bankrupt and was purchased in the 1890–91 season on a shareholder principle by a group of its contributors. Among them were Liubov Iakovlevna Gurevich (1866–1940) and Akim Volynsky (pseudonym of Khaim Leibovich Flekser, 1861–1926). Gurevich and Volynsky were serious critics, by contrast, and left behind interesting evaluations of *On Life*.

4. The author takes issue with Protopopov's aside in a footnote to chapter 17 of his final article on the "'philosophy' of Tolstoy," as he puts it (*SV* 12 [December 1889]: 25). The works of the populist writer Gleb Ivanovich Uspensky (1843–1902), and remarks uttered in these works by dense characters representing the ruling regime, were a favored polemical weapon used by democratic and also Marxist critics, including Lenin, against their opponents.

5. Ivan Andreevich Krylov's (1786–1843) verse fable "The Elephant and the Lapdog" [Slon i mos'ka] describes a brazen lapdog, Mos'ka, yelping at an elephant during a procession of a traveling circus through the streets of a town.

6. The author cites a portion of Protopopov's belated and backhanded compliment to Tolstoy that he reserved for the very last paragraphs of his final article: "It is time to finish. As I was getting ready to put in a full stop, and in the process of going over my articles, I could see clearly that I have not said a tenth of what one may and must say of Tolstoy . . . Such is the power and depth of this colossal talent whose works will for a long time yet serve as an impulse for criticism and a subject of study for readers" (M. Protopopov, *SV* 12 [December 1889], part 2:35–36).

Vladimir Soloviev's
Unsent Letter to Tolstoy

(circa 1889–91; 1894)

Our entire disagreement can be focused on one particular point—the resurrection of Christ.[1]

I think that in your own worldview—as long as I correctly understand your latest compositions—there is nothing that could prevent acknowledging the truth of resurrection; more so, there is something there that compels one to acknowledge it. I will speak about the idea of resurrection in general to begin with, and then I will speak of the resurrection of Christ.

(1) You admit that our world undergoes a progressive modification, transitioning from the lower forms and stages of being to higher and more perfect ones. (2) You admit the interaction of inner, spiritual life and the higher, physical life.[2] And (3) on the ground of this interaction you admit that the perfection of a spiritual creature is expressed in that his own spiritual life subjugates his physical life to itself and gains control over it.

Taking one's cue from these three points, I think it necessary to arrive at the truth of resurrection. As matters stand, in its relation to material existence, spiritual force[3] is not a constant but an increasing value. In the animal world, it is present, generally speaking, only in a latent, potential state; in humanity, it is released and becomes manifest. But this release takes place only in the ideal form *of reasonable consciousness*:[4] I see my distinction from my animal nature, I become aware of my inner independence from it and of my superiority over it. But can this *consciousness* transform itself into *deed* [?][5] It not only is able to do so but also does in part do so. Just as in the animal world we find some beginning or some glimmers of reasonable life, so in humanity those beginnings of that higher and perfect state do exist in which the spirit subdues material life in fact and in deed. It fights against the dark strivings of material nature and subjugates them to itself (and it does not only make a distinction between itself and them). The greater or lesser fullness of this victory depends on the degree of inner perfection. The extreme triumph of the hostile material element is death—that is, the liberation of the chaotic life of material parts and the destruction of their reasonable, purposeful connection. Death is the apparent victory of meaninglessness over meaning, of chaos over cosmos. It is especially true in relation to living creatures of the highest order. The death of man is the destruction of a perfect organism—that is, the destruction of a purposeful form and tool of the higher reasonable life. Such a victory of the lower over the higher, such a disarming of the spiritual element demonstrates, evidently, the insufficiency of its power. But this power is *increasing*. Immortality for man is what reason is for animal; the meaning of the animal kingdom is reasonable animal—that is, man. The meaning of mankind is *the immortal*—that is, Christ. In the same way as the animal world is drawn to reason, so is humanity drawn to immortality. If the struggle against chaos and death is the essence of universal process[6] whereby the luminous, spiritual side doth indeed win, albeit slowly and gradually, resurrection, then—that is, the real and final victory of a living creature over death—is the necessary moment of this process, which, with that, arrives in principle at its conclusion.[7] The whole subsequent progress, strictly speaking, bears only an extensive character, and it consists in the universal embrace of this individual victory or in the spread of its consequences across the entire human race and the entire world. [. . .]

Since the time that I accepted that the history of the world and of mankind has meaning I personally have not had the slightest doubt in the resurrection of Christ, and all objections only reinforce my faith with their weakness. The only original and serious objection that I know of belongs to you. In a recent conversation with me, you told me that to accept resurrection and consequently to accept the unique supernatural meaning of Christ would force Christians to rely more on the mysterious force of this supernatural creature for their salvation than on their own ethical work. But this abuse of truth is in the end only the exposure of the abusers. Because in reality, even Christ resurrected can ultimately accomplish nothing without us; there is no danger of quietism here for sincere and conscientious Christians. If the resurrected Christ possessed visible reality to us, then it might be granted that he could accomplish things without us, but the actual, personal connection with him can be spiritual only under present conditions, and this presupposes man's own ethical work. Only hypocrites or scoundrels could cite grace [*blagodat*] *to the detriment* of ethical duties. And besides, God-man is not the all-consuming absolute of Oriental mystics and the unification with him cannot be one-sidedly passive. He is the firstborn of the dead, the one who shows [us] the way, the conductor and the banner for active life, for the struggle and the achievement of perfection, and not for the immersion in nirvana.

At any rate, whatever the practical consequences of the resurrection of Christ, the question of its truth is not resolved by these consequences. It would be extremely interesting for me to know whatever substantive thoughts you could share with me a propos this topic.

Notes

This excerpt is from Vl. Soloviev, "Iz pis'ma Vladimira Sergeevicha Solovieva k grafu L'vu Nikolaevichu Tolstomu" [From the Letter of Vladimir Sergeevich Soloviev to Count Lev Nikolaevich Tolstoy], VFP 79, no. 4 (September–October 1905): 241–46. The letter was published by Soloviev's friends Lev Lopatin and Evgeny Trubetskoy in the issue commemorating the passing of Prince Sergey Trubetskoy. The story with Soloviev's letter is complex. Apparently, he kept revising it and still hesitated to forward the last known edited copy of it in 1894. Ernest Radlov published the longest redaction of the letter with a range of dates between July 28 and August 2, 1894, in volume 3 of his edition of Soloviev's correspondence (which appeared in 1911 and thus after Tolstoy's death): Pis'ma Vladimira Sergeevicha Solovieva, *3 vols., ed. E. L. Radlov (St. Petersburg: Obshchestvennaia pol'za, 1908–11), 3:38–42. The letter is not listed among the received letters in Tolstoy's papers. I am here translating an excerpt from the version of the letter made public in Tolstoy's lifetime.*

1. The word "resurrection" is not capitalized in the original.

2. Here Soloviev is wrong: Tolstoy holds inner spiritual life higher than the physical. For Tolstoy, the reformed inner life that posits the commonness and unity of all life above itself is what he means by the highest form of life.

3. This is a Hegelian argument shared by Soloviev with Tolstoy and Strakhov.

4. Although Soloviev would not be supportive of Tolstoy's concept developed in *On Life*, he adopted it after 1887 for the purposes of his polemic against Tolstoy.

5. There is no question mark in the original.

6. The original has here *sushchnost' mirovogo protsessa*.

7. Soloviev's chiliasm is Hegelian just as it is patristic, and neither is embraced by Tolstoy.

Nikolai Grot's Comparison of *On Life* with Nietzsche's Writings

(1893)

Nietzsche [is] a materialist and an atheist. The soul and God are superstitions. And this is what explains Nietzsche's leap from man-animal toward Overman [*sverkh-chelovek*], by skipping the stage of "man" in the true sense of this word. It is not surprising that this consistent materialist, atheist, and moral evolutionist repeats—completely without any skepticism or diffident shame—the famous phrase of Ivan Karamazov so brilliantly justified by Smerdiakov, that if anyone does not believe in God and in the immortality of the soul then "everything is permitted" to him.

Lev Tolstoy professes a completely different worldview. Anyone familiar with Tolstoy's piece *On Life* (see volume 13 of his *Complete Works*)[1] would know what a deep gulf lies for him between animal and reasonable consciousness, between beast and man, and what passionate efforts he undertakes to justify the immortality of the soul and the idea of eternal life. [He would know][2] that shifting occasionally from the idea of the personal immortality of the "soul" in favor of the idea of impersonal immortality of the "spirit,"[3] he [Tolstoy] nonetheless consistently defends the thought about the eternity of spiritual life and about the impossibility of complete death. Does Tolstoy believe in the living God? Yes, he does, he does deeply. He even believes in prayer and the mysterious communication[4] of the eternal being with the souls of living human beings. Tolstoy believes in the will of the One who sent us here—into the world of eternal truth and absolute good. At the same time, Tolstoy does not believe in external—that is, material and technical—progress. He proclaims the return to "man" instead of inventing a winged and feathered "overman." "The Kingdom of God Is within You."[5] It is already fully given in the great potencies of the human soul; it has more than once shone brightly and manifestly for the edification of all mortals. The whole of development and evolution boil down to the growth of the spiritual and moral person of man. For it is necessary to return to the purity of the Gospel teaching, "Love your enemy and render good [*blagotvorite*] unto the ones hating you."[6] The world of the soul, the abdication of all and any vanity and not the external progress concerned with the organization of personality and society—this is the true aim of man, his happiness,[7] the source of his moral satisfaction.

Despite all the hatred and disgust that Nietzsche feels toward the contemporary industrial and bourgeois civilization, there is an inkling of an echo of the incessant clatter and racket of the machines of an enormous west European or American factory in his teaching, of the countless pistons and anvils invented by man, which have conquered him and yet are so appealing to him. All these machines and this whole production have as their final ideal the making by mechanical-chemical-physical-anatomical-physiological ways of a new animal creature—the flying and winged overman who is organically producing great ideas by means of the upgraded hemispheres and convolutions of the brain. The sound of soft, expansive, virginal spaces of the steppes of our motherland, of infinite melancholic fields of black soil, of the quiet and concentrated seclusion of the village in which the feeling of the "power of the earth" and the "freedom of a healthy spirit mighty in its seclusion" echoes in the teaching of Tolstoy.[8] Leave him alone, leave him to himself and he will be great without any machines, flying artillery shells, factories and manufactories, without chemistry, medicine, and histology.

Man who is a tamed beast and man who is the fullness of divine reason in the flesh on earth are the mutually opposing principles and ideals of both thinkers.

It goes without saying that the moral teachings of Tolstoy and Nietzsche reflect all merits and all shortcomings of the theoretical worldviews that they both profess.

The main accomplishment of both consists in that they bring their theoretical views to a conclusive end.

[...]

[For Nietzsche,] no absolute or obligatory morality exists; hence there is no morality at all. This is an empty invention and a teaching of certain people. People are beasts, and the sole foundation of their life is the struggle for existence, for power and for might. Let this struggle to the very end[9] be *openly* elevated to the status of the sole law of life.

Count Tolstoy is equally consistent in his teaching. If man is solely reason and spirit, then the law of his life, his inner law, is the *moral* law. If he is not a beast, his principle of existence then is not the struggle for existence but love. One must sincerely and honestly acknowledge the law of love as the only possible law of human life. [. . .]

Notes

This is an excerpt from Grot's article "Nravstvennye idealy nashego vremeni (Friedrich Nietzsche i Lev Tolstoy)" [Moral Ideals of Our Time (Friedrich Nietzsche and Lev Tolstoy)], VFP 4, no. 16 (January 1893): 129–54. It would be reprinted numerous times in brochures in Russian and in a German translation.

1. Grot means the selections from *On Life* published in the seventh edition of Tolstoy's *Collected Works*, reprints from *Nedelia*.

2. I have broken down an overly long sentence that would not be tenable in English into two separate ones.

3. Grot uses quotation marks around these words, "soul" and "spirit," perhaps in order to underscore the fuzziness in the division between the two in the philosophical discourse about the humanities at the time.

4. Grot most obviously overstates this point.

5. Grot here references Tolstoy's famous work of the same title (1890–93).

6. Grot is attempting to adjust Matthew 5:43 to the vocabulary used by Tolstoy.

7. The word used by Grot is "happiness" proper (*schast'e*), rather than *blago*.

8. The quotation marks are Grot's: Tolstoy never used and never could have used any of these adorned phrases. The whole passage tells us more of Grot's own sense of the use of artistic device.

9. The Russian expression *bor'ba ne na zhizn' a na smert'* cannot be translated idiomatically with the retention of the contrast between life and death: this is not the struggle for life but the struggle until one or both of the opponents should die.

Letter to the Editor from
P. K. Novitskaya

(1895)

In 1894, P. K. Novitskaya, a twenty-year-old governess from Bessarabia, wrote to Tolstoy with questions about the meaning of life. She wrote to him three times, on September 9 and then again on November 16 and 20. Tolstoy responded with a detailed explanation on December 11, 1894, from Moscow: "*What is the essence of that endeavor that should go parallel with a meticulously practiced life?* you ask. The endeavor that we are called upon to undertake in life is a double one, although it is achieved by means of one and the same action: the external endeavor consists in giving aid with our individual life to the establishment of the kingdom of God on earth—that is, it consists in replacing hostility, struggle, and separation with accord, mutual assistance, and unification . . . We can assist this service of truth with the truthfulness of thoughts, words, and deeds . . . The inner endeavor consists of self-perfection, of getting nearer to God" (67:285–86).

Tolstoy explained that getting nearer to God coincides with growing love toward the world from within. "To grow love" is to let one's soul become more receptive to goodness. Love hidden within has a tendency to grow of its own accord. And all the temptations that cause obstructions to this growth ("hostility, struggle, and separation") ought to be resisted and overcome. It is in this connection that Tolstoy elaborates most interestingly on *blago*: "This very growth of love provides such happiness [*blago*] to people that it replaces all the dark joys coming from temptations—which it precludes. And it does not behoove one to think that the life dedicated to the growth of love[1] is a dark life, which has as its aim the welfare gifts[2] of one's animal individuality. These are my answers to your questions in brief. I would be very glad if they proved satisfactory to you" (67:286). Novitskaya quoted Tolstoy's letter in her letter to *VFP* with his permission before offering her criticism of Kozlov, which follows.

Disputing A. A. Kozlov's Interpretation of Tolstoy's *On Life*

My dear sir Mr. Editor,

I have just read "Pis'ma o knige gr. L. N. Tolstogo"[3] by A. A. Kozlov, and I would like to prove that Mr. Kozlov does not quite correctly understand the teaching of Lev Nikolaevich. I would be very grateful to the editorial board for publishing the lines that follow below.

It seems strange sometimes that one and the same thing could be understood differently. What might seem simpler, clearer, and more comprehensible than the teaching of L. N. Tolstoy! But how variously it is being interpreted and how few understand it really. It might be that L. N. Tolstoy is in the wrong from the scientific and philosophical point of view—I cannot judge that, because my knowledge in that sphere is too limited—but one thing I do know is that all that Lev Nikolaevich is teaching us is so simple, clear, and comprehensible, so accessible to all people, that one could not desire anything better. If there are minor blemishes, infatuations, some contradictions, these are such trifles compared with the great and the good that the great teacher has done for us. I keep open in front of me the book by Professor Kozlov, "Letters on the Book by L. N. Tolstoy on life,"[4] and it seems strange to me that such a deep and comprehensively educated mind is so far from a true understanding of this serious and at the same time simple teaching.[5] [. . .]

Novitskaya makes the following summary of Kozlov's accusations against Tolstoy:

> The one who loves as we find him in Tolstoy is giving away to others not because he, out of love for them, desires the happiness and enjoyment for the others but only because happiness and enjoyment are impossible for himself, and therefore he does not need any sort of conditions for happiness—he is indifferent to them. Love in Count Tolstoy is in essence the principle of asceticism, the mortification of the flesh, the mortification of all desires." [. . .]

Novitskaya then quotes Tolstoy's letter to herself as evidence against Kozlov's accusations:

> It would be arrogant on my part to add anything to such a letter:[6] it speaks so well and so simply for itself, there is a profound moral teaching in it, but there is none in it of *asceticism, mortification of the flesh, or the*

mortification of all desires,[7] and there cannot be because Tolstoy's ideal is a greater possible happiness for men—not for some select few but for all men in general, beginning with the most plain and common and ending with great artists, geniuses, philosophers, and scientists. Lev Nikolaevich Tolstoy is a "man" in the deep sense of the word, and this is why he is great. —P. Novitskaya.

Notes

1. The phrase "growth of love" was changed by Tolstoy to "the service to truth" in the version published in *VFP* 32, no. 2 (March–April 1896): 167–69, in which Novitskaya provided quoted passages from his letter to her.

2. "Happiness" in the plural in Russian (*blaga*) has as its first meaning the material gifts that improve welfare. To distinguish this from the meaning of the highest happiness, one ought to say "spiritual gifts" (*dukhovnye blaga*).

3. "Letters on the Book by Count L. N. Tolstoy" (on Kozlov's review of *On Life*, see the editor's introduction).

4. Tolstoy's book title is transcribed in this way by Novitskaya.

5. Like all serialized articles, Kozlov's letters concerning Tolstoy's *On Life* also appeared in a brochure offprint in Moscow, in 1891.

6. Novitskaya means Tolstoy's letter to herself of December 11, 1894, quoted at the beginning of this entry.

7. Novitskaya is referring here to Kozlov's frequent charges against Tolstoy.